THE PILGRIM'S GUIDE
TO ROME

THE
PILGRIM'S GUIDE
TO
ROME

For the Millennial Jubilee Year
2000

BARRETT McGURN

Illustrated by Curtis Tappenden

VIKING

A GINIGER BOOK

VIKING

Published by the Penguin Group
Penguin Putnam Inc., 375 Hudson Street,
New York, New York 10014, U.S.A.
Penguin Books Ltd, 27 Wrights Lane, London W8 5TZ, England
Penguin Books Australia Ltd, Ringwood, Victoria, Australia
Penguin Books Canada Ltd, 10 Alcorn Avenue,
Toronto, Ontario, Canada M4V 3B2
Penguin Books (N.Z.) Ltd, 182-190 Wairau Road,
Auckland 10, New Zealand
Penguin India, 210 Chiranjiv Tower, 43 Nehru Place,
New Delhi 11009, India

Penguin Books Ltd, Registered Offices:
Harmondsworth, Middlesex, England

First published in 1998 by Viking Penguin,
a member of Penguin Putnam Inc.

1 3 5 7 9 10 8 6 4 2

LIBRARY OF CONGRESS CATALOGING IN PUBLICATION DATA
McGurn, Barrett.
The Pilgrim's Guide to Rome for the millennial jubilee year 2000 /
Barrett McGurn
p. cm.
Includes bibliographical references.
ISBN 0-670-87627-5
1. Christian pilgrims and pilgrimages—Italy—Rome.
2. Rome (Italy)—Description and travel. 3. Christian shrines—Italy—Rome.
4. Holy Year, 2000. I. Title.
BX2320.5.I8M37 1998
263'.04245632—DC21   98-29027

This book is printed on acid-free paper.

Printed in the United States of America
Set in Minion

To Jan and the children
Bill, Betsy, Andrew, Lachie, Martin, and Mark

CONTENTS

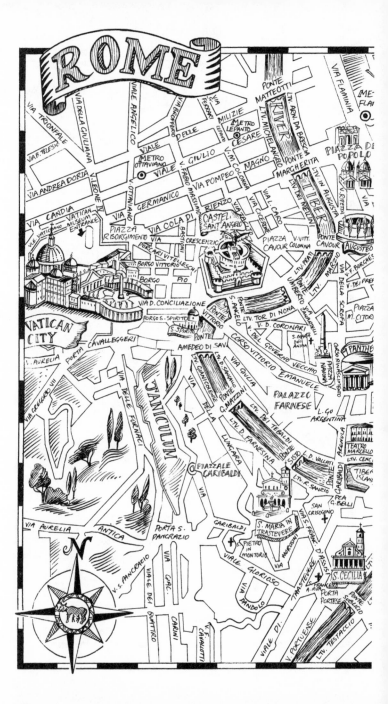

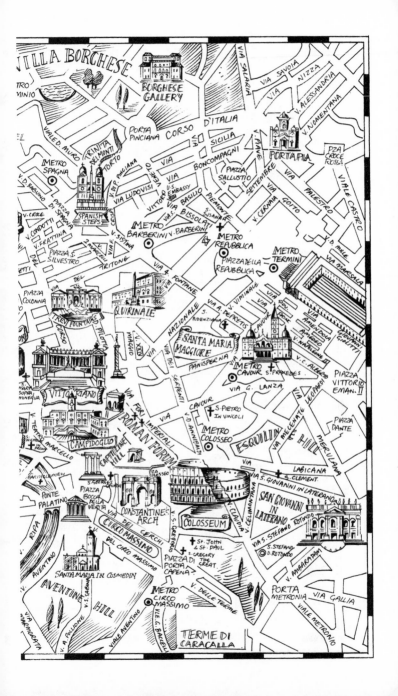

MADONNA OF LOURDES

LEONEN WALLS

VATICAN RADIO

VIA AURELIA

VIALE VATICANO

RAILWAY

VIALE DELL' OSSERVATORIO

STAZIONE FERROVIARIA

COMMISSARY

S. STEFANO

ELECTRIC OFFICE

VIA AURELIA

VATICAN CINEMA

TRIBUNAL

VIA D. STAZIONE VATICANA

ST. PETERS BASILICA

D. CROCIFISSO

VIA PAOLO II

VIA STAZIONE

VATICAN CITY

PORTA CAVALLEGGIERI

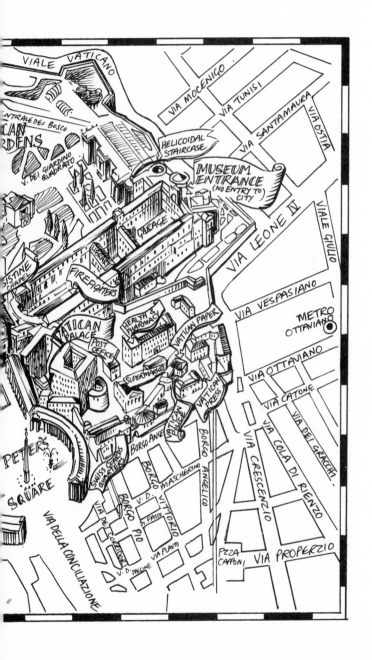

THE PILGRIM'S GUIDE
TO ROME

ROME IN 2000

VISITORS TO ROME at the start of the new millennium can expect a unique experience.

They will walk the same streets and visit many of the same monuments that were there two thousand years ago at "year zero," the time when the Gospels tell us that the emperor of Rome ordered a census, causing Joseph and Mary to make a pilgrimage to a manger in Bethlehem.

They will see ample remains of the pagan temples that were in place nearly one thousand years before the Christian era, and they will set foot where the first Christians died as martyrs, shedding blood that was the seed of a new faith so powerful that a billion people now embrace it across the globe.

The millions of year 2000 pilgrims will pray in the very basilicas that, seventeen centuries ago, saw the tumbling of the shrines to Venus, Apollo, Diana, Mars, Jupiter, and the plethora of other ancient deities while taking their own places as huge new edifices in honor of a Galilean fisherman.

Rome's visitors will also see a modern city of three million people, not without faults, to be sure, but nonetheless ready to welcome them good-naturedly, as they have done to the many generations that have preceded them. They will see why poets and philosophers have been awed by Rome through the ages.

Most of all, the visitor in 2000 will be absorbed by a unique spiritual experience. Rome will be celebrating the twenty-sixth in a series of Holy Years dating from the start of the fourteenth century, the first of these jubilees to welcome a new millennium of the Christian era. Launched in the heart of the Middle Ages, the "age of faith," the series has continued with few exceptions through the Renaissance and the Enlightenment up to this dawn of the third millennium.

While many of the earlier Holy Years were dramatic, this promises to be the most ambitious and most spectacular. All Holy Years have seen throngs of pilgrims joining Romans in seeking reconciliation with God while praying at the tombs of Saints Peter and Paul, but this one, at the direction of the indefatigable and innovative Pope John Paul II, will reach for a higher goal, seeking to bring back the splintered Christian community as nearly as possible into a once again united family, while extending the hand of friendship to other great religions and reaching out through cooperative welfare efforts to those with no religious faith.

An estimated twenty million pilgrims and tourists are expected to make their way to Rome, many of them overnighting in Naples and Florence and making day trips into the city. There will be housing problems, especially for the poorer pilgrims from liberated Eastern Europe; there will be traffic jams; and, at many places, long waiting lines. But there will also be great recompenses as the Holy Year visitor takes part in a series of events seeking to embrace all humanity.

Joining a long line of pilgrims reaching back seven centuries, those of the Catholic religion, those of other Christian faiths, and those of other religions or of none who travel to Rome to pray at the beginning of a millennium will not pray alone.

CHAPTER I

HOLY YEARS

THE FIRST HOLY YEAR, in 1300, happened virtually by accident, although theologians find antecedents now in the first books of the Jewish Old Testament of three millennia ago (see Leviticus 25 : 2–13).

Europe had been tormented in the thirteenth century by wars and epidemics. There was exhaustion and also fear that the end of time predicted in Saint John's Apocalypse might come in the new century, beginning with the number thirteen. It was a dread that had already swept Europe at the turn of the millennium and again in 1200.

Word spread that peace with God could be found by traveling to Rome to pray at the tombs of Saints Peter and Paul, and that Pope Boniface VIII, the Italian Benedetto Caetani, who reigned as Peter's successor from 1295 to 1303, would use his priestly primacy to invoke an indulgence from God on each penitent, thus waiving the after-death punishment for sins.

There was some precedent. Papal indulgences had been granted to those making pilgrimages to Jerusalem or to the great shrine of Santiago de Compostela in Spain, and to Crusaders seeking to liberate the Holy Land from Muslims.

With a throng of pilgrims pouring into the old city, Boniface consulted with the cardinals of the Roman curia, and, two months into the new century, on February 22, a papal bull was issued granting the desired grace but requiring that each penitent pay prayerful visits to the basilicas of Peter and Paul, fifteen times for those from outside Rome and thirty for local residents.

Thus, in the heart of the Middle Ages, began a dramatic religious phenomenon that has endured for seven centuries and is expected to reach its greatest climax in 2000, with full global television coverage and many millions of direct participants—what Pope John Paul II, its enthusiastic promoter, has called "the great jubilee."

Boniface VIII launched the jubilee as something to recur only at the turn of centuries, but the decision quickly was made by 1350 to repeat the jubilee at intervals of fifty years, to allow more generations to take part. Now it occurs at least every quarter of a century.

The description of the Holy Year as a jubilee makes reference to what is seen as an Old Testament precedent—the references in Leviticus (25 : 8–55 and 27 : 17–21) and in Numbers (36 : 4) to a "jubilee year," an event to occur one year after "seven weeks of years . . . seven times seven years," a special period of debt forgiveness. Leviticus said a trumpet should be blown. The horn of a ram, a *yobel*, was among the trumpets in use; hence, perhaps, the origin of the word "jubilee."

From the very first Holy Year there were logistical problems. Indeed, Romans expect them again in 2000 as cars and huge buses weave their way through ancient streets, as crowds converge on Saint Peter's and the Vatican, and as throngs squeeze into such special places as the Holy See's Sistine Chapel. In 1300, the supplies of bread and wine, meat and fish held up and were available at fair prices, but lodging and hay for horses were expensive. There was profiteering. Questions arose that caused concern to later popes and to civil authorities and still preoccupy Holy Year committees today. Organizers at the Vatican have pleaded with Rome labor unions to call no strikes in 2000. They have been hard at work setting up bed-and-breakfast arrangements in private homes, something new to Romans. Much work has gone into converting empty convent and monastery space into simple but adequate lodging, especially for pilgrims with scant funds.

Difficulties of many kinds have beset Holy Year celebrations across the centuries, but the spiritual demand for these jubilees has never ceased.

Although much of the life had gone out of Rome with the transfer of the papal curia to France, a request arose in the mid-fourteenth century for a repetition of Boniface's jubilee, and the Avignon pope, the French Pierre Roger, Pope Clement VI (1342–1352), agreed. He did not attend himself, but he sent two cardinals to represent him, Guido da Boulogne and Annibaldo de Ceccano. He granted the customary indulgence, but he raised to three the number of churches at which to pray. His addition was Saint John Lateran, the second of

Constantine's great churches and the particular church of the pope as Rome's bishop.

What the cardinal delegates and pilgrims found was shocking. Brigands preyed on the travelers. The city was in a state of collapse. Cows grazed and pigs rooted in the Forum, the very heart of the ancient empire. The plague had struck in 1348 and an earthquake had followed in 1349. Monuments were tumbling and looters were using them as a source of building supplies. Prices soared and housing was short. Some visitors slept eight to a room.

Gregory XI, the French Pierre Roger de Beaufort (1370–1378), at an appeal from Saint Catherine of Siena, moved from Avignon to Rome and called for a Holy Year without waiting for 1400, but he died, at forty-seven, before he could organize the celebration. His death caused a crisis. In an election that the Vatican recognizes, the Neapolitan Bartolomeo Prignano, Urban VI (1378–1389), became pope, agreeing that there should be a Holy Year in 1390, but the French clergy disagreed, choosing Robert of the Counts of Geneva to become the Antipope Clement VII (1378–1394) back in Avignon. At Urban's death, the Neapolitan Pietro Tomacelli, Boniface IX (1389–1404), took over as the pope of the 1390 Holy Year, adding the Madonna's main church, the basilica of Saint Mary Major, as the fourth place of worship to be visited for the indulgence. The four churches remained the pilgrims' goal thereafter.

The actions of European governments hampered the 1390 celebration. Kings took sides with either the Roman or the Avignon incumbents—England, Portugal, Poland, and part of Hungry agreeing with the pope of the Holy Year, while France and the kingdoms of Naples, Savoy, Castille, and Aragon in Spain backed the Avignon claimant, blocking the passage of pilgrims.

The 1390 jubilee was one of two for Boniface IX. In 1350 it had been decided that the spiritual celebration should be at the start and middle of centuries, so, despite a lapse of only ten years, he called for a 1400 Holy Year. It was tragic. Throngs of white-robed and hooded penitents, barefoot, carrying huge crosses and some bearing a crown of thorns, descended from Provence in France, often flagellating themselves until blood flowed. Filthy from the road, carrying no change of clothing, they fell ill of the black plague, spreading the disease. There were accounts of six hundred to eight hundred persons dying each day in Rome.

Urban VI had explained the 1390 Holy Year as a commemoration of the thirty-three years of Christ's life, even though more than thirty-three years had elapsed since the celebration of 1390, so, in 1423, thirty-three years after the first Boniface IX Holy Year, the Roman Oddone Colonna, Martin V (1417–1431), announced the fifth jubilee.

For the first time, use was made of a "holy door," a wall opening in the basilica of Saint John Lateran through which pilgrims entered for the jubilee visit. Symbolizing an entry into purification, opened at the start and closed at the finish of the year, the "door" had no hinges but was merely a temporary penetration of the church wall. It was an innovation soon imitated in all four of the Holy Year basilicas as a principal jubilee ritual, with the pope presiding at Saint Peter's, using hammer and trowel. As the pontiff taps three times with an ornate hammer, the previously prepared opening falls clear, and the pope is the first to enter. A year later the pontiff lays the first bricks for the resealing. It is a ceremony now nearly a half millennium old that TV watchers around the world will see on their home screens in 2000.

Because of another onslaught of the plague, Martin V shortened church services and cut back on the number of church visits required for the indulgence. At the 1450 Holy Year, returning to the fifty-year cycle, Nicholas V (1447–1455), the northern Italian Tomasso Parentucelli, adjusted the number of visits required to the four basilicas. Although Romans were still held to the requirement of a month of visits and other Italians to fifteen, eight now sufficed for those from beyond the Alps.

Again problems beset the celebration. Crowds exceeded those of 1300. Lodging was inadequate. Many had to sleep in the open. Some fell ill, some died. In November the Tiber, in our era well walled in, overflowed, causing injuries. Worst of all, on December 19 pilgrims returning from benediction in Saint Peter's were involved in a nightmare incident on the bridge in front of the Castel Sant' Angelo. Crowding was dense on what is still a narrow structure. A mule and four horses panicked, kicking wildly. Some pedestrians were thrown into the river. Two hundred died.

Paul II (1464–1471), the Venetian Pietro Barbo, established the present rhythm of a Holy Year every quarter of a century when he ordered the celebration of the 1475 jubilee, although he did not live to see it. Presiding instead was his successor, Sixtus IV (1471–1484), the northern Italian Francesco della Rovere. Like John Paul II, he was

Holy Year Door

an up-to-date man of innovations who made use of Gutenberg's then recent invention of movable type to print announcements of the jubilee. He relieved pressure on the Ponte Sant'Angelo, the jinxed bridge of 1450, by adding a new structure downstream, now named for him, the Ponte Sisto. In a city swarming with such artists as Luca Signorelli, Perugino, Ghirlandaio, Verrocchio, and Botticelli, he made another central addition to Rome's patrimony, also bearing his name, the Sistine Chapel, a mecca now for art lovers as well as the place where generations of popes have been elected.

The 1475 jubilee was yet another with troubles. Wars among France, Spain, Germany, and Hungary blocked the way for many who might have come. Turkish and Saracen pirates infested the sea. An autumn cloudburst caused Tiber floods and a new epidemic.

Fifteen hundred was the Holy Year of Alexander VI (1492–1503), the Spanish Rodrigo Borgia. Borrowing from the example of the 1423 Holy Year at Saint John Lateran, Alexander ordered that a special jubilee entranceway, a "holy door," be opened and at year's end closed in all four jubilee basilicas, a practice followed ever since. Using a golden hammer, now in the Louvre in Paris, Alexander read a prayer in Latin: *"Aperite mihi portas justitiae. Introibo ad domum tuam, Domine. Aperite mihi portas, quoniam nobiscum Deus."* (Open to me the door of justice. I will enter your house, O Lord. Open the door because God is with us.)

Mindful of pilgrim perils on the highways and seas, the Borgia pope threatened to excommunicate local authorities who did not combat brigandage, and stationed warships along the Tyrrhenian Sea to do battle with pirates.

The Holy Year of 1525 saw relatively few pilgrims, but Clement VII (1523–1534), Giulio de' Medici, persisted with it. The Europe of the Middle Ages was changing rapidly. Martin Luther had launched the Protestant Reformation. Henry VIII of England had broken with Rome. Turkish Muslims swarming north through the Balkans were near Hungary. Roman residents were unruly. Pope Clement attempted to deal with one problem by granting the indulgence to pilgrims who were unable to make it all the way to Rome or who died after arrival. As for Romans abusing pilgrims who did reach the city, the pope as the civil ruler of the community promulgated fines, confiscations, floggings, and even long confinements in the papal state jails. It was a low point for the Church-governed state, and two years later was lower still. Fourteen thousand mercenary troops from Germany sacked the Eternal City, and Clement VII fled for safety into Castel Sant'Angelo, which had entered history as the tomb of Emperor Hadrian (117–138).

The pope of the 1550 Holy Year was the Roman Giovanni Maria Ciocchi del Monte, Julius III (1550–1555). Unabashed by the woes of Clement VII, he was hard at work with the help of the omnicompetent Michelangelo in putting to rights what the invaders of 1527 had damaged. He and Michelangelo were also pressing ahead with the rebuilding of Saint Peter's Basilica, replacing the decayed 1,200-year-old structure of Constantine. As a side job, Michelangelo was redesigning the top of the Capitoline hill in the form it has now.

Clement tackled the usual lodging crisis by blocking rentals for the year and, to protect residents from profiteering landlords, forbade evictions. To fight a food shortage he imported extra grain from Spain. Feeding stations were set up for poor pilgrims, and a special indulgence was granted to sailors who rid the Tyrrhenian Sea of Dragut, a notorious Barbary corsair.

The story is told that Michelangelo decided to seek the indulgence. Worn out at seventy-six, he was in no condition to walk barefoot to the Holy Year churches, as thousands had done before him; the pope assured him it was all right to go on horseback.

The jubilee of 1575 had special importance. The split in Christendom that had occurred just after the start of the second millennium, when the Orthodox Church separated from Rome, was duplicated now, with Protestantism victorious in much of northern Europe. Ugo Buoncompagni of Bologna was Pope Gregory XIII (1572–1585), a take-charge person who gave the world its present calendar. The ecumenical council of Trent, Italy, had launched a Catholic Counter-Reformation, reestablishing ascetic values undermined by Borgia scandals. Clement urged rulers of states still friendly to the papacy to make the Holy Year pilgrimage. The number of churches to be visited rose temporarily to seven, the then traditional four plus Santa Croce in Gerusalemme (Holy Cross in Jerusalem), San Lorenzo fuori le Mura (Saint Lawrence Outside the Walls), and San Sebastiano on the Appian Way. In line with revived austerity, carnival festivals were prohibited.

Participation was strong; some four hundred thousand of the faithful arrived from the far parts of Italy and from France, Spain, Germany, and Hungary. Again there were problems. Rainstorms were frequent, and the plague broke out in Trent and in Sicily. Gregory closed some gates in the third-century walls so that plague bearers could be kept out of the old city.

With the new scientific and democratic world of the printing press, astronomic discoveries, and overseas explorations in collision with some of the traditions of the medieval past, the Holy Year of 1600, summoned by the Florentine Ippolito Aldobrandini, Clement VIII (1592–1605), was marred by an event still causing repercussions. Giordano Bruno, a Dominican friar, accused of revolutionary religious and philosophical ideas, had been jailed for seven years in

Venice and had been brought to Rome to be tried for heresy by the Inquisition. Found guilty, at age fifty-two, he was burned at the stake on February 17 in Rome's Campo de' Fiori (the Field of Flowers).

One of Rome's liveliest and most pleasant plazas, filled with flowers, open-air markets, and delightful sidewalk eating places, and a few yards from where Julius Caesar was stabbed to death, the Campo de' Fiori has been dominated since 1887 by a heroic bronze statue of the hooded Bruno. The monument was erected by anticlericals and was used by Communists after World War II as a rallying place. Bruno's story so upset Morris West, the best-selling Australian Catholic novelist and a former monk, that he wrote a play about it. It may have been one of the episodes of Holy Year history that Pope John Paul II had in mind when he proposed as a year 2000 theme that apologies be made for many past actions of Church leaders. The pontiff specified that both anti-Semitism and the Inquisition be restudied in an effort to set straight the historical record and to seek social reconciliations at the start of the third millennium.

Clement VIII labored to make the Holy Year an edifying experience. He visited the traditional four basilicas repeatedly, walked barefoot in processions like others of the faithful, washed the feet of pilgrims as Christ humbly had done for his disciples, invited twelve of the visitors each day to dine with him, paid visits to the sick, and heard confessions.

Maffeo Barberini of Florence, as Pope Urban VIII (1623–1644), was the host of the 1625 Holy Year. With a great Tiber flood again blocking the way to the Pauline basilica, he substituted the church of Santa Maria in Trastevere as one of the Holy Year four, thus increasing to eight the number of places of worship that have had jubilee honors.

Urban added an indulgence, granting it to those who would couple the customary visits to the four churches with prayers at each of them for European peace; France, England, the republic of Venice, and the kingdom of Savoy were at war with Spain and Austria. Thought was also given to those who could not get to Rome—the old, the ill, those in jail, and the monks and nuns in cloisters. The indulgence was extended to each of them. For those reaching Rome, however, conditions were not easy. Thirty sets of visits to the four churches were required.

The 1650 jubilee of the Roman Giovambattista Pamphili, Innocent X (1644–1655), came in an era when Saint Peter's cupola was illuminated for the first time, a dramatic bit of nighttime magic now a commonplace of after-dark Rome. For the jubilee, the architect Francesco Borromini redid the Constantinian basilica of Saint John Lateran in its present Baroque form. Attendance was measured at seven hundred thousand.

The Holy Year of 1675, inducted by the Roman Emilio Altieri, Clement X (1670–1676), drew 1,400,000 persons. Prominent at many ceremonies was Christina, a former queen of Sweden and a convert from Protestantism to Catholicism. Wool blankets showed up on charity beds for the first time. With nations across Europe aware of the health problems that had beset earlier participants, on hand were twenty hospitals, set up variously by the English, Scots, Bohemians, Hungarians, Flemish, and Portuguese, some of them still ready for service in 2000.

Bullfights in the Colosseum were banned. Partly in memory of a pious activist, one Almachius, who had been killed while trying to stop bloody shows inside the old structure of Vespasian and Titus, the Colosseum was consecrated to the cult of the martyrs.

The 1700 jubilee was the first with two popes, Antonio Pignatelli of southern Italy, Innocent XII (1691–1700), to start it and, after his death in September, Giovanni Francesco Albani of central Italy, Clement XI (1700–1721), to close Saint Peter's holy door.

Rome by then had a population of 135,000, a mere remnant of the million at the time of the Caesars, but an improvement over the scant 15,000 at the heart of the Middle Ages. Six percent of the population were clergy: 8,327 priests, members of religious orders and monks, including forty-two bishops. Innocent forbade nepotism in the assignment of Church offices, opened the original papal palace at Saint John Lateran's to house those unable to work, and, as in 1625, had to use Santa Maria in Trastevere as a Holy Year church because of more flooding at Saint Paul's. Innocent ordered streets to be cleared of litter, especially those leading to the jubilee churches. Marble plaques threatening punishment for dumping garbage in the streets, signed by a monsignor, are still to be seen on walls near the Piazza di Spagna, the Spanish Plaza, hard by the office of American Express.

Benedict XIV, Prospero Lambertini of Bologna (1740–1758), was the pope of the 1750 Holy Year. An ascetic person, he prepared for it with a personal ten-day spiritual retreat. The year focused in good part on the preaching of two clerics who were later canonized, Alphonsus Liguori in the Naples area, who received Benedict XIV's permission to found the Redemptorist Order, and a Franciscan friar, Leonard of Port Maurice, who brought throngs to tears in Piazza Navona, in Piazza Santa Maria sopra Minerva next to the Pantheon, and in the square in front of Santa Maria in Trastevere.

The Holy Year of 1775 saw the papacy on the threshold of one of its most diminished periods. Within a century, the thousand-year-old central Italian papal kingdom with the pope both its spiritual ruler and its temporal sovereign would be suppressed, and, for an additional seventy years, each successive pontiff would pass the whole of his reign as a voluntary prisoner inside the Vatican.

The 1775 jubilee was summoned by Giovanni Vincenzo Antonio Garganelli of Rimini, Clement XIV (1769–1774). He died on the eve of the jubilee, but, before he did so, he abolished the two-century-old Jesuit Order, which, by then, administered the greater share of Catholic higher educational institutions. Fellow sovereigns, including those of Portugal, France, and Naples, complaining that the Jesuits were exercising too much political power, had insisted on the suppression, and, in 1773, Clement had complied. The Jesuits, stripped of their organization, became simple disunited diocesan priests, and the general of the order, Father Ricci, pleading innocence during his few remaining years, was jailed in Castel Sant'Angelo.

There were repercussions even in the young United States of America. The Jesuit Father John Carroll, a native of Prince George's County in Maryland, on the outskirts of the present Washington, D.C., and a member of a family of patriots who gave signers to both the Declaration of Independence and the Constitution, had been one of those who had accompanied Benjamin Franklin north in the 1770s in an unsuccessful effort to bring Canada into the Revolution. Dismissed from his order but still a priest, Father Carroll, at Franklin's urging to the papacy, became the first American Catholic bishop, founding in 1793 the first American Catholic college, Georgetown, in Washington.

Not until a half century later, after the fall of Napoleon, did the Vatican revive the Jesuits, but it was too late by then for Archbishop Carroll. Georgetown, however, with a Foreign Service School supplying staffs to American embassies, its law school producing judges for courtrooms, and its school of arts and sciences contributing William Jefferson Clinton to the presidency, is back as a premier Jesuit institution.

With Clement dead in 1774, Giannangelo Braschi, of Ravenna, Pius VI (1775–1799), opened Saint Peter's holy door, launching a 1775 jubilee attended by only three hundred thousand. Again there was the sight of some barefoot pilgrims carrying great crosses to the basilicas and the spectacle of the fountains of Rome gushing wine rather than water on the day when the pope, on horseback, took symbolic possession of Saint John Lateran in his role as "the supreme priest and the venerable visible head of the Church."

The turn of the century for the first time in half a millennium saw no Holy Year. Barnaba Chiramonti, Pius VII (1800–1823), was pope. With Clement under arrest in revolutionary France, Italy had broken up into a cluster of republics, one of them in Rome. To meet the spiritual needs of the faithful, Pius assigned a two-week summertime period during which an indulgence was offered under certain pious conditions but with no need to visit Rome.

Pius was another jailed by France's Corsican emperor. He suffered five years of internment in Italy and France. With the French defeat at Waterloo, he regained civil control of much of the old papal states, but, within decades, that was to be gone again forever.

Annibale Sermattei of the Counts of Genga in southern Italy, Leo XII (1823–1829), was the pope of the 1825 Holy Year, the last in a century to be celebrated in full traditional form. In his bull of May 27, 1824, Pius urged the faithful to come for "a year of expiation, of pardon, of redemption, of grace, of remission and indulgence." Come, he said, to "this Holy Jerusalem, this royal priestly city which has become the capital of the world as the sacred see of Blessed Peter," a place whose "soil, walls, monuments, churches, sepulchers of martyrs and everything else inspire souls with the sense of the sacred."

The centuries-long effort to keep unruly locals from interfering with a spirit of prayer was renewed. Barriers were placed at hostelries, often the scene of unseemly language and even of occasional knifings, so that no wine could be consumed on the premises but had to be taken out. Preaching was arranged for plazas during the first half of August and singing, dancing, and loud talk by young people were forbidden at such times. Modest dress was decreed for women. Repairs were made on the Colosseum and the Forum's Arch of Titus. Distantly reminiscent of the captives of the conquering emperors, the notorious gang of kidnappers of Giovan Battista Gasparone were marched in chains to the Castel Sant'Angelo prison.

Two plotters against papal temporal sovereignty were hanged. Many nobles, friends of church-state unity, came, but there was a notable paucity of representation of the emerging democratic middle class.

Giovanni Maria Mastai Ferretti of Senigallia, Italy, Pius IX (1846–1878), the last of the papal kings, called for no Holy Year in 1850. Revolutionaries in 1848 had besieged him in the Quirinal Palace and had announced the establishment once again of a Roman republic. Rescued in 1850 by French and Bourbon troops, the pope eschewed a regular Holy Year, granting indulgences instead during a three-week summer period for those participating in specified novenas and other church services.

Pius summoned an ecumenical council, the first in three hundred years and the last until that of Pope John XXIII in the 1960s. The council rallied behind him, asserting a new dogma that popes are infallible when speaking ex cathedra, from Peter's chair, on matters of faith and morals.

It was a suddenly interrupted concilior meeting. Midway, the

The Tomb of Saint Peter

troops of the red-shirted Garibaldi and of the Savoy king, Victor Emmanuel, marched into Rome as the creators of united modern Italy. Pius IX withdrew into the Vatican Palace as a voluntary prisoner as did all of his successors until 1929; Popes Leo XIII, Saint Pius X, and Benedict XV up to Pius XI stayed there for the duration of their pontificates. Election in the cardinals' conclave meant life in confinement.

Pius IX served longer than any other pope, thirty-two years, and was succeeded by another pontiff of long service, Gioacchino Pecci of Anagni, Italy, Leo XIII (1878–1903). As a fifteen-year-old seminarian, Gioacchino Pecci had been invited to read a greeting in Latin to Leo XII in the 1825 Holy Year, so, perhaps with that still in mind three-quarters of a century later, the Vatican Palace internee called for a 1900 Holy Year. There were no outdoor ceremonies. Some 350,000 persons came. There was an indulgence for Romans who prayed at the four basilicas twenty times and for out-of-city visitors who performed the exercise ten times. No longer confined to making their way on foot, many of the year 1900 pilgrims hopped streetcars or hailed buggies. The newly installed royal government took a hands-off but faintly benign attitude, although foes of church political power organized a commemoration of the three-hundredth anniversary of the burning of Friar Bruno, and one group called for visits to the "four laic basilicas—the Pantheon, where the assassinated Savoy King Umberto was now buried; the Janiculum hill, with its great statue of Garibaldi; the Porta Pia, where the king's troops entered through the Aurelian wall in 1870; and the Capitoline hill, where the Rome municipal government now has its offices. Among the year's pilgrims was a seminarian from Sotto il Monte, the genial John XXIII of 1958–1963.

The Holy Year of 1925 drew a half million participants, no longer just Europeans but even Australians, Argentines, Africans, and Asians. The pope was Achille Ratti of Desio in northern Italy, the former cardinal of Milan, Pius XI (1922–1939). Still a prisoner in the Vatican after three generations, he took office and summoned a Holy Year at a time when a consensus was developing that something had to be done about the split loyalties of the peninsula, all its citizens subjects of the Savoy king and virtually all of them, including members of the royal family, Catholic.

New and old were intermingled in the year's celebration. The hammer used to tap on Saint Peter's holy door was a work of art, ivory and gold studded with rubies and emeralds. Electric lights illuminated the basilica dome at night. Ordinances were put into effect against those who disturbed the religious atmosphere by foul speech or immorality, although this time it was the new civil authorities and not the papacy who imposed the restrictions. A huge cross that had been removed from the Colosseum after the Savoy victory was reinstalled, and fourteen stations of the cross, places of prayer commemorating Christ's ascent to Calvary, also were placed in the ancient arena. From April to July, there were many beatifications and canonizations, men and women of recent times raised to the church altars as blesseds and saints.

Within twenty-four months of the end of the Holy Year and in a new political climate, secret talks began between the Vatican and the by then Fascist government of Italy, culminating in 1929 in a treaty ending the state-church standoff. Signed at the old papal palace at Saint John Lateran's, it involved mutual concessions. The pope renounced all claims on a broad, earthly kingdom and Italy agreed that a 105-acre State of Vatican City, with a few additions, including the Holy Year basilicas and the pope's hilltop summer residence east of Rome at Castel Gandolfo, should be a miniature country of its own with a right to negotiate internationally, receive its own corps of diplomats, issue its own postage stamps, and even coin its own money. Gone were the days when the Roman popes filled the civic vacuum left by the departure of the emperors, but in exchange the popes were left free, without the seductive and compromising need for their own tax collectors, police, and prisons, to devote themselves wholly to matters spiritual.

The pope of the 1950 Holy Year was the Roman Eugenio Pacelli, Pius XII (1939–1958). A member of an old papal state family, his grandfather had been minister of the interior for Pius IX prior to 1870. Trained as a Vatican diplomat, he had served as nuncio to Munich and as Pius IX's secretary of state. The Holy Year was again a mixture of new and old. The slender pontiff was carried on the shoulders of footmen in the *sedia gestatoria,* the last of the popes so treated. (The pope of 2000 will use a specially built Jeep.) At the same time the Vatican's own up-to-date radio transmitter, designed by the wireless inventor Guglielmo Marconi, gave instant reports of the jubilee events to audiences far beyond Italy.

For the first time, two hundred news reporters and photographers, perched on the steps of a huge temporary stand in the porch of Saint Peter's, watched as the pope hammered the signal to the San Pietrini, the Vatican's labor force, behind the "door," that they should pull down the already largely severed barrier. Such intimate media coverage was new; it had been only twenty-six years since a young priest on the Vatican staff, the future Cardinal Francis Spellman of New York and a graduate of the Jesuit Fordham University, had made the revolutionary suggestion that the Holy See have a press office.

Pius XII suppressed the earlier requirement that foreigners make fifteen visits to each of the four jubilee basilicas and that Romans perform thirty. Once, he said, would suffice to receive "a full indulgence and a pardon for all punishment due to sin" on condition that the petitioner confess his sins, receive Communion, and, at each church, recite once the Apostles' Creed. and four times the Lord's Prayer, the Hail Mary, and the "Glory be to the Father, Son, and Holy Spirit," one of the four in behalf of the pontiff's special intentions.

Europe was still recovering from the devastations of World War II, but there was a distribution of 1,100,000 pilgrim passes providing for reduced rates on many services. Group pilgrimages arrived with the leader bearing a tall bare cross. Among the first to come in the chilly days of late winter was one led by the same Cardinal Spellman—men in neat, conservative dress and many women in fur coats. Side by side with the cross bearer was a husky New York policeman holding aloft the United States flag. It was one of the first times in the jubilee and certainly the last that a national emblem was carried through the holy doorway. The basilica's forceful administrator, Monsignor Ludwig Kaas, the former head of the German Catholic political party, announced the very next day that no more national emblems would be tolerated inside Saint Peter's.

Airlines responded to the needs of the midcentury pilgrims. Trans World Airlines boosted its New York–Rome service to sixty a week. Air France went up from three times a week to daily flights. Inside Rome, a Vatican agency, the Peregrinatio Romana ad Petri Sedem, the Roman organization for pilgrimages to the see of Peter, set up campsites and other reception centers with a five-thousand-person capacity. Again there were many canonizations and, in addition, a rare phenomenon, the proclamation of a new dogma, an essential article of belief, that the Virgin Mary was assumed bodily into heaven just as was Christ. Hundreds of bishops attended as the pope made the declaration. The names of each are inscribed now on marble tablets just inside the basilica entrance. In the last act of the jubilee year, on Christmas Day, Pius XII extended the grant of the indulgence to all Catholics across the world for the duration of 1951.

The twenty-fifth in the Holy Year series was in 1975, with Giovanni Battista Montini of Brescia, Italy, presiding as Paul VI (1963–1978). Son of a Catholic political leader, Father Montini, as spiritual adviser to the young members of the Catholic Action organization, had helped form a number of the prime ministers and cabinet members of post–World War II Italy. Paul VI used the jubilee to attempt to restore interfaith relations with the Orthodox and with Anglicans and Lutherans and other Protestants and to create them afresh with Shintoists, Buddhists, and other non-Christian faiths. He used an encyclical, *Populorum progressio* (the Progress of Peoples), to urge more sharing between rich and poor nations. An unprecedented ten million pilgrims arrived, including two thousand Gypsies, to whom the polyglot pope spoke a few words in the Gypsies' own language. There were six canonizations and thirteen beatifications, and crowds of one hundred thousand were a commonplace at regular Wednesday papal audiences. An estimated 350,000,000 watched Holy Year events on television. It was a new chapter in the two-thousand-year story going back to popes Melchiadus and Silvestro and to Peter.

It was a long step toward even further innovations in the jubilee of 2000.

CHAPTER 2

JUBILEE 2000

TENS OF MILLIONS of pilgrims and tourists are expected to visit the Eternal City for ceremonies beginning on Christmas Eve with the solemn opening of the holy doors in the basilicas of Saint Peter, Saint Paul, Saint John Lateran, and Saint Mary Major.

During the year, participants will descend beneath the Roman terrain to pray in the same catacombs where the first Christians worshiped and, after the martyrdom of many of them, were buried. They will explore churches seventeen centuries old and will take part in ceremonies raising new blesseds and saints to the altars of the Catholic Church. Penitents will seek special graces that for seven hundred years others before them have sought at the tombs of Saints Peter and Paul.

Immense preparations began for the jubilee in the middle 1990s, spurred in part by a warning from the much-traveled papal nuncio and initial director of the Holy See program, Archbishop Sergio Sebastiani, that, so far as housing, buses, parking spaces for vehicles, rest rooms, first aid arrangements, and other basic facilities needed for the awaited influx, Rome was "a second class city." The Italian government budgeted millions of dollars for a score of municipal improvements, including the widening of the highway from Leonardo da Vinci international airport.

Nine or ten huge events are expected to attract at least half a million participants, while a couple of them are counted on to draw one million. There will be rallies, beatification of new blesseds, canonizations of saints, musical and theatrical performances, and unprecedented interfaith celebrations.

As the final years of preparation began, the one remaining inhibiting factor in setting some of the dates was the health of Pope John Paul II, the tireless promoter of ambitious plans for what he called "the Great Jubilee." As Elena Bartoli, the director of the Jesuit Order's visitor center at 8 Borgo Santo Spirito, pointed out, the universal desire of Holy Year pilgrims will be to see the pope presiding at a great majority of the year's ceremonies, and "his health has been shaken badly."

Considered by some of his fellow churchmen as the greatest pope of the fifty since 1500 and, without compare, the most traveled of the 264 pontiffs of history, John Paul II nonetheless would be eighty in 2000, suffering from the effects of a failed assassination attempt, repeated surgeries, and what Vatican staffers called "pyramidal" difficulties, accumulating disabilities possibly including Parkinson's disease. Bent forward, hands trembling, tiring easily and preferring in off hours to revert to his native Polish rather than use Italian or any other language, the pope, nevertheless, was determined, if possible, to live through the Great Jubilee experience.

Raymond Flynn, Boston's former mayor and President Clinton's first ambassador to the Holy See, a strong admirer of the pontiff and one who knew him from shared journeys, was certain of John Paul II's keen desire to share in the Holy Year. "A difference between him and our politicians," Flynn said, is that "even when people agree with our political figures they don't respect them, while even people who don't agree with the pope do respect him." Regardless of John Paul II's longevity, Flynn added, based on his observations of the Holy See as the American envoy, "Though we may not know who will be the players, we do know they will field a good team." For himself, he would be back for the Holy Year, the retiring ambassador added.

Put differently by Mrs. Bartoli, should a new pope be in office in 2000, a change such as happened both in 1700 and in 1775, more papally presided events will be possible. Even so, much of the year 2000 program was clear many months in advance. In addition to opening Saint Peter's holy door, the pontiff of the final days of 1999 will ring a gigantic new jubilee bell, designed by the sculptor Angelo Marinelli and cast in the thousand-year-old Fondaria Marinelli in the small Apennine city of Agnone in Italy's Molise district, the oldest such bell-making factory in the world.

One of the events expected to attract one million participants will be a youth rally in late June at the Sanctuary of Divine Love on the Via Ardeatina just outside the automobile beltway and seven miles south of the center. Dating from 1744, the church honors Mary as the protector of Rome and houses a fresco of the Madonna that is popularly considered miraculous. Special ceremonies are held at the shrine every spring on Pentecost Monday.

The youth rally will occur at a time of mild weather, one of the pleasantest periods of the Roman year. The plan is to have an evening mass celebrated by the pope with the throng of young men and women camping overnight in the ample surrounding fields. A second papal mass at 9:00 or 9:30 next morning will close the meeting. Based on the programs of previous such assemblies and at preparatory meetings at which John Paul II presided, it will be no surprise to observe rap singers performing original pieces on religious themes, television stars explaining their personal faiths, dancers and sports figures demonstrating their skills, all of it against a backdrop of exhibits on interreligious themes.

The assembly will be the thirteenth in a series begun in Rome in 1987 by John Paul II in line with his pontificate's constant concern with what church officials lament as "youth in an ethically neutral society." The pontiff followed the initial meeting with attendance at six others: Buenos Aires in 1987, Santiago de Campostela in Spain in 1989, Czestochowa in Poland in 1991, Denver in 1993, Manila in 1995, and Paris in 1997. Hundreds of thousands of youths took part in each.

Ambassador Flynn has a vivid memory of the rally in Denver. A drive-by shooting was in the news, distressing the pope. "Have American youths changed?" he asked Flynn.

"Not at all, it was an aberration," the ambassador sought to assure him.

Six hundred and fifty thousand well-behaved boys and girls with slim pocketbooks took part, troubling shopkeepers who had hoped for more business. Quipped one, "They came with a ten dollar bill and the Ten Commandments and didn't break any of them."

"You were right," the delighted pope told the ambassador as the two flew back to the Vatican.

Addressing a crowd of youth estimated at close to one million at the Paris rally, the pontiff reminded them of the Holy Year rendezvous. "We'll meet in Rome," he said. "I am sure you will be numerous at that extraordinary meeting. In the course of the Great Jubilee of 2000 we will live together an experience of spiritual communion which certainly will make a mark on your lives. "*Chi vivra, vedra,*" the pope added in an Italian expression meaning "Those who live to see it, will see it."

Calculating that one person in one thousand in huge gatherings needs some medical attention, and remembering two births at one of the earlier rallies, organizers of the youth event were busy round-ing up at least one thousand health workers to provide first aid and even more serious medical support. Other immense events will in-clude those for families, for the unemployed, for workers, and for people in military service.

Among other plans are these:

• A two-day January conference of members of various national legislatures on how the international debts of underdeveloped coun-tries can be canceled or at least reduced, a goal John Paul II has set for the jubilee.

• The fifth in an annual series of meetings bringing together as many as possible of the 261,000 parish priests of the world and of the 142,000 others who are members of orders such as the Francis-cans, the Dominicans, the Benedictines, and the Jesuits. Sponsored by the Vatican's Congregation of the Clergy, the first assembly was in Fatima in Portugal in 1996, followed the next years in the Ivory Coast in Africa, Guadalupe in Mexico, and Jerusalem in 1999.

• Already determined will be repeated events focused on those who have dedicated their lives to the service of the Church: a mass ordination of bishops on January 6; a jubilee on February 2 for those in the consecrated religious life; a jubilee on February 20 for deacons who have made a permanent commitment; another on February 22 for members of the Roman curia, the pope's immediate staff; a May 18 jubilee for all the clergy; and an October 8 jubilee for bishops, with an emphasis on Mary's role in the Church.

• An international Eucharistic Congress, in the June 18–25 pe-riod, the first since one in Bratislava in 1997 and the forty-seventh since Maria Tamisier, a thirty-seven-year-old French woman, ob-tained the approval of Pope Leo XIII for the one in Lille, France, in 1881. The meetings focus on worship of the Eucharist as the body and blood of Christ but also include discussions of the practical ap-plication of religious values to civil life. An Italian national eucharis-tic congress convinced the country's Catholics in 1895 to end a twenty-five-year boycott of political life, and one in Bologna in 1997 prepared the way for the Holy Year by a discussion of youth prob-lems, social justice, bioethics, and the relationship between philoso-phy and theology.

• A conference on science and religion, set for September 10, to be attended by seven thousand priests, teachers, and professors from both Catholic and secular universities. Overseeing the event will be Cardinal Pio Laghi, the Holy See representative in Washington during the 1980s and the head of the congregation for worldwide Catholic education since 1990.

• A series of cultural events, with a display of new works of art and music emphasizing religious themes.

Beyond that, there will be already scheduled special celebrations for almost all aspects of society. (See also the Calendar of Events, pp. 199–200.)

• January 2 will be Children's Day.
• January 9 will see a mass baptism of infants.
• On January 18 there will be an ecumenical service aimed at closer relations between the Orthodox, the Anglicans, and Protestants.
• February 11 will be the day for the ill and for doctors, nurses, and other health care workers.
• March 20 will be for practitioners of the various workaday crafts; plumbers, carpenters, masons can all expect a welcome.
• March 25 will be women's day, with an emphasis on Mary.
• April 10 will focus on migrants and refugees.
• May 1, May Day, which often saw Communist parades in postwar Europe, will be dedicated to all working people.
• May 25 will welcome scientists, a group often seen in the nineteenth century as skeptics about religion.
• June 4 will be for journalists, a group often treated with suspicion at the Vatican, until the time of John XXIII.
• On July 9 there will be services for convicts in prisons.
• September 17 will focus on the elderly.
• October 3 has been set aside for a dialogue between Jews and Christians.
• Families and marriages will be the center of attention on October 14–15.
• Mission work will be the October 20–22 theme.
• Athletes and others of the world of sports will have October 29 as their day.
• Public officials will follow on November 5.
• Farmers will be honored on November 12.
• Soldiers and policemen will be saluted on November 19.
• Laymen will have their jubilee November 24–26.

- Entertainers of the world will be welcomed December 17.
- The "year" will begin on Christmas Eve of 1999 and end on January 6 of 2001, the holy doors opened at the start and sealed at the finish.

Just as in earlier Holy Years, there will be beatifications and canonizations, but, extraordinarily, this time several popes may be among the new blesseds and saints. Though the Catholic Church considers all but three of the first fifty-seven popes from Peter to Saint Silverio in 536–537 to have been saints, only six pontiffs since the 1300 Holy Year have been raised to the altars, Blessed Innocent XI (1676–1689) and Saint Pius X (1903–1914) the most recent.

Under lively consideration at the four-century-old Congregation for the Cause of Saints are Popes Pius XII (1939–1956), John XXIII (1956–1963), and Paul VI (1963–1978), with some mention also of Pius IX (1846–1878), the last civil sovereign of the vanished papal states.

Pius XII, trained as a Vatican diplomat, steered the Catholic Church in Europe through World War II. A theme of his pontificate was that science and religion were compatible. While many Jews were hidden from the Nazis in Catholic institutions in Rome, the pontiff drew postwar criticism from those who felt he could have done more to oppose the Jewish Holocaust.

John XXIII, a humble peasant from the Italian Alpine foothills, was known in his lifetime as "Good Pope John" and was aware of it. When the writer of a *Reader's Digest* article so entitled presented an album of round-the-world editions repeating the thought in a dozen languages, Pope John handed it back to a monsignor behind him, saying, "Hold on to it; I'll have a better look later," and then told his visitor, "You're a writer. If on your last day you can say you have always served what is true, you will be able to die happily."

Paul VI, a strong defender of the church's stand against contraception, was a tireless worker to bring people of all faiths and of none together. Even without further action the church already lists Paul as a Servant of God.

Collection boxes placed in recent years at the tombs of Pius XII and John XXIII on the lower level of Saint Peter's Basilica are a measure of how far in advance the preparations for some of the papal beatifications have been made. Heavy expenses are involved in the meticulous investigation into the lives of the altar candidates and into miracles attributed to them, so visitors are invited to help with the cost. There has been no such box at the tomb of Paul VI, but funds have been raised in his home area of Brescia in northern Italy.

By 1997, Edith Stein, a Jewish woman who became a Carmelite nun and was killed in 1942 in an Auschwitz gas chamber, was listed as a certainty for Holy Year or even earlier canonization. Church officials were satisfied that at least one miracle took place through her influence.

Mother Katherine Drexel, a Philadelphia nun, is one American expected to be given altar honors in 2000 and, if so, large pilgrimages from the United States are expected for the occasion.

Among others under accelerated study in the late 1990s at the Congregation for Saints and a strong possibility for 2000 is a Capuchin monk, Padre Pio da Pietrelcina, of San Giovanni Rotondo, in the heel of the Italian boot. Barely literate, for fifty years he displayed wounds resembling those of the crucified Christ, the stigmata. He was sought out as confessor by thousands, including, in 1947, the then recently ordained Karol Wojtyla. By 1997, a long step toward beatification was taken when the Vatican concluded that Padre Pio was a person of heroic virtues. Throngs from throughout Italy made pilgrimages to the friar during his lifetime, some visitors even convinced that the priest had the miraculous power of bilocation. An illustration of the appeal of Padre Pio was a sermon one Sunday morning in Montelepre, the Sicilian home village of Salvatore Giuliano, Italy's most notorious postwar brigand, slayer of one hundred policemen and soldiers. "If you people would just make it up to this communion rail, it would do you even more good than going off all the way to Padre Pio," the exasperated priest told the bandit's family members and accomplices. Padre Pio died in 1968.

Although virgin lives dedicated to God's service have been among church ideals since the time of Saint Paul, a married couple are two others who may be lifted jointly to the altars in 2000. It will not be wholly unprecedented, for Aquilan and Priscilla have long been considered saints for risking their lives to help Saint Paul in the first century, but similar cases since then have been rare. An ardent beatifier and canonizer who proclaimed 757 blesseds and 277 saints in his first eighteen years in the papacy, John Paul II said, at the end of the International Year for the Family in 1994, that he hoped to see a husband and wife so honored by the time of the Holy Year. The two being considered are Luigi Beltrame Quattrochi, of Catania, Sicily, who served as vice attorney general of Italy, and Maria Corsini, of Florence, a writer and educator. They married in 1905, when he was twenty and she a year older. The couple had four children. A large collection of letters survives; the letters, according to Cardinal Camillo Ruini, the vicar general of Rome, establish that "the history of grace of the one spouse finished with identifying itself in very high percentage with the history of grace of the other." That conclusion meant a long step toward beatification of the couple.

Monsignor Josemaria Escrivá de Balaquer (1902–1975), the priest-founder of Opus Dei, God's Work, an association of dedicated lay persons living in the general society, is another possible Holy Year honoree.

Mother Teresa, the Nobel prize–winning angel of the Calcutta gutters, is mentioned prominently in the official jubilee announcements of the Holy See, where she has been described as "a person of extraordinary charisma, an exceptional witness of Christ's love," but a mere three years after her 1997 death is considered a very short time for what is usually a lengthy process. Christopher Columbus was under consideration for centuries after the Congregation for Saints was established in 1588, although favorable action never was taken in his case.

Among candidates for beatification whose cases are still in an early stage and considered premature for the millennium jubilee is a monk, Savonarola, who died at the stake as a heretic on May 23, 1498. Dominican friars in Florence are pressing his case.

Also on the schedule for 2000 in Rome and across Europe are proud and hopeful ordinations of many new priests, some of them graduates of the North American College, who are destined to work in the parishes, colleges and, in some cases, eventually, the bishoprics of the United States. A significant number of those ordained will be African. After a low point in the 1970–1975 period, when a decline of 17.6 percent in vocations to the Catholic priesthood was listed in the *Annuario Statistico della Chiesa,* the official Church record, there has been a rebound, especially in Southeast Asia, where the number rose 152.5 percent by 1994; in South America, where the rise was 253.3 percent, and in Africa, with a striking expansion of 393.5 percent. By 1995, the number of seminarians worldwide was an impressive 105,075, but Church worries continued with regard to the reduced number of seminarians and clergy in Europe, the United States, Canada, and even in almost totally Catholic Italy. In Europe, from 1978 to 1995, the number of Catholic priests declined from 251,033 to 217,275, a shrinkage of 13.45 percent, while in Italy the fall-off was 10.98 percent. A measure of what the church saw as the Italian problem was provided by a poll of 1,500 teenagers at the time of the 1997 national eucharistic congress in Bologna. Only two-thirds of the youths in the street called themselves Catholic and of them merely 40 percent regularly attended Sunday mass. Three-quarters had no belief in an afterlife.

Cultural events have been assembled by Archbishop Francesco Marchisano of Turin, the head of both Vatican departments concerned with antiquity and the arts: the Pontifical Commission for Sacred Archaeology, which Pius IX set up in 1852 to take care of the catacombs and Rome's oldest churches, and the Pontifical Commission for the Cultural Patrimony of the Church, a 1993 creation of John Paul II with the double competence of preserving all art works and archives in the Vatican's possession while encouraging religious values in all the areas of art—painting, sculpture, music, the theater, radio, television, motion pictures, and the printed word.

Among exhibitions will be one on Boniface XIII and the Holy Year of 1300. Another will feature the pilgrimages of the Middle Ages. A third will focus on religious art.

A competition for new spiritually oriented works in art, literature, music, theater, and cinema was launched. It was the hope of Archbishop Marchisano's committee that each would produce "at least one significant work as a Jubilee gift to Rome and humanity." Hundreds of projects promptly were proposed. Guidelines were clear. In Archbishop Marchisano's view, "Contemporary art suffers from the disorientation of Western civilization." The art he sought would "get away from subjectivism," returning to an earlier vision of the fine arts and "speaking a more understandable language." Works chosen would "document the spiritual." Theatrical works performed as part of the year's program would be those that "direct souls to noble moral values." Sponsored television scripts would help "those who seek God and will not promote moral disorder and the rejection of religion." As for new music introduced into ceremonies of worship, none would be accepted that were "pantheistic," seeing God in the various aspects of nature. One idea under consideration was

Saint Mary Major

to award an "Oscar of the Church" for the best spiritual film. Promoting the idea was Father Hank Hoekstra, a Carmelite, president of OCIC, the international Catholic cinema organization.

The usual Roman year includes a weekly appearance of the pope at noon on Sunday mornings, when a maroon cloth is lowered as a signal from the window of his apartment toward the right end of the top floor of the Vatican Palace. Scores of thousands crowd the plaza, listening through loudspeakers to a brief spiritual address from the

pontiff and holding up rosaries and medals for the blessing with which he closes. The prayers of the Angelus are recited. The huge plaza has space for tens of thousands; no tickets are required. On Wednesdays, there is a general audience attended by similar thousands, for which tickets are needed. For the Holy Year, an expansion of papal appearances is planned, with the pontiff appearing at his apartment each evening to bless the expected crowds. The exception will be on the few days of the pope's absence from Rome.

As much as possible of the usual practice can be expected. Few moments of the year will be without interest. Alongside the special jubilee activities, there will be the customary calendar of church events, many of them centered on Saint Peter's: Epiphany, celebrated on January 2; Ash Wednesday, on March 8, and the forty days of Lent; Holy Week, beginning April 17, in which it has been a papal custom to wash the feet of twelve seminarians in a service at Saint John Lateran on Holy Thursday; Good Friday, when popes often in the past have carried a great wooden cross at the Colosseum; Easter Sunday, April 23, with a great celebration at Saint Peter's; Pentecost, on June 11; June 29, when Romans enjoy a great holiday in honor of Saints Peter and Paul; August 6, the feast of the Transfiguration; August 15, *Ferragosto*, the Italian feast of August and the Catholic feast of Mary's Assumption into Heaven (the day when every Roman who can afford it heads for the beaches of the Tyrrhenian or Adriatic seas or for the Apennines or the Dolomites, leaving Rome to the shopkeepers, restaurateurs and visitors); December 8, the Feast of the Immaculate Conception, when it has been a papal custom to pray beside the 1856 column and statue in honor of the Virgin in Piazza di Spagna; and the days of Advent, which begins December 3, followed by the Christmas celebration of December 25.

For those hoping to avoid great crowds, the chilly but snowless days of January and February are usually among the quieter. Huge crowds can be expected from March through June, especially in Holy Week and at Easter. July and August will see some thinning out of the local population, but, coinciding with vacations, expected throngs will encounter painful moments in the stifling heat of the streets. The thick walls of the churches as a defense against the sun's rays and the cool depths of the catacombs, however, will provide some respite. With September, workaday Rome will revive, and October, with the *Ottobrate,* the bright, clear days of Rome's version of Indian summer, can be counted on to provide some of the most radiant and pleasant periods of the year.

The pope can be expected to be in Rome most of the year as the pilgrims' most sought-after personality, but John Paul II added to the agenda at least one trip out of the city, a brief journey to the Middle East. If it could be arranged he would like to have a religious summit on Mount Sinai with leaders of the Jewish and Muslim faiths at the place where Moses received the Ten Commandments from God. From there the pontiff would like to travel the "road to

Damascus," where Saul, the persecutor of Christians, had a mystical experience that converted him into Paul, the phenomenally effective Apostle to the Greeks, to other Gentiles, and to the hundreds of millions of Christians today. A visit to the biblical Holy Land would fit naturally into the parameters the innovative John Paul II set for his Great Jubilee. No longer centered on Rome alone, the year and its graces will focus also on the Holy Land and on every local diocese around the world as well.

Three great issues faced the Holy Year planners as the final months of the twentieth century passed. Should a new dogma be added to the Catholic faith, that Mary was the co-redeemer of mankind? How intimately will Protestants, Orthodox, Jews, Muslims, and those of other great faiths and of none be involved in the year's ceremonies? What place will there be for a commemoration of the many new martyrs, Catholic and Protestant alike, who died in the tumultuous century just ending?

Urging the year 2000 proclaiming of the dogma of Mary as co-redeemer of mankind is an American group, Vox Populi Mariae Mediatricis. With their help and that of others, more than 4,300,000 signatures from 157 countries and all continents except Antarctica have been collected urging the pope affirm infallibly that Mary, who has already long been venerated in such great churches as Notre Dame in Paris, the Hagia Sophia in Constantinople/Istanbul, and Saint Mary Major in Rome, is the Co-Redemptrix, Mediatrix of all Graces and Advocate for the People of God.

Cardinal John O'Connor of New York and forty-one other cardinals as well as the late Mother Teresa supported the appeal, but it was rejected unanimously by twenty-three Mariologists, experts on Mary, who were assigned by the pope to study the suggestion. Opponents of the idea said that Catholics would be puzzled about whether the Trinity had been expanded to include Mary and that Protestants and Orthodox would have problems with an invocation of infallibility implying that Christ's death on the cross was not a sufficient act of Redemption. Church theologians have found references to Mary as Mediator as far back as the fourteenth century but not before that. Benedict XV, the pope of World War I, and Pius XI, who succeeded him, spoke of Mary the co-Redeemer, although Pius XII and Paul VI did not. The dogma declaration would be a major feature of the 2000 jubilee, but the likelihood of its occurring seemed to fade. Christ's mother, however, will be far from neglected. The March 25 day for women will focus upon her, and so will the international marialogical congress in the September 15–25 period and the bishops' day on October 8.

What does remain as one of the most interesting items of the Holy Year agenda is the effort to include some recognition of Christianity's new martyrs, Protestant, Orthodox, and Catholic alike, who died at the hands of Nazis, Communists, and others in the century now ending. John Paul II was determined to find a place in the calendar for them.

Even more dramatic would be joint ceremonies with Orthodox, Protestants, those of the other major faiths, and those with no religion. Vatican committees have been set up to accomplish all that.

CHAPTER 3

QUEST FOR UNITY

A CLIMACTIC EVENT of the 2000 jubilee, if the Holy See achieves the objective set by Pope John Paul II, will be "an all-Christian meeting to enable Christians to make a solemn public profession of their common faith in Jesus Christ and in the Most Holy Trinity."

The realization of a papal dream would be to have all three branches of Christianity "completely united" in 2000. Short of that distant goal, as he said in the apostolic letter of 1996, *Tertio Millennio Adveniente* (The Coming of the Third Millennium), it was his hope that the three be "at least much closer to overcoming the divisions of the second millenium." Christian interfaith discord, he added, was "a scandal to the world."

One reference to second millennium divisions was to 1054, when an argument over theological formulas severed relations between the Catholic and Orthodox churches, each of them tracing their faith to one of Emperor Constantine's two capitals, Rome, where his fourth-century reign began, and Constantinople/Istanbul, where it ended. Each branch of the common Christian faith in the eleventh century anathematized and excommunicated the other. A second reference was to Germany's Martin Luther, England's King Henry VIII, and other reformers creating Protestantism in the sixteenth century.

Beyond that, as it was expressed by Archbishop Sergio Sebastiani, the chairman of the Vatican Holy Year committee, the Holy See set about seeking contacts with the major non-Christian religions and with nonbelievers, "making known our sincere desire to share with them our joy at celebrating the two thousandth anniversary of the birth of Christ but also to persuade them that in certain aspects the events concern them." Only as the events of the year unfold will it be clear how successful the Herculean effort will be.

To make the try, Pope John Paul II set up a series of committees. Cardinal Edward Idris Cassidy, a native of Sydney, Australia; Bishop

Paul-Werner Scheele, of Wursberg, Germany; and the Italian monsignor Eleuterio Fortino, were assigned talks with the Orthodox, the
Anglicans, and the Protestants. They did not have to start from
scratch. Helping them were more than a third of a century of reconciliation talks going back to John XXIII. Two years into his pontificate, in 1960, he had created a Secretariat for Christian Union,
specifying that it should look both east and west, to the Orthodox
and to the Protestants. It served as a tentative reply to a 1937 Protestant move in the same direction taken with the formation of the
World Council of Churches.

Simultaneously with the establishment of the outreach secretariat, John summoned the Vatican II ecumenical council to open
church windows on a changed world. The thousands of Council Fathers from all continents and scores of nations followed John's lead,
issuing an open-armed decree called *De Oecume,* from the Greek
word *Oikoumenh,* meaning literally "the inhabited land," but, in a
broader sense, universality. Building on that, in 1967, John's successor, Paul VI, strengthened the unity secretariat, adding a new feature,
relations with the Jewish religion. John Paul II in 1988 took it all a
step further by elevating the secretariat to the Pontifical Council for
the Promotion of the Unity of Christians.

With the necessary Vatican organizations in place there were several decades of talks with Orthodox, Anglicans, Lutherans, Presbyterians, Baptists, Methodists, the Disciples of Christ, the Pentecostals,
the Evangelicals, the Waldensians, and other Christians. Playing a
central role was Pope John Paul II, by far the most traveled of the 264
popes of history and, in the view of some of his fellow churchmen,
the greatest of the fifty popes of the past five hundred years. He identified several major stumbling blocks, including his own official titles
as not just the Bishop of Rome, Archbishop of the Church's Province
of Rome, Primate of Italy, and Patriarch of the West but also Supreme Pontiff of the Universal Church, Successor of the Prince of
the Apostles, and the Vicar of Jesus Christ. The pope's further title,
"servant of the servants of God," suggested an answer to the con-
tested question of primacy, and, in an encyclical letter of May 30,
1995, *Ut Unum Sint* (That All May Be One), he appealed to non-
Catholic Christians to "rethink" with him the papal role as perhaps
"the first among equals" or, as in early Christian centuries, a unifier
and moderator where discord arises.

Evident in his journeys to many nations was the way bitter historic memories poison local Catholic, Protestant, and Orthodox relations, sometimes even to the extent of bloodshed. Apologies, he said, are often due on both sides and, to set the example, he listed nearly one hundred on the Catholic side: the burning of Giordano Bruno; misunderstanding of the reformer Martin Luther; the massacre of Huguenot Protestants beside the Louvre in Paris on August 24, 1572, for which an exultant Te Deum had been sung at the time; the condemnation of Galileo Galilei for saying correctly that it is the earth that goes around the sun and not vice versa; crimes committed by papally sponsored Crusaders in the twelfth and thirteenth centuries; participation in the African slave trade; sins of anti-Semitism; the mistreatment of Indian natives in America; the failure of so many Catholics in Germany to resist Hitler; and male domination of women.

Where the feminist issue was concerned, in a Church of all male priests, arrangements were made to add three women to the list of twenty-eight cardinals, archbishops, bishops, and male laity on the central Holy Year committee: Mother Giuseppina Fragasso, the president of the union of superiors of female religious orders; Professor Mary Ann Glendon of Harvard University; and Mrs. Marie-Ange Besson, an expert advisor to the Pontifical Council for Justice and Peace, the Holy See department cooperating with international efforts on behalf of human rights, assistance to labor, and religious liberty. The latter was set up on a tentative basis by Paul VI in 1967, was made permanent by him in 1976, and was then given an Apostolic Constitution by John Paul II in 1988.

Taking the question of mutual apologies a step further, John Paul II assigned one Holy Year committee member, Monsignor Rino Fischiella, to conduct a full-scale historic inquiry into two of the most controversial episodes of Church history, anti-Semitism and the Inquisition, which caused suffering and death for many. Results can be expected to be announced as part of the jubilee effort at reconciliation.

Unity talks with Protestants achieved broad concord on questions of public policy such as measures to promote justice and peace and to defend the environment. With many there was concurrence on baptism as a common bond. The Lord's Prayer was another. The United Baptists, Presbyterians, Methodists, and the Reformed Church had moderators or superintendents rather than bishops as their seniors, but the episcopacy claiming descent from Christ's

Apostles offered an additional tie to the Church of England, the world Anglican Communion, and the Orthodox. George Cary, the archbishop of Canterbury and primate of the Anglican Communion, made several trips to the papacy, on one occasion with his wife, Ellen, staying as the Vatican's guest at the Venerable English College, the seminary founded in 1579 to train new generations of Catholic priests for England after Henry VIII helped launch the separate Anglican communion. The conferees found many common points, but the Vatican balked at the ordination of women.

With the Orthodox Church and the Patriarchs of Istanbul/Constantinople and of Moscow, several decades of conferences and meetings resulted in the lifting of the nine-century-old anathemas. Paul VI and Patriarch Athenagoras of Constantinopole exchanged visits to one another's cities, worshiping together in one another's churches. For the first time since 1054 the pope was mentioned before the patriarch in a liturgy in the Istanbul cathedral, while the papacy was so pleased by Athenagoras' presence at a service in Saint Peter's that a marble plaque inscribed in Latin and Greek is now to be seen next to the holy door, commemorating the event as important history. The two churches took note that they had shared for a thousand years the same line of bishops dating back to the apostles and that they agreed on the faith pronouncements of the first seven ecumenical councils, including the first, which Emperor Constantine convened in Niceae, the council that produced the Nicene Creed, the basic statement of belief that is recited at Catholic masses. Not accepted by the Orthodox, however, and a continuing point of separation, are the subsequent councils, including the nineteenth, at Trent, after the start of the Protestant Reformation; the first Vatican Council of 1870, which proclaimed papal infallibility; and the councils in Saint Peter's, from 1962 to 1965, which gave significant impetus to the Holy See's outreach efforts.

There could be a basis for improved Catholic-Orthodox relations, John Paul II suggested in a meeting with Orthodox Serbs in the spring of 1997. Fratricidal conflict in a Yugoslavia made up of Orthodox Serbs, Catholic Croatians, and Muslims emphasized, he said, "the urgency of a real reconciliation among Catholics and Orthodox" to accomplish "a more perfect following of Christ, the Supreme Priest and the Sole Shepherd." Once again the pope underlined that Christ was the leader, not particular churchmen.

When it came time to restore Rome's Chapel of Redemptorist

Mater (Mother of the Redeemer), the pope chose Russian artists, calling them "a sign of what unites us, Rome, Moscow, and Constantinople, West and East," the same effort to be the church of Christ.

By mid-1998 partial progress on various of the objectives was reflected in the first announcement of Holy Year events. The Holy See specified:

• In the first month of the Holy Year, on January 18, during a week of prayer for Christian Unity there will be an "ecumenical service," Christians of various faiths joining in prayer with Catholics.

• On March 8, the Church in Rome will ask pardon for wrongs that various of its followers, including high officials, have committed across turbulent centuries.

• On March 25, Rome will salute "the dignity of women," with special mention of Mary as "the mother of God."

• On August 5, a suggestion made by Patriarch Bartholomew of Istanbul, a foremost leader of Orthodoxy, will be carried out in the form of a prayer vigil for the feast of Christ's Transfiguration, a hand outreached across the divide that has separated Catholicism and Orthodoxy for most of the second millennium.

As the countdown to 2000 continued, it was not yet clear how successful the Holy See would be in bringing together in Rome the leaders of other Christian churches, each in their own ecclesiastical robes, each loyal to their own time-honored traditions and the faith of their fathers. The blood of the martyrs was the seed of the early faith, as the third century theologian Quintus Septimius Florens Tertullianus (Tertullian) had observed. Why not recognize that the century just ending has been another era of martyrs, not just of Catholics but of other faiths? There was a bond of common suffering. The pope ordered for 2000 a new martyrology listing, if possible, every person, Catholic, Protestant, and Orthodox alike, slain for his faith in the century just ending.

CHAPTER 4

MARTYRS

ONE OR MORE of the most moving events in Rome during the Holy Year will be the celebration of the memory of Protestants and Orthodox as well as Catholics who died as martyrs to the Christian faith during the twentieth century. A great many will be victims of the Communists and Nazis in Eastern Europe and the Soviet Union, but others will be included from dozens of other countries on all five continents. The event will be held on May 7 in the Colosseum, a site tied from its earliest days in antiquity to human suffering.

These, said the pope, were "God's unknown soldiers," martyrs as deserving to be identified and honored as the early Christian saints to whom scores of Rome's basilicas and churches are dedicated. These "new martyrs," the pope said in repeated speeches, are "a light to the Church and humanity," a "community of saints" serving both as an inspiration and as a bridge, closing the gap between divided Christian churches.

"The community of the saints," the unity-seeking pontiff added as he summoned the jubilee observance, "is perhaps what is more convincing than anything else. It speaks with a louder voice than that of division."

As a part of the Holy Year committee the pope appointed a "commission for the new martyrs," assigning a bishop of Ukrainian ancestry to head it, Canadian-born Michael Hrynchyshyn, the spiritual overseer of the Ukrainian Catholic community in France. The bishop was taxed with the task of assembling for the Holy Year as complete as possible a catalogue of all who have been killed since 1900 because of their allegiance to Christ or to the Gospel values. More than forty countries were identified as centers of such persecution during the century, beginning in the first decades with the assault on the Armenians in the Middle East and continuing to the many slaughters in Algeria in the century's final years.

By early 1997, 3,200 files of martyrdom cases were already under study by Bishop Hrynchyshyn's staff. The world Union of Superiors General by itself assembled four hundred dossiers of European, Latin American, and African cases. "We already have a common martyrology" of Christians of many denominations," the commission was convinced.

Prompting the work was evidence of what happened in the Siberian gulags. In a place where evil seemed to have triumphed, Orthodox, Catholics and others separated by doctrinal differences were drawn together by a common hope in Christian salvation, Bishop Hrynchyshyn said. Hampering the study of what happened under Stalin was the ban forbidding the Orthodox Church to canonize Moscow's victims but, since 1990, the identification of martyr saints has begun in Moscow. Among a few quickly hailed as saints were Metropolitan Vladimir of Kiev, who was shot in 1918, and Metropolitan Veniamin of Saint Petersburg, who was executed in 1922 after a farcical trial. As the Vatican's catalogue of martyrs was assembled, the case of the two new Orthodox martyr-saints was noted.

Austria, Ukraine, Rumania, Greece, the Czech republic, Slovakia, Lithuania, and Spain, Mexico and Guatemala, Laos and Cambodia, Algeria and Central Africa all drew Vatican attention as the search for the names and stories of "the new martyrs" began. One of the first cases noted was that of seven French Trappist monks arrested at their monastery in Tibherine, Algeria, in the spring of 1996, held prisoner for a month, and then killed. The seven had been approached at Christmas in 1993 by an armed band demanding that they support the Muslim fundamentalist revolution against the secular government in Algiers, providing economic, logistical, and health support. The Benedictine-Cistercian oath the friars had taken committed them to remain for life in their monastery with friendship for all people, especially the poor. The seven were aware of what had happened in recent similar cases at brother monasteries. In Mokoto, in Zaire, the friars left, but those in Huambo and Bela Vista in Angola, in Butende in Uganda and in Banja Luka in Bosnia stayed firm. The seven refused to take sides in the civil war, agreed only to providing medical help inside their monastery, and decided that if the Algiers government expelled them they would not return to France but would wait out the Algerian war in adjacent largely Muslim Morocco pending a return to Tibherine.

Father Christian drafted a letter to Sayah Attiya, leader of the

Bernini's Baldachin

armed band, to explain the monks' refusal: "Brother, let me speak man to man, believer to believer. We cannot take sides. We are foreigners. We are monks, *ruhban.* That binds us to the choice God made for us, to live a life of prayer, a simple life, one of manual labor, hospitable to everyone, especially the poor. This was our free choice and binds us to the death. I do not think God wants us to die at your hands. We love everyone, you included. Forgive me for using my native tongue. May the one God guide all our lives. Amen." It made no difference.

Among the countries quickly answering the commission's appeal was Lithuania, asking canonization for three bishops, Matulionis, Borusevicius, and Reinys. Guatemala sent seventy names, but drafters of the catalogue sought further information to be sure that politics rather than persecution of the faith had not caused the killings.

The files in other Vatican sections provided material. An example was a list of slain Catholic missionaries. In the first months of 1997 alone, sixteen missionaries of the Church were killed in various parts of the world. In 1996 the toll was forty-six, of whom forty-one were slain in Africa. In 1995 the number was thirty-two. In 1994, in a Rwanda massacre, 248 persons were murdered, among them twenty-five missionaries. From 1964 to the first months of 1997, 594 Catholic missioners were killed.

Even before Pope John Paul II called for a general listing of twentieth-century martyrs, some dramatic cases had become known and had resulted in beatifications and canonizations. Between 1982 and 1996 John Paul II canonized one priest, Father Maximilian Kolbe, a Franciscan killed in Auschwitz in 1945, and beatified 266 of the twentieth-century martyrs. He beatified 218 who died in the Spanish civil war of the 1930s.

Many of those beatified were part of groups:

Seventeen sisters of Christian Doctrine of Mislata, several of them in their eighties, shot in Valencia, Spain, in 1936.

Fifty-one young seminarians of the Claretian Order shot with their superior elsewhere in Spain the same year.

Seventy-one Brothers of the Order of Saint John of God, most of them young, also shot in Spain in 1936.

Twenty-two priests and three of the laity shot in Mexico between 1926 and 1937.

Eight worker priests shot in Spain in 1936.

Twenty-six members of the Passionist Order of Daimiel, most of them young students, shot in Spain in 1936.

Bishops Diego Vantaja of Almeria, and Manuel Medina of Guadix, along with seven Brothers of the Christian Schools, murdered in Almeria, Spain, in 1936.

There were many widely differing individual cases:

Father Otto Neurerer, a parish pastor in the Tyrol, hanged by his feet, tortured and killed in the Buchenwald concentration camp in 1940.

Father Karl Leisner, a German, who was ordained secretly during six years in the Dachau death camp, dying of exhaustion just after the Allied liberation and after celebrating only one mass.

Isidoro Bakanja, a lay teacher of religion, tortured and killed in Zaire in 1909.

Peter To Riot, a lay catechist, father of a family, killed in Vunaiara, Papua, New Guinea, in 1945 by two Japanese soldiers.

Three virgins killed while resisting rape: Karolina Kozka, 17, in Wal Ruda, Poland, in 1914; Angelina Mesina, 16, in Orgosolo, Sardinia, in 1935; and Pierina Morosini, 26, in Bergamo, Italy, in 1957.

Father Maurice Tornay, a Swiss of the Great Saint Bernard monastery, killed as a missionary by local lamas in Tibet in 1949.

The catalogue of twentieth-century martyrs of many Christian faiths will take its place in Church annals alongside the *Depositio Martyrum* of 354, which chronicled third-century martyrdoms. It will serve as outreach to fellow Christians at the same time that the Vatican seeks to reach even beyond them to all the other great religions and to humanitarians of no religious allegiance.

CHAPTER 5

ALL MANKIND

THE MOST EXTRAORDINARY feature of the Great Jubilee of 2000 may be seen only in limited fashion in Rome. It will be the effort to bring together in a joint celebration of the two thousandth anniversary of Christ all the major religions of the world, those of the Jews, the Muslims, the Buddhists, the Hindus, and the African ancestor worshipers, and in addition the nonreligious friends of the environment and of international economic aid.

In the early stages of the Holy Year preparations, recognizing difficulties, a limited initial goal was set by Pope John Paul II, a Jewish-Muslim-papal summit meeting in 2000 at such places as Bethlehem, Jerusalem, and Mount Sinai, the site where Moses reported receiving from God the Ten Commandments as the proper standard for human behavior. Beyond that, local joint celebrations with those of other faiths or none also would be sought.

To make the arrangements with those of other faiths, Pope John Paul II assigned Bishop Michael Louis Fitzgerald, who was born in 1937 in Birmingham, England. Like the Australian Cardinal Cassidy who was working with the Anglicans, the Protestants, and the Orthodox, Bishop Fitzgerald had a head start. He was already a member of several interfaith Vatican sections dating from John XXIII and the hand of friendship that the Vatican II ecumenical council had extended to those outside the Catholic faith. He was secretary of the Pontifical Council for Interreligious Dialogue, a consultor of the Commission for Religious Relations with Hebrews, vice president of the Commission for Religious Relations with Muslims, and consultor for the Pontifical Council for Justice and Peace. All four had their origin in Pope John's Secretariat for Christian Union, which he founded on June 5, 1960, and which the Vatican Council adopted as one of its own instruments on January 14, 1963. With the death of Pope John in midcouncil in 1963 and the election of Pope Paul VI, the latter vastly expanded the effort to establish ties of friendship with others. In 1964 the new pope broadened the competency of John XXIII's Christian unity secretariat to enable it to seek cordial relations with other faiths. The council approved with its document *Nostra Aetate* (Our Age). John Paul II went further, setting up the interreligious dialogue council in 1988 as a unit of its own.

In similar fashion, Paul VI in 1967 expanded the Christian unity secretariat to include relations with Jews on matters of religion. That, too, in 1974 became a commission of its own, with the expressed aim of bringing other Christian faiths eventually into similar contact with leaders of the Jewish faith. Simultaneously, Paul VI created a like commission for Muslim contacts.

A pontifical commission for justice and peace to work with international organizations and others on questions of human rights was set up by Paul VI on a temporary basis in 1967, made permanent by the same pope in 1976, and then elevated to its present council status by John Paul II in 1988.

As he set about the task of bringing non-Christians into the Holy Year celebration, Bishop Fitzgerald commented in *Terzio Millennio,* the Holy See's magazine for the jubilee, that his assignment was twofold, first "to convince Christians of the value and indeed the necessity of this interreligious dimension of the Jubilee" and after that "to show people of other religions that they are concerned."

For Christians, the bishop drew on thoughts expressed by John Paul II in announcing the Holy Year: Christ is the Lord of history; the incarnate word fulfills the yearning expressed in all religions; Christ identified himself with all humans.

For non-Christians, Bishop Fitzgerald said, a different approach would have to be used. He outlined it: "Those who do not share the Christian belief in Jesus as Son of God, Lord and Savior, may yet be willing to join in the anniversary of a great spiritual leader.

"Or perhaps it may be possible to say to them: 'We Christians are celebrating the anniversary of the birth of Christ. We do not want to celebrate without you. Would you like to join us?' "

The bishop added: "The promotion of justice and peace is a task in which people of all religions should join. Some themes that could be studied together are: the use of the world's resources both from the point of view of respect for the environment and that of an equitable distribution of the world's goods; techniques for conflict resolution and the specific contributions of the religions for building up peace; respect for life; the rights of minorities."

To seek to arrange joint Holy Year events, Bishop Fitzgerald assembled five dossiers, one each on Jews, Muslims, Hindus, Buddhists, and African animists. Special attention was given to the Jews. John Paul II had set the tone in an April 13, 1986, address to the small Roman community inside the main synagogue in the onetime ghetto between the Capitoline Hill and the island in the Tiber. The pope said: "Jews and Christians are the trustees and witnesses of an ethic marked by the Ten Commandments, in the observance of which humanity finds its truth and freedom. To promote a common reflection and collaboration on this is one of the great duties of the hour. . . . The Jewish religion is not 'extrinsic' to us, but in a certain way 'intrinsic' to our own religion. With Judaism therefore we have a relationship which we do not have with any other religion."

In addressing the synagogue audience, the pope was speaking to a community with bitter memories reaching across two thousand years. One of the main Roman monuments surviving from antiquity is the arch of Emperor Titus in the Forum with friezes boasting of his sack of Jerusalem in A.D. 70, an event driving Jews into exile across Europe and into Rome itself. A more recent memory was of October 16, 1943, when 1,022 Jews were rounded up in the narrow streets just around the synagogue to be deported to the concentration camps, a disastrous blow to one of Europe's oldest Jewish settlements, a group well known in almost wholly Catholic Rome and Italy as a rare exception to Catholicism. How unusual it was came home to one foreign correspondent at the time of the 1938 census. Don Minifie, a Canadian Protestant, Rome bureau chief for the New York and Paris *Herald Tribune*, was asked whether he was Catholic. "No," he said.

"Ah, Jewish!"

"No."

"Forgive me, I thought you said you were not Catholic!"

Minifie explained about Protestants.

Although the Jewish presence in Rome was small, there was no doubt in the minds of a succession of late-twentieth-century popes that centuries of anti-Semitism loomed large as a problem for Christian consciences. By removing from the Holy Friday liturgy a reference to "perfidious Jews," John XXIII set in motion in the 1960s a Christian-Jewish dialogue that continued through the following decades, fostering Holy See hopes for some jubilee sessions in common.

Working from his dossier, Bishop Fitzgerald developed talking points for fellow negotiators: Jesus was born, lived, and died a Jew. The key concepts of his teaching cannot be understood apart from the Judaism of his time and apart from his Jewish heritage. Jesus loved the ancient Scripture and also the synagogue. Even after the Resurrection, Jesus' followers understood the "Christ Event" through essentially Jewish tradition and liturgy. The first Church members were Jewish Christians, even though Gentiles soon joined the expanding community.

According to the bishop's research there was little Jewish opposition to Jesus as a man during the first two centuries, hardening only in the third with Christian insistence on Christ's divinity. After several centuries of indifference, there was a change in Jewish attitudes after the year 1000 as persecutions against them mounted; they saw Christ as the fountainhead of their sorrows. The twelfth to the fourteenth centuries saw a further change, some Jewish sages perceiving Christ as a saint, helping "to prepare the whole world to venerate God in a heartfelt community." Since then, in the bishop's analysis, while declining to accept Christ as the Messiah, many Jews consider Jesus as an ethical and religious leader, a reformer and a man of faith.

In all the increasing documentation, the Vatican made a distinction between Jews and Hebrews, the latter seen as the followers of the old religion. Jews, considered as members of a racial group, were already members of the College of Cardinals and thus "papabili," potential popes. One was Jean-Marie Lustiger, the cardinal of Paris, a convert at fourteen, son of a mother killed in Auschwitz, and another was the son of a mixed marriage, William Wakefield Baum, of Kansas City, Missouri, the former Archbishop of Washington, D.C., and Apostolic Penitentiary of the Catholic Church, the supreme judge in matters of conscience. By mid-1998, enough progress had been made in the interfaith effort to announce an October 5 Holy Year date for a Jewish-Christian dialogue.

In jubilee-focused talks with both Hebrews and Muslims, Catholic representatives emphasized existing points of agreement, each worshiping the one God and all claiming Abraham as religious forefather. In approaches to Muslims, John Paul II summoned a synod of the Catholic bishops of Lebanon, a country recently torn by Christian-Muslim conflict. On December 14, 1995, the pope told the Lebanese episcopacy: "Because of the religious roots of the national and political identity of Lebanon, this assembly seemed appropriate after the sad period of war, a synod in which we could seek a renewal of faith, better collaboration and a more effective common witness in seeking the reconstruction of society." The pope added, "I am certain that my view of this is shared by our Christian brothers who do not belong to the Catholic Church and also by Muslims."

From his dossier on Mohammedanism, Bishop Fitzgerald drew several conclusions: The appeal to Muslims to join in the jubilee should concentrate at the outset on Christ's message and only later on his person and on "the mystery of Christ." The Koran speaks of "the Word" and "the Spirit that came down from God," but the broad thrust of the Muslim holy book is a denial of Christ's divinity. The Koran describes Christ's birth of the Virgin and hails him as a prophet, but one less than Mohammed. The Muslim holy book denies there was a Crucifixion, insisting that Christ was rescued from his pursuers and then rose to heaven.

To Catholics in areas of large Muslim populations, especially Indonesia, but also Malaysia, the southern Philippines, and parts of India, Bishop Fitzgerald's aides have recommended that invitations to share in the Holy Year activities emphasize that both religions share "a God of justice." The virtue of Islam, in the Muslim belief, is justice, these aides have advised.

In outlining the approach to Muslims, Bishop Fitzgerald's commission may also have kept in mind that Mohammedanism has become Italy's second religion. Ninety-eight percent of Italians consider themselves Catholic, but, thanks in large part to immigration from former French North Africa, Egypt, Senegal, Iran, and Iraq, there are now three hundred thousand Muslims in the country, fifty thousand to one hundred thousand of them served by five mosques in Rome.

Bishop Fitzgerald's dossier on the Hindus included these points: Only a few have become Catholics, but many have admired Christ, finding it easier to see him as God, as an example of full self-realization, the goal of Hindu dharma. What was harder for Hindus to believe was that Christ was a human being, a part of history, rather than an ideal. The dossier cited Mahatma Gandhi as a great admirer of Christ's teaching, especially the Sermon on the Mount.

To Catholics in predominantly Hindu and also Buddhist regions such as India, Sri Lanka, Thailand, Cambodia, Taiwan, and Japan, Bishop Fitzgerald's assistants advised that the emphasis in Holy Year discussions be on shared concepts of spirituality. They urged "stress on the notion of individual search for salvation, self-cultivation in the moral sense, in brief, the call to sanctify oneself and others." They added: "Meditation and sharing of mystical experiences could be used. All this, of course, should lead to involvement in justice issues in view of attaining peace for all." The identical approach, the commission suggested, could be used in those parts of Asia where the Sufi tradition influences Muslims.

In announcing the Holy Year, Pope John Paul II gave it as his opinion that both Hinduism and Buddhism have a "clearly soteriological character," each seeing salvation through Christ although in different ways Where Buddhism is concerned, Bishop Fitzgerald concluded, there is one fundamental difference not to be ignored in the search for a common jubilee observance: "They accept Jesus as a wise Master but not as a divine person." He added in his advice to Catholic conferees, "Buddha deliberately avoided talking about the existence or nonexistence of God, so it is obvious that Buddhists have a difficulty with the Christian faith in Jesus, Son of God, true God and true man."

Even so, he said, some Buddhists have shown a great interest in Jesus Christ. He cited a contemporary Japanese, Masao Abe, who took note of chapter two, verses five to eight, in Saint Paul's Epistle to the Philippians, in which the apostle spoke of Christ "emptying himself" of divinity to take on human form and suffering, a concept Masao Abe saw as a parallel to the self-emptying of Buddhist sunyata. Talks with Buddhists, the bishop suggested, might well emphasize self-abnegation with Christ as a bodhisattva, renouncing his own interests out of compassion for others. He noted that the Dalai Lama expressed appreciation of Christ's focus on other people.

A jubilee dialogue with the Buddhists was opened by Chiara Lubich, a consultant of the Pontifical Council for the Laity, an agency founded in 1967 by Paul VI. She met with the supreme patriarch of Thai Buddhism in January 1997 and lectured to young monks in Thailand's second city, Chiang Mai. Some Vatican staffers favored further contacts on a basis of monastery to monastery, Catholic monks on the one side, Buddhists on the other. Inside Italy itself there were 32,000 Buddhists by 1995, an increase of 7,000 in four years.

With regard to Japan and its many Shintoists and Buddhists, John Paul II made suggestions in a February 25, 1995, talk to Japanese Catholic bishops. The Catholic community, which traces from the 1549 arrival of the Jesuit missionary Saint Francis Xavier, has representatives now all through Japanese society, so that a dialogue with the other faiths on human life issues "springs naturally" from such contacts. The pope urged Tokyo's Cardinal Peter Seiichi Shirayanagi to seek interdenominational jubilee celebrations with other Japanese Christians and at the same time attempt dialogue with Japan's other great faiths.

Where Africa is concerned, Bishop Fitzgerald recommended to jubilee organizers that they build on widespread native ancestor worship, pointing out that Christ is the giver of life, as the Gospel of Saint John (10 : 10) expresses it, and thus "the ancestor par excellence."

In attempting to achieve such an unprecedented union of so many religions and so many peoples, the Vatican recognized key problems. Bishop Fitzgerald addressed one of them as a fear in much of Asia that the West and its culture might again be attempting to "colonize" the East with its ideas. In seeking cooperation with the Christian jubilee in Malaysia and in some other parts of Asia, especially in Turkey and India, the bishop said, "The idea of human dignity could be used." What was well to avoid, he said, was "the term 'human rights,' " since "many in East Asia think of human rights as culturally imposed by Westerners." Speaking of "human dignity," he continued, "leads inevitably to the rights of a person, of a community, and of a country" and avoids any misunderstanding to the effect "that Christianity is coming again in a different form to 'colonize' Eastern values."

Another concern of some Vatican theologians was that the effort to reach agreements with those of other faiths might lead to syncretism, the merging and lessening of faith. The Nigerian Cardinal Francis Arinze, president of the Pontifical Council for Interreligious Dialogue, warned that in talks with Muslims there should be no diminution in the faith in Christ as the sole Savior "yesterday, today and tomorrow." The Holy Year Pastoral Commission, headed by Ivory Coast Archbishop Bernard Agre, emphasized that the Incarnation, the divine Christ becoming man, "is not a myth or a legend (but) an historical and saving fact of which biblical and profane literature bears reliable witness." Bishop Michel Moutel, of Nevers, France, in February 1996, counseled French priests working on Holy Year plans that Christ must not be presented merely as "a prophet or great sage of humanity."

Cardinal Roger Etchegaray, the overall director for the jubilee, agreed that "Christianity obviously must preserve its own identity," stating that "Christ is the sole Savior" even though in interfaith dialogue respect for other religions is appropriate. Supporting him was the Vatican II Council document *Nostra Aetate,* which emphasized universal brotherhood. Monsignor Eleuterio Fortino, the vice president of the ecumenical commission for the Holy Year, agreed: "We will celebrate according to our ideas but that includes a strong ecumenical concept."

Bishop Fitzgerald summed it up: "There are many ways to come close to Christ. As Christians, we believe in Jesus as the Son of God, the Lord and Savior, and in our love for Him. It is that faith and that love that allows us to approach others. We must realize that, although these others do not believe in Christ and our commitment to Him, there is a part of the road they can travel with us. This impels us to invite them to join with us in celebrating the two thousandth anniversary of the birth of Christ."

Apart from the approaches to other religious faiths, one final item remained on John Paul II's agenda for 2000, cooperative ventures with those of all religions and of none in behalf of peace, justice, the protection of the environment, and economic aid to those in need. To arrange them, a commission on social issues was added to the Holy Year organization with an Irishman, Monsignor Diarmuid Martin of Dublin, as its president.

Never in the previous seven centuries of Holy Years had there been anything similar, but there were some precedents in the Church's recent past—the labor encyclicals of Popes Leo XIII and Pius XI, *Rerum Novarum* (Of New Things) and *Quadragesimo Anno* (On the Fortieth Anniversary). There was also Paul VI's Pontifical Council for Justice and Peace, with its assigned role to work with other groups, whether or not religious, to foster religious and other human rights, to work for justice and peace, and, especially, to lend support to "the world of labor." A Holy Year goal, Monsignor Martin said, will be "some form of debt cancellation, if only partial" to ease the economic burdens of the poorer nations, most of them in Africa. One form it could take, he indicated, was appeals from Catholic

Church leadership in the wealthier countries for forgiveness of all or part of their nation's loans to developing nations. He applauded London's Cardinal Basil Hume as one who has already done something similar. He was encouraged by signs that the World Bank and the International Monetary Fund "realize that a start must be made" with regard to monies owed to them.

Is this a question in which the Church should be involved? Why should an office of the Holy See speak on such technical, economic questions? This, said Monsignor Martin, was asked a decade ago when his pontifical commission published the document "At the Service of the Human Community: An Ethical Approach to the International Debt Question." That statement, he said, was in response to appeals from local hierarchies, many of them in Latin America. With the problem still unsolved, he said, it is especially appropriate to be addressed in a jubilee that traces its distant origin to the ancient Jewish fifty-year period of debt forgiveness described in Leviticus in the Old Testament.

The year 2000 visitors to Rome are likely to see only partial successes in the Holy See appeals for prayer services with Orthodox, Anglicans, and Protestants, conferences with youth, scholars, family members, and military personnel, joint celebrations with Jews, Muslims, Hindus, Buddhists, Shintoists, and those of other religions, and cooperative international efforts to relieve debt pressure on the world's poorest, but they are likely to take part in dramatic, however partial, activities in each.

Beyond that they will have the opportunity to pray in the same churches and catacombs where the first Roman Christians worshiped and gave their lives. They will be able to walk the same streets and see the same monuments that were there in the "year zero" of our era, when the Galilean carpenter took Mary to Bethlehem in response to the emperor's summons. They will enjoy an ancient city that has thrilled generations of poets. They will experience as well the modern life of a continental capital.

For pilgrim and tourist alike Rome in 2000 promises an experience to remember.

CHAPTER 6

SAINT PETER'S

THE COMMON GOAL of the many millions visiting Rome for the turning of the millenium and the year 2000 jubilee will be Saint Peter's.

Like all the millions who have preceded him for twenty centuries, the pilgrim of the Holy Year will embrace the opportunity to pray at the tomb of the Prince of the Apostles, the most important shrine dating from the Apostolic era. Like the especially numerous throngs that flocked to the Petrine area after Muslim control in the eighth century shut off pilgrimages to the Holy Land, those visiting Vatican Hill will see an enormous basilica, not the immense one of the eleven centuries from Emperor Constantine to the Renaissance but an even greater one erected on the same foundations in the 1500s and 1600s. Like the pilgrims of the first twenty-four Holy Years prior to the mid-twentieth century, the year 2000 visitor will see in Saint Peter's memorials of Peter and of popes of the intervening centuries. But the turn-of-the-millenium traveler will see even more.

For one thing, the ever-changing Saint Peter's now enshrines not only some of Christianity's most ancient memories but the stuff of yesterday's newspaper headlines and television broadcasts. There are many such examples:

Both Pius XII, the austere pope of World War II, and amiable John XXIII, without waiting for possible beatification in the year 2000, are already honored inside the great nave. The statue of Pius XII is on the right side of the nave, a few steps beyond Michelangelo's *Pietà*. Sculpted in bronze, it depicts the tall, slim, bespectacled pontiff of 1939–1958 with an expression of horror, his right arm twisted to the left as if to fend off evil. The reference is to the fruitless efforts he made during his first half year as pope to avoid the start of World War II. The statue is above the tomb of Blessed Innocent XI of 1676–1689, one of the few popes entombed in the basilica nave. Innocent, a campaigner for morality in public life, is remembered as a defender of Vienna in 1683, when the Turkish surge through the Balkans was arrested at the city's near approaches.

Pius, like John XXIII and Paul VI, all three potential Holy Year blesseds, is interred in a plain white marble sarcophagus in the grottoes below the nave floor. Pius XII is depicted also on the Holy Year door in the atrium. He is shown tapping open the door of the 1950 jubilee. Not shown on that panel are the dozens of reporters and cameramen who were perched on a small temporary grandstand just behind him as he rapped on the door. The ages-old arm's-length Vatican relationship with the media had been relaxed for the occasion, a prelude to the pontificate of John Paul II, who was to say in his era that "if it doesn't happen on television, it doesn't happen." Prominent on the same current holy door is a depiction of the Crucifixion, with the knees of Christ already burnished to gold after merely a few decades of caresses from worshipers.

John XXIII's monument is directly across the nave from that of Pius XII, just to the left of the chapel of the choir. It is a bronze plaque showing "good Pope John" visiting people in jail, one of the first things he did as Pius XII's successor in 1958. At his feet is a scrawny dog, his snout upraised in a gesture of appeal, a symbol of mankind's starvation for justice and peace.

Both Pius XII and John are commemorated more than once in the atrium. In the center of the pavement is John's coat of arms, with a tower as its centerpiece, a reminder that he called into being the modernizing ecumenical council, Vatican II of 1962–1965. John is depicted also on one of the five basilica doors, the "door of the dead," in a modern bronze work of Giacomo Manzu. The pontiff is shown opening Vatican II on October 11, 1962. The door is just to the left of the centerpiece, itself a fifteenth-century work, the sole such survivor from the first basilica.

On the atrium walls on marble slabs are the names of the hundreds of bishops who were present, lending implicit approval, when Pius XII invoked rarely used papal infallibility in the 1950 Holy Year to proclaim as a new dogma and required article of faith that Mary, like Christ, was assumed bodily into heaven.

Most important, the visitor of 2000 will be able to enter in Saint Peter's a crucial area no pilgrim saw across fifteen centuries, from the time of the construction of Constantine's basilica until after the first Holy Years of this century. It is the cemetery of about the time of the birth of Christ in which Peter is believed to have been buried.

Known as the Scavi (the Excavations), the ancient cemetery is two floors below the pavement of the nave. It can be visited by passing through the Vatican gardens entrance at the left of the basilica and going forward to a point midway on the side of the basilica. For those who have time, a visit to the *Scavi* is recommended.

The rediscovery of the cemetery under Saint Peter's was a 1939 accident. Pius XI, who had negotiated the reconstitution of a miniature independent papal state, had died in February 1939, and the

Saint Peter's

basilica laborers, the *sampietrini,* seeking a burial place, had punctured a hole in the side of the grotto. They found a wall of the ancient original basilica and asked the newly elected Pius XII for permission to explore further. Pledging that they would not damage the stability of the present basilica, the diggers were allowed to proceed. Removing hundreds of truckloads of earth from beneath the grotto, they made an astonishing discovery.

For centuries there had been a tradition that Peter had been crucified upside down next to Emperor Nero's stadium. A cruel despot who blamed the small newly arrived Christian colony as the arsonists who set the devastating fire of A.D. 74, Nero had used the stadium for the slaughter of the accused. These were some of the first Christian martyrs, Peter among them.

Roman custom forbade burial inside the city walls, so cemeteries, including catacombs, had sprung up outside the walls along such roads as the Appian Way and also across the Tiber, away from the left bank's seven hills. One such burial ground had developed beside a road running north from the Tiber's right bank through what is now Vatican City. It was within it that a small wall was constructed in the second century. Dated by the stamp of the current emperor on the bricks, the wall's apparent purpose was to protect the otherwise undistinguished area from Vatican Hill drainage. Subsequently small altarlike structures were added one atop the other, all still to be seen. Graffiti collected on the walls, including a reference to Peter. Tribute coins were dropped, there to remain for a millennium until *sampietrini* picked them up. Bone fragments were found, but the Vatican concluded that there was no way they could be identified as those of the Apostolic Prince to whom Christ gave heaven's keys.

What is certain is that Constantine, the first Christian emperor, gave his architects and engineers a startling assignment, to build a huge papal basilica with its high altar centered on the retaining wall and the little altars and to do this on the side of a hill and atop the burial chambers of many generations of pagan families and of a few Christians. The spot was the same one now just below the present basilica's high altar and directly under the center point of Michelangelo's dome.

To obey the emperor and create a level space, the builders of the first Saint Peter's had to gouge deeply into Vatican Hill on the one side while dumping an immense amount of fill on the east. The visitor can still see the builders' problem as he observes the tilt of the plaza and the steep staircase leading up to the basilica and the sharp rise of the Vatican gardens out beyond the structure.

The *Scavi* visitor can walk through the long-lost cemetery, peering into the ornately decorated burial chambers, most of them pagan, a few showing the signs of a burgeoning Christian faith. The second-century retaining wall is still struggling against the hillside drainage, but it is a battle hard to win. Beneath the spot a well still collects the oncoming flow.

One tomb inscription speaks of the incumbent resting near Nero's stadium, a support for the traditional belief, although all traces of the Neronian structure have long since vanished beneath Vatican pavements and buildings. The one surviving Neronian object is the first-century Egyptian obelisk that stood to the left of the basilica as the stadium centerpiece until 1585, when Pope Sixtus V moved it to its present position in the broad plaza in front of Saint Peter's.

Whether Peter lived and died in Rome as the imperial city's first bishop and as the initial pope, thus giving Christian leadership and authority to the succession of pontiffs, long has been a subject of interdenominational debate, but the *Scavi* visitor underneath the basilica will see that there could have been no more logical a place for the apostle's interment than just such a nearby cemetery.

The visit to Saint Peter's begins at the Tiber at the east end of the Via della Conciliazione—"Conciliation Street"—which the dictator Benito Mussolini carved out of a medieval neighborhood to celebrate the 1929 peace pact with the Holy See. That was the agreement ending the fifty-nine-year protest of the papacy over modern Italy's abolition of the thousand-year-old central Italian kingdom of the papal states. Pius XI agreed that popes should no longer rule the space between the Po Valley and Naples, and the Italian government recognized the independence of the Vatican entity.

The Vatican state henceforth had its own national identity, complete with freedom from Italian taxes; its own international passports, currency, and postage stamps; membership in the International Postal Union and other international organizations; its own diplomatic corps, eventually including an ambassador from the United States; its own foreign service, including a representative at the United Nations in New York City; its own little army, made up of Swiss Catholic volunteers from the German-speaking cantons; its own railroad station linked into the European rail network; its own helipad; its own radio transmitter; a national population of one thousand; and even its own pharmacy, supermarket, and gas station, all the latter with prices well below those in surrounding Rome.

Dominating the horizon as the visitor turns into the Via della Conciliazione is Saint Peter's Basilica, the world's largest church, with Michelangelo's dome soaring above it. It is an imposing sight that none of the Holy Year pilgrims prior to 1950 were able to enjoy. Their first glimpse of the dramatic structure was after they had wended their way through the narrow streets of the old Borgo neighborhood and finally entered the vast plaza embraced by the arms of Gianlorenzo Bernini's colonnades of 1656–1666. By then, with the basilica so close, Michelangelo's magnificent dome, designed for a church in the shape of a Greek cross with four naves of equal length, was hidden by the present vast facade of 1607–1614, the terminus of the structure's final Latin cross design.

Although they could not see the soaring summit of the basilica, the pilgrims since the eighteenth century were able to enjoy much of what the visitor of 2000 will see. Standing at the exit of Via della Conciliazione amid city buses, taxi stands, and horse-drawn carriages, the visitor is already in the aura of the Vatican. Although he is still on the soil of the Italian republic, he is in a plaza named for Pius XII, a space flanked on either side by matching structures housing many Holy See offices, including some for the Holy Year.

To reach the open frontier into the Vatican state one must cross a heavily traveled street to a line of white travertine paving stones connecting the tips of the Bernini colonnades. Except for crowd control barricades erected on busy days, there is no other indication that one is now a temporary immigrant into the pope's own country. The peaceful crossing is a far cry from World War II, when Axis personnel patrolled the border.

The great colonnades are the first to demand attention. They enclose a space 643 feet across at the widest point, large enough to hold a quarter of a million people and, on many occasions, including perhaps some in 2000, serving merely as the introduction to a throng of one million reaching the full length of Via della Conciliazione.

The colonnades consist of 284 columns, forty-eight feet tall. Lined four abreast and roofed over, they provide a welcome passageway and escape from the sizzling summer noontime sun. The perfect alignment of the twin semicircular structures can be tested on either side of the obelisk by standing on either of the two circular stone markers. The tangle of four columns, as you observe them, dissolve into one.

The 84-foot-tall, 312-ton granite obelisk is the object of a fanciful Roman tale. According to the yarn, Sixtus V was so worried when he ordered it moved from beside the sacristy and raised to its present prominent position that he threatened capital punishment for anyone who made a sound during the delicate raising of the shaft. A hundred men and fourteen oxen strained at the ropes, and a sailor in the crowd was appalled to see smoke curling from the strands. Unable to contain himself, he screamed a warning: *"Acqua alle funi!"* Water on the ropes! Buckets flew, the ropes were drenched, the obelisk rose, and the temerarious tar received a commendation.

Along the left side of the plaza are a cluster of Vatican facilities aimed to meet many tourist needs: a pilgrim and tourist information office, a gift shop, a money exchange center, one of the Vatican's three post offices, from which mail can be sent bearing the Holy See's own postage stamps, a medical first aid station, rest rooms, and a bus stop for rides through the Vatican gardens and to its museums. The bus ride can spare the visitor a quarter-mile walk around the outer walls of the little state to the main museum entrance on the north. Other rest rooms are across the plaza just beyond the Bernini colonnades.

From the plaza, directly ahead, high on the facade, is the balcony on which a newly elected pope appears for the first time, giving his blessing *"urbi et orbi"* (To the city of Rome and to the world). Nearby, not many steps away, to the right of Saint Peter's, is the Sistine Chapel, a rectangular building perched on a ledge of Vatican Hill, the place where the cardinals elect the head of the church.

Inside the atrium two equestrian statues on either side point up the extraordinary papal history, Constantine of the fourth century behind glass on the right and Charlemagne on the left. The millennium year will mark the precise twelfth centenary of Charlemagne's consecration as emperor at Saint Peter's, the first of twenty emperors to arrange for the same.

Inside Saint Peter's, on the right, the inevitable first stop for every visitor is the *Pietà,* one of the many extraordinary works of genius Michelangelo created for Vatican Hill. A remarkably youthful mother gazes with serene resignation at the dead young Redeemer held tenderly in her arms. Carved from a single block of marble in 1498–1499, when the sculptor was only twenty-four years old, the work bears his name chiseled along a ribbon running across the Madonna's body from the left shoulder, the only work the Renaissance master ever signed. A glass enclosure now protects the statuary group. It was placed there after a vandal used a hammer to attack the masterpiece in 1974. Skillful repairs conceal the damage.

The immensity of Saint Peter's is one's first impression. It covers a six-acre area. It has a visitor capacity of sixty thousand. How vast it is can be judged by the cherubs at the holy water fonts. Carved to match the basilica's dimensions, they are as bulky as fullbacks. Another way to estimate the structure's great size is to take note of the pavement plaques running down the center of the nave, comparing the length of the Petrine sanctuary with those of other great Christian edifices. Saint Peter's is 606 feet long, the length of two football fields. Saint Paul's in London comes nearest, with 514 feet. Then, in descending order, as marked in the pavement, come the Florence Duomo, Brussels's Sacred Heart of Jesus church, the National Shrine of the Immaculate Conception in Washington, D.C., the cathedrals of Rheims, Cologne, and Seville, Notre Dame in Paris, the basilica of Saint Paul's Outside the Walls in Rome, Saint Vitus cathedral in Prague, the primatial church of Toledo, Saint John Lateran in Rome, the cathedrals of Mexico City, Antwerp, and Esztergom in Hungary, Saint Mary of the Angels in Assisi, and the not very impressive 356-foot Santa Sophia in Constantinople, not much lengthier than a single football field. Santa Sophia, as marked on the floor, reaches from the rear of Saint Peter's just past the papal altar to the beginning of the nave. New York's Episcopal/Anglican Saint John the Divine, 602 feet, is not shown.

The floor plaques were the subject of an exchange in midcentury between two patriots whose countries had been on opposing sides in World War II, New York's Cardinal Francis J. Spellman and the supervisor of the *sampietrini* and basilica maintenance, Monsignor Ludwig Kaas. The monsignor had been the head of the Catholic political party in Germany until Hitler suppressed it.

"Where is Saint Patrick's?" the former shortstop of the Fordham College baseball team asked about his New York City cathedral.

"I know Americans pride yourselves on being always the biggest," was the casual response. "Saint Patrick's is not on the floor because it would be the smallest!"

"Monsignor," came the firm reply, "put it down."

It is there now to be seen, listed in Latin with "Neo Eboracen" for New York, a paltry 326 feet in length, the least shrine of all. A few feet shorter it would have vanished into the confession, the well in front of the papal altar and the place of reverence of Peter.

Much history has been made in Saint Peter's, and much of it is recorded inside the structure at every turn. Only two ecumenical councils, teaching assemblies of the church, have occurred in the past four centuries, both of them inside Saint Peter's. That of 1870, twentieth in the series and a rather restricted one, took place in the right transept, the right arm of the Latin cross. It proclaimed that the pope was infallible when speaking officially on questions of faith and morals. John's council, with more than two thousand bishops, theologians, and interfaith observers, was far greater in size, occupying two huge temporary grandstands along the length of the nave. One uncommon sight as the four-year council proceeded was a snack bar on the left in front of the Chapel of the Choir displaying a salesman's dream, a sign reading "Drink Coca-Cola."

Near what was the council's place for refreshments is a footnote to English royal history, a monument to the son and grandsons of the Stuart king, James III of 1633–1701, Britain's last Catholic monarch. The Stuart descendants and claimants to the British throne ended their days as exiles in Rome and are honored on the monument, James III (1688–1766) and his sons, Charles Edward (1720–1788) and Henry, Duke of York (1725–1805). Henry became a cardinal, the bishop of Frascati, Ostia, and Velletri in the Rome area and, after 1788, proclaimed himself King Henry IX of England, never, however, ascending the distant throne. The monument honoring the three was created by Antonio Canova in 1820. As a good sport and one seeking dynastic peace, Britain's King George III contributed to the cost of the monument.

At the far end of the nave, on the right side near the confession, is the most honored statue in the basilica, a thirteenth-century bronze showing Saint Peter as a seated, bearded figure beneath a halo, his left hand clutching the keys to the Kingdom, and his right raised in a two-fingered blessing. On June 29, the feast day of Peter and Paul, the statue is clothed in full papal vestments.

Entering the crossing, the pilgrims and tourists are at the heart of the basilica. In the center is the altar reserved for masses said by the pope. Raised above the level of the basilica pavement, it is centered on the Petrine memorial and is squarely beneath the towering dome. The altartop is a single marble slab once part of a first-century imperial forum. Hovering over the altar is the stupendous bronze canopy created in the seventeenth century by the 26-year-old Gianlorenzo Bernini. Tall as a five-story building, it would rate in any other setting as a dramatic structure of its own, but as it is, the baldachin is dwarfed by the Michelangelo dome above it, a "Pantheon sitting atop a Greek cross."

The dome, topped by a lantern, rises 335 feet above the basilica floor, the equivalent of a thirty-story building. The lantern, piercing the top of the dome, is fifty-eight feet tall, with God the Father shown in its ceiling with arms outstretched. Below the lantern there are six circles descending to the rim, the topmost depicting the first sixteen popes buried in the basilica; the second, Christ, Mary, John the Baptist, Paul, and the Twelve Apostles; and the lower four, a series of angels and cherubs in postures of worship. There are ninety-six figures in all. Encircling the rim, in letters five feet high, is a quotation in Latin from Matthew 16 : 17–19: "Thou art Peter and on this rock I will build my church and I will give unto thee the keys of the kingdom of heaven."

Supporting the dome are four huge pillars sixteen feet square depicting saints with relics of Christ's passion: the Roman centurion and later convert Saint Longings with the spearhead with which he pierced Christ's side; Saint Andrew, the brother of Peter; Saint Veronica with the veil with which she wiped Christ's face; and St. Helen, the mother of Constantine, with a fragment of Christ's cross that she brought back from the Holy Land. What are believed to be the actual relics are preserved in a recess at the Veronica statue and are displayed for veneration in Holy Week. Absent from them now is the head of Saint Andrew. Originally an object of Eastern Christian veneration, it was returned to the Orthodox diocese of Patras in 1963 as part of the effort to reunite Western and Eastern Christianity.

Prominent throughout the crossing and the two transepts are confessional boxes where pilgrims seeking the traditional Holy Year indulgence can make the required admission of sins. A red light burning at various of the confessionals is the indication that a confessor is inside. Each box lists the languages in which confessions can be heard. On a day chosen at random thirteen Franciscan, Carmelite, Jesuit, Servant of Mary, and Augustinian priests, many of them multilingual, were prepared to listen in Italian, French, English, Polish, German, Spanish, Slovene, Portuguese, Ukrainian, Czech, and Russian, in that descending order of frequency.

Saint Peter's abounds with fifty altars and 450 statues. Few visitors will have time to see it all, but in the nave, transepts, and apse they may note these:

• In the apse is the dramatic throne of Saint Peter in glory. It is a chair of bronze created by Bernini from 1658 to 1666. Supporting it are four doctors of the Church, great leaders of the Christian community, Saint John Chrysostom and Saint Athanasius for the East and Saint Ambrose and Saint Augustine for the West. Encased in the metalwork is a wooden chair said to have been used by Peter. It was a gift to Pope John VIII from Emperor Charles the Bald in 875.

• One hundred forty-seven popes and other eminent personalities are buried in Saint Peter's, almost all of them in the grotto beneath the nave floor and above the ancient cemetery. Two popes are an exception, Saint Pius X of 1904–1914 and Blessed Innocent XI of 1676–1689. Both are in the nave on the left side, Saint Pius X just forward of the tall Stuart memorial and Blessed Innocent a short distance further on beneath the altar of the Pius XII monument.

• Several Holy Year popes are honored. In addition to Pius XII of 1939–1958, there is a monument on the right side of the nave near the crossing recalling Gregory XIII, who walked barefoot to the jubilee churches in 1575, one to Urban VIII of the 1625 Holy Year, to the right of the Petrine chair in the apse, and one to Pius XI, the mountain-climbing pope of the 1925 Holy Year. This latter is near the tomb of Blessed Innocent XI. There is also a monument to a pope who had to forgo a jubilee, Pius VII of 1800, Napoleon's prisoner.

• Two popes called "the great" are memorialized, Saint Leo of 440–461, who dissuaded Attila the Hun from invading Italy, and Saint Gregory of 590–604, whose initiative in sending missionaries to England helped create a unified Western church. Leo is honored by a large seventeenth-century marble relief in the far left corner of the apse and Gregory in an altar on the left of the nave near the transept. Another Gregory, the thirteenth (1572–1585), is also commemorated. His monument is on the right of the nave just before the crossing. He was the pontiff who gave the world its present calendar. The monument shows the seated figure of the pope looking on as the goddess of knowledge uncovers an urn disclosing the length of each year.

• The place of greatest reverence is the sunken confession at the foot of the papal altar. Faced with multicolored marble and surrounded by seventy gilt oil lamps that never cease to burn, the well faces the site of the Petrine memorial and the successive altars raised over that spot by Gregory the Great, by Pope Calixtus of 1119–1124, and by the creator of the present high papal altar, Clement VII of the 1600 Holy Year.

Two sets of exits from the crossing lead to other major areas of interest. At the left of the crossing is the entrance to the basilica treasury. Looted by the Vandals in 455, the Saracens in 846, the Normans in 1084, the Spanish in 1527, and Napoleon in 1798, it nonetheless still has a nine-room exhibit of silver, gold, and jeweled religious articles of interest. A puzzle for the curators of the treasury for some time has been what do with a bust of himself that Lyndon Johnson bestowed on Paul VI.

The other twin exits are beside the statues of Saint Longinus and Saint Andrew in the crossing. They lead down to the grottoes, where there are the tombs of Pius XII, John XXIII, John Paul I (the pope of only one month, September 1963), Paul VI, and scores of other pontiffs, including the one Englishman, Nicholas Breakspear of the twelfth century. Part of Constantine's original basilica walls can be seen.

Just outside the grottoes' exit in a courtyard to the right of the basilica is the entrance to the rooftop of Saint Peter's and to the top of the dome. For those making the ascent, dramatic views are the reward. An elevator goes to the roof, where there is a gift shop, toilets, and a striking view down Via della Conciliation to Castel Sant'Angelo and the Tiber. From there a narrow, seemingly endless, sloping staircase with 332 steps opens into two successive walkways around the inside of the dome and, finally, to the outside base of the lantern. The first walkway is 160 feet above the basilica floor, shrinking people below to little more than specks. Acoustics are superb. A whisperer on one side of the railed-in void can be heard clearly at the opposite side. It is no place, however, for anyone suffering from vertigo, especially if he or she undertakes the four-hundred-foot walk around the inside of the shell. The immensity of the dimensions is indicated by the size of the nearby four evangelists, each of them twenty-six feet wide, and those of the angels in the dome mosaics, their arms yards long. For the adventurous there is a second walkway just under the ceiling, two hundred twenty feet above the floor.

Twisting up between the two shells of the dome, the climber goes out into an open-air walkway at the foot of the lantern. At a height of 394 feet above the ground, there is a magnificent panoramic view of all Rome.

Practical Information

The basilica is open daily from 7:00 A.M. to 7:00 P.M., April to September, and from 7:00 A.M. to 6:00 P.M., October to March. Proper dress is required—no short pants, miniskirts, undershirts, or similar ultra-casual attire. Guards in the atrium enforce the regulation. ATAC bus 64 goes to Saint Peter's.

The hours of the basilica are 9:00 A.M. to 6:00 P.M., April to September, and 9:00 A.M. to 5:00 P.M., October to March. There is a 5,000-lire admission charge.

Admission to the basilica grottoes is free of charge. The hours are 7:00 A.M. to 6:00 P.M. in summer and 7:00 A.M. to 5:30 P.M. in winter.

The dome is open from 8:00 A.M. to 6:15 P.M., April to September, and from 8:00 A.M. to 4:45 P.M., October to March. The entrance is from the hall of the basilica on the far right side of the church. The charge is 6,000 lire if the elevator is used, 5,000 lire for the climb on foot.

For a visit to the excavations under Saint Peter's, tickets are required. The phone number is (06) 698 85318. By mail, tickets may be obtained by writing to the Reverenda Fabbrica di San Pietro, Ufficio Scavi, 00120, Citta del Vaticano. Required is the number of persons in the party, the language spoken, the address and telephone number in Rome, and the dates of the visit. Multilingual guides lead the tours.

There is a free guided tour of Saint Peter's every afternoon at 3:00 and on Sundays at 2:30 P.M. It begins at the information desk to the right just inside the portico. It is a service instituted at the time of the 1975 Holy Year.

Masses are celebrated daily from 8:00 A.M. to 1:00 P.M. at the Blessed Sacrament chapel midway on the nave on the right, and also at the altar of Saint Piux X in the right center of the nave, in the left transept, and in chapels on either side of the high altar. Communion is distributed at the Blessed Sacrament altar from 6:30 A.M. to 1:30 P.M. on weekdays. There is a mass in Latin at 10:30 A.M. on Sunday.

Papal Audiences

The person every pilgrim wishes to see is the Holy Father. It is the custom for him to appear at noon on Sundays and on holy days at the window of his library in the papal palace, the building just beyond the colonnades on the right of Saint Peter's plaza. The pope's window is second from the right on the top floor.

The arrival of the pope is signaled at the window by the lowering of a maroon drape, as mentioned earlier. It is the custom for the pope to lead the recitation of the Angelus prayers, following that with a brief address carried over loudspeakers. In addition to the window appearances, it has been a recent papal custom to lead the recitation of the Rosary at the Vatican at 8:30 P.M. on the first Saturday of each month.

Admission to papal audiences and ceremonies is free of charge, but tickets are required. There are general audiences on Wednesdays at 10:30 A.M. in summer and 11:00 A.M. in fall and winter. Depending on the size of the crowd and weather conditions they are held either in Saint Peter's plaza or in the modern Paul VI Audience Hall, designed by Pier Luigi Nervi in 1971. The latter is at the southeast corner of the Vatican state to the left of Saint Peter's.

The audiences in the plaza seat twenty thousand. Tens of thousands more can stand, but the pontiff becomes a tiny figure. To meet the needs of the distant, it is the pope's custom to drive out toward them in a specially built jeep. On one such ride, John Paul II survived a gunshot attack, later visiting prison to express forgiveness to the would-be assassin. The audience hall has seats for 6,500 and provides for 4,000 standees. When the hall is used, it is wise to submit ticket requests early. Audiences generally last two hours, with the pope blessing the visitors and such religious articles as they carry. It is the pope's custom to address the throng in several languages, English among them. In addition to the weekly audiences, the pope also presides at liturgies on holy days, especially at Christmas, during Holy Week, and at Easter. Tickets for these special masses are also required.

An excellent source of tickets and also for information on papal appearances apart from Wednesdays and first Saturdays is the United States Bishops' Center for Visitors to the Vatican, where Monsignor Roger C. Roensch is director. He is the former pilgrimage director of the National Shrine of the Immaculate Conception in Washington, D.C. The center is in the graduate house of study for American priests, the North American College, at Via dell'Umilta 30, at the corner of Via dell'Archetto near the Trevi Fountain. To get special seating near the papal throne, a letter from one's pastor or, even better, from the local bishop is helpful. All members of the party need to be identified, and advance notice by letter or fax to Via Umilta 30, Rome, Italy 00187 is requested. The fax number is 011 396 679 1448 and the telephone 690 011.

Monsignor Roensch submits his requests to the Vatican a week before each papal event and receives the invitations, the *biglietti*, on the morning before the ceremony. Special seating is available, and there are places close to the papal throne reserved for newlyweds and those who are ill. Letters of introduction from local pastors or, even better, from bishops, are a help. Wheelchairs are given a space close to the pontiff, and, hard to believe, some able-bodied visitors, untroubled by scruples, have been known to hire chairs on wheels just to exploit that opportunity. For those such as choirs, orchestras, bands, and dance groups who wish to go beyond a merely silent audience participation, putting on a brief number of their own, there are provisions. They need to give the monsignor word in advance of what they propose. Tickets to the audiences can be picked up at the monsignor's office on Tuesdays between 2:00 P.M. and 7:30 P.M. on the day before the Wednesday audiences, or after 7:00 A.M. on the day itself. For those unable to meet the deadlines, the monsignor's staff will go the extra mile trying to help.

Other sources of tickets are these:

The American Catholic church of Santa Susanna at Via XX Settembre and Largo di Santa Susanna, telephone 488 27 48; or

The Jesuit Curia, Borgo Santo Spirito, 00193 Roma, near the plaza of Pius XII, telephone 678 58 00 (especially for those with Jesuit connections), and

The Prefettura della Casa Pontificia, Citta del Vaticano, 00120 Roma. A letter of introduction from the local Catholic diocesan chancery, sent two months in advance, is helpful. The Prefettura is just inside the Vatican bronze doors under the right colonnade in Saint Peter's Plaza. The office generally is open Tuesdays from 9:00 A.M. to 1:00 P.M. and on Wednesdays from 9:00 A.M. on. *Biglietti* are available there.

For audiences in the plaza during the warmer months, head covering against the unpitying sun is a necessity.

Photography is permitted, but flashes are discouraged close to the pope in the audience hall.

During the hotter summer months, the pope often helicopters from the Vatican gardens to his lakeside villa at Castel Gandolfo, sixteen miles south of Rome. When there, the pontiff speaks from a balcony on Sunday.

CHAPTER 7

VATICAN STATE

SAINT PETER'S is the centerpiece and reason for the existence of the independent kingdom of the state of Vatican City, but the minute papal nation, only 105 acres including Saint Peter's, would be worth a visit even if there were no basilica. Some of the greatest art of the Renaissance as well as sculpture treasures of antiquity and unique documentation of the Middle Ages are within its surrounding walls.

Tours of the state and its gardens are provided by the Vatican. They begin from the Pilgrim and Tourist Information Bureau on the left-hand side of Saint Peter's plaza, a few yards in front of the Swiss Guard post at the Arch of the Bells. An intimate look at the tiny world of the ecclesiastical state is provided.

The tours go through the Arch of the Bells, passing on the left a ninth-century cemetery, which is still in use. Swiss Guards were buried there after the troops of Emperor Charles V decimated their ranks in a 1527 attack. The guards' sacrifice gave Clement VII of 1523–1534 the time he needed to escape into Castel Sant'Angelo.

Also on the left is one of two national seminaries inside the state, this one devoted since the time of Pius IX to German-speaking clerics. The other, higher up the hill and also passed on the tour, serves Ethiopian students for the priesthood.

Opposite the rear of the basilica, also on the left, is a newly equipped structure to house cardinals at the time of papal elections. No longer will they have to endure the harsh temporary living conditions they experienced at such earlier conclaves as that in which Pius IX was elected in 1939. Fitted into palace corridors, with a narrow bed, a wash stand, a table, a chair, and little else, the seventy Princes of the Church had Spartan accommodations not experienced since seminary days, if then.

A few yards further is the state's railroad station, built in 1930. The facade has bas-reliefs of the New Testament's miraculous draft of fishes, and of the Old Testament's Prophet Elijah and his fiery chariot.

A few yards to the south of the station tracks, there is a link-up with the Italian railway system and, from there, to all points across Europe and Asia. The station is employed mainly for cargo, but John XXIII made use of it in October 1962 for a trip to the shrines at Assisi and Loreto, and Pope John Paul II has also journeyed from the station.

In midcentury the station was also used to carry out the terms of a prophecy. The modest patriarch of Venice, Giuseppe Sarto, had assured his people on the eve of the 1903 conclave, "I will return," but he did not. Elected as Pius X and now a canonized saint, he lived the remaining eleven years of his life as a voluntary prisoner in the Vatican and is entombed in Saint Peter's nave. Determined that the promise be kept, Vatican officials took the pontiff's remains, now sacred relics, to the railroad station and on to Venice for a few days before a return to Saint Peter's.

Near the same area is the Palace of the Tribunal, the security office of the state and the residence of many of the priests who hear confessions in the basilica. Beyond it is the large administrative office of the state, another 1930 building. Near it is a bed of flowers depicting the coat of arms of the reigning pope.

High on the top of Vatican Hill, at an altitude of 254 feet, is the helipad from which John Paul II makes flights to the summer residence on the hills at Castel Gandolfo. From there one has a splendid view of Saint Peter's, nestled on the slope below. Also nearby is a stretch of the wall Leo IV (847–855) erected to protect the Vatican from the recurring waves of attackers, a barricade reinforced by Nicholas V (1447–1455). In the same area is the Vatican's first radio transmitter. Another feature of that part of the upper gardens is the Tower of Saint John. It was used as his summer residence by John XXIII. John Paul II stayed there while work was done on his private apartments. Many visitors also have been housed there, including Constantinople's Orthodox patriarch, Athenagoras.

Circling back down the north side of the hill, the visitor passes a copy of the grotto of Lourdes, France, where Saint Bernadette Soubirous reported visions of the Madonna in 1858. The original Lourdes altar is installed there now, a gift to John XXIII.

Completing the circuit, the visitor passes the English gardens, where the vegetation is allowed to grow naturally, a contrast to many manicured places of verdure. Near them is Amalia Dupre's 1887 statue of Saint Peter in chains, a tribute to the voluntarily imprisoned Leo XIII and the first work of a woman artist to be included in the gardens. Close by is a Chinese pavilion, given to Pius XI by Chinese Catholics in 1933 on the occasion of the nineteenth centenary of Christ's death. It was one of John XXIII's favorite spots. Just ahead is the Tower of the Winds, where astronomical observations gave Gregory XIII the information he needed to create the present calendar.

Further on, to the right of the basilica, is the complex of Vatican museums and archives and also the papal palace. Beyond them, at the northeast corner of the papal kingdom, is a private area, not included on the regular tours. It has its own entrance to the Vatican state, the Saint Anne Gate, on Via di Porta Angelica, just to the right of the Bernini colonnades, and has the atmosphere of a country village. Businesslike and workaday, it offers a contrast to so much else that is monumental.

Those with business in the area see on their left, just inside the gate, the barracks of the one hundred Swiss Guards and a complex of eleven apartments for the officers' families. It is a little corner of Switzerland. One officer fitted out his rooftop patio with potted plants, a beach umbrella, and a child's rubber swimming pool, all of it out of sight from the ground and just a few yards across the tops of buildings to the Bernini colonnades. Opposite the Swiss is the Vatican's own parish church, Saint Anne's, dating from 1572.

Straight ahead a few dozen yards further is the state's main post office, handling four million letters and fifteen million postcards a year. The pope receives two thousand letters each day. They are carried up to him in a mailbag labeled *Poste Vaticane, Santo Padre:* (The Vatican Mails, Holy Father).

The state's postage stamps are collectors' items, as are the country's own coins, which are interchangeable with the money of Italy. Although the post office claims its origin in the pontifical couriers of the fourteenth century, the stamps of the papal state go back only to 1852, a few years after the first stamps appeared elsewhere. Many of them depict religious works of art. The stamps are printed for the Vatican in Italy and in Switzerland.

The post office is next door to the Vatican's Polyglot Press, so named because it publishes books in thirty languages. Nearby is the office of the Vatican's newspaper, the one-and-one-half-century-old *Osservatore Romano* (The Roman Observer). It comes out daily in Italian, once a week in five other languages, and once a month in Polish. The newspaper was the bane of the Nazis during World War II with its constant leaks on what was happening in Germany. An unsuccessful search was made for the paper's German correspondent. He was inside the Vatican, a young Italian, Federico Alessandrini, a member of *Osservatore*'s staff. Through the neutral Secretariate of State, he had a subscription to every local German paper. Working his way through the stack, he put together tidbits for his scoops.

Also near the *Osservatore Romano* is a tapestry repair shop. White-clad French sisters, Franciscan Missionaries of Mary, working with scissors, needles, and threads of a vast range of colors, make repairs on the Vatican's rich array of Belgian and Flemish tapestries designed by Raphael and others in the sixteenth century.

Rounding out the area are grocery stores, a huge car park, a pharmacy, a machine shop, a power plant, and one of the Vatican's oldest buildings, the church of San Pellegrino, dating from the pontificate of Pope Saint Leo III (795–816). It is a place of some fascination and charm but, for visitor interest, does not compare with the stupendous museums that loom on Vatican Hill just above it.

Practical Information

There are 10:00 A.M. guided tours of the Vatican gardens from March 1 to October 31, all days except Wednesday and Sunday. Tickets may be obtained at the Holy See's Pilgrim and Tourist Information Bureau on the left side of the plaza in front of Saint Peter's and should be picked up a day in advance. The telephone numbers are (06) 698 4466 and (06) 698 4866.

The bureau is open 8:30 A.M. to 6:30 P.M. all days except Sunday and important religious holidays. Buses start from out front of the bureau. They carry the license plates of the state beginning with the letters CV for City of the Vatican (some vehicles carry SCV for State and City of the Vatican). All tours start at 10:00 A.M. There is a choice of three:

• The city and gardens, two hours. This is available on Friday, March through October, and on Tuesday, Thursday, and Saturday during the four cooler months.

- The city, the gardens, and the Sistine chapel, three hours. March through October on Monday and Thursday.
- The city, the gardens, and Saint Peter's, three hours. The eight warmer months, Tuesday and Saturday.

There is also a daily Vatican shuttle bus from in front of the bureau. It runs every twenty minutes from 9:00 A.M. to 12:30 P.M., going to the Vatican museums and the Sistine Chapel. It offers a welcome relief from the quarter-mile walk from the plaza around the Vatican walls to the museums' entrance on the state's north side. The bus schedule is posted at each of the stops. Tickets can be purchased aboard the bus.

CHAPTER 8

VATICAN MUSEUMS

IN THE YEAR 2000 jubilee, those who come will be able to see not just the magnificent works of Michelangelo and Raphael inside the extraordinary papal museums but also the creations of painters, sculptors, and other artists who are the visitors' own contemporaries or part of the recent past. Five hundred works are on display in the Holy See's new collection of modern religious art. The assemblage of current objects of art was begun in 1973 by the indefatigable Paul VI, a modern man of his time. He said, at the inauguration of the collection on the feast of Peter and Paul, June 29, that "even in our arid secularized world there is still a prodigious capacity for expressing beyond the truly human world what is religious, divine, Christian."

All the works were gifts either from the artists themselves or collectors. Among them there is an entire room given over to the French expressionist painter Georges Rouault (1871–1958), as well as areas for the art of Pablo Picasso, Salvador Dalí, Bernard Buffet, Ben Shahn, Paul Gauguin, Maurice Utrillo, Marc Chagall, Georges Braque, Paul Klee, Wassily Kandinsky, Fernand Léger, and others.

The exhibit is now part of nearly a dozen great collections and museums strung out along hallways more than four miles long. They have accumulated just northeast of Saint Peter's Basilica over a fifteen-century period starting with the first palace construction in the time of Pope Symmachus of Sardinia (498–514). Popes at that time lived in the palace next to the basilica of Saint John Lateran, but the need for support facilities at Saint Peter's had been recognized.

With that beginning, Nicholas III (1277–1280) built much of what is there now, while more was added when in 1377 the popes ended their thousand-year stay at Saint John Lateran, moving their residence to Vatican Hill. Impressive art appeared with Fra Angelico's frescoes in the chapel of Nicholas V (1447–1455) and, a generation later, Sixtus V (1471–1492) built the Sistine Chapel, giving it his name. Finally, with Julius II (1503–1513) the Vatican art collection began in earnest. The visitor in 2000 will walk the same historic corridors and view the same masterpieces that a succession of popes down to the present pope have added ever since.

Still prominent among exhibits are two pieces of statuary with which Julius began the Vatican collection. They are the *Apollo Belvedere* and the *Laocoön*. The *Apollo* is a second-century copy in marble of a Greek bronze of 330–320 B.C. A radiant, noble, youthful figure, it has been said to be one of the finest representations of the highest ideals of art to have survived since antiquity. The other portrays the Trojan priest Laocoön and his two sons dying in the coils of two snakes. Carved in marble in the first century by sculptors from the island of Rhodes, the work is a copy of a second-century B.C. bronze. It was lost for more than one thousand years and rediscovered in January 1506 in Nero's palace next to the Colosseum. Michelangelo was impressed, emulating it in his own work.

The two pieces are now in a vastly expanded Vatican collection of ancient sculpture that Clement XIV (1769–1774) and Pius VI (1775–1799) assembled and which is now called the **Pio-Clementine Museum**. Housed in the eighteenth-century **Belvedere Palace**, the

The Heliocentric Staircase in the Vatican Museum

collection also boasts a headless muscular figure known as the *Belvedere Torso*, another piece of ancient statuary with which Michelangelo was much taken. Found in the fifteenth century, it was carved in the first century B.C. The same museum has busts and statues of Sophocles, Epicurus, Euripides, Plato, Socrates, Homer, Pericles, Julius Caesar, and the emperors Augustus, Titus, Trajan, Marcus Aurelius, Commodus, Caracalla, Hadrian, and Claudius.

Two more museums of ancient statuary were the creation of Pius VII (1800–1823), the pope of the omitted 1800 Holy Year, who passed part of his pontificate as Napoleon's prisoner. One is named for his family, the **Chiaramonti Museum**. It includes colossal heads of Augustus and Tiberius along with another one thousand ancient sculptures.

The other Pius VII collection is known as the **Braccio Nuovo** (the New Arm), named for its location in a recently added wing. The "new arm" houses objects Napoleon looted from the Vatican in 1797, only having to return them by order of the 1815 Congress of Vienna.

Two museums were the work of Gregory XVI (1831–1846): the **Etruscan Museum,** in 1837, and the **Egyptian Museum,** in 1839. The Etruscan Museum has an immense collection of vases, jewelry, terra-cotta bas-reliefs, and bronze statuary illustrating the high civilization of the vanished Etruscans of central Italy. Some items date to the Iron Age. Much of the material came from mid–nineteenth-century excavations in the papal states north of Rome. Much of the contents of the Egyptian Museum is statuary taken out of the Nile Valley by the ancient Roman conquerors.

The **Pinacoteca,** an art gallery, is one of the fairly recent creations. It dates to 1932 under Pius XI (1922–1939) and embraces masterworks of Italy across eight centuries—paintings by Giotto, Fra Angelico, Filippo Lippi, Benozzo Gozzoli, Leonardo da Vinci, Titian, and Guido Reni, plus a roomful of Raphaels.

John XXIII added three more museums to the rich Vatican patrimony, each of them formerly in a less prominent place in the Lateran Palace: the **Gregorian Profane Museum** of Gregory XVI of 1844, another vast collection of ancient Roman and Greek statuary, reliefs, friezes, and sarcophagi; the **Pio Christian Museum** of Pius IX of 1854; and the **Missionary-Ethnological Museum** of Pius XI of 1926.

The **Gregorian Profane Museum** includes bits of sculpture from the Parthenon of Athens, a bronze head of Sophocles, one of Cleopatra, and a representation of Diana of Ephesus, whose cult caused Paul problems described in Chapter 19 of the Acts of the Apostles.

The **Pio Christian Museum** includes sarcophagi from the catacombs of the third and fourth centuries, including one signed by Crescentianus and inscribed to "my dearest wife Agapene," who, he said, lived with him "fifty-five years, one month and seven days." In less careful lettering, there is a note that the mourning husband was "buried 30 August at the age of 101."

The **Missionary-Ethnological Museum** displays artifacts of other religions, assembled from eighty-five nations, including the United States and Canada. The North American exhibits focus on the Eskimos and various Indian tribes—the Sioux of Mississippi, the Winnebagos, and the Creeks. In the collection are items of the Hindu, Buddhist, Shintoist, Confucianist, Lamaist, Polynesian, Melanesian, Australian aboriginal, North African Coptic, Islamic, African, and Latin American Indian faiths, philosophies, and traditions. Among odd items are central African fetishes used in magic cults, painted human skulls from New Guinea, and Tibetan Bond-po religious flutes made from human bones.

Rivaling the museums as items of interest are elements of the **papal palace** itself:

• A gallery of Brussels tapestries woven from cartoons by Raphael.

• The 390-foot-long gallery of maps built in 1578–1580.

• The four Raphael rooms of 1508–1517, including the master's frescoes of the miracle of Bolsena when a priest who doubted the doctrine of the real presence, in 1263 saw blood on the consecrated host, and of Saint Peter being freed from prison (both in the room of Heliodorus); and the *School of Athens,* with the faces of fellow artists Michelangelo, Leonardo, and Bramante depicted among the philosophers.

• The Borgia Apartment, with murals of Pinturicchio of 1492–1494.

• The greatest triumph of all, the Sistine Chapel, with Michelangelo's Last Judgment and his ceiling portraying the Old Testament, and its side wall paintings by other Renaissance masters—Perugino, Botticelli, Ghirlandaio, Luca Signorelli, and others. The Sistine Chapel in its present brilliant state is another Holy Year opportunity that no one in the jubilee since the Renaissance could have enjoyed to the same extent. Decade by decade the brilliant original reds, greens, yellows, and blues had grown darker, sinking under a coat of soot from burning candles and from the brush used in a corner metal stove to signal the progress of papal elections (wet brush with black smoke out the chimney to announce failed votes; dry brush with white fumes to hail an election). Eighteen years of careful cleaning with bicarbonate of soda and ammonium, reaching into the early 1990s, have restored the chapel to the way the Renaissance geniuses designed it.

Practical Information

In early planning for the expected heavy invasion of visitors in the more popular months of late spring, early summer and early fall, Vatican authorities have discussed the possibility of opening a second entrance to the Vatican museum complex and the Sistine Chapel in addition to the existing one on Viale Vaticano on the north side of the state. Subject to modifications, the museum rules and facilities are these:

• The museums are open daily except Sunday from 8:45 A.M. to 1:45 P.M. From April to mid-June and in September and October the museum hours are extended on Monday to Friday until 4:30 for the five weekdays, while closing as usual at 1:45 P.M. on Saturday. The last admissions are forty-five minutes before closing time. One exception to the above is that the museums are open free of charge on the last Sunday of each month unless that day is Easter, the June 29 Feast of Saints Peter and Paul, Christmas, or the day after Christmas.

• Religious feast days on which the museums are closed are New Year's Day, the day of Mary, Mother of God, January 1; the Epiphany, January 6; Our Lady of Lourdes, February 11; Saint Joseph's Day, March 19; Easter Sunday and Monday; Saint Joseph the Worker, May 1; Ascension Day, June 1; Corpus Christi, June 25; the Assumption, August 15; All Saints' Day, November 1; Lateran Basilica Dedication Day, November 8; and Christmas and its following day.

• A convenient way to reach the museum entrance on Viale Vaticano is to take the bus in front of the Pilgrim and Tourist Information Bureau near the Arch of the Bells in Saint Peter's plaza. There is round-trip service. Inside the museum entrance at the top of a spiral ramp, there is the ticket office and many facilities: a self-service restaurant, rest rooms, a currency exchange office, a post office, a shop with books, maps, guides, and greeting cards, telephones, a cloak room, and a writing room. First aid stations are there and at two other points along the visitors' route.

Days would be needed to savor all that the Vatican museums and palaces have to offer, but the Vatican has suggested four possible itineraries, indicated by signs along the way. The quick look (the violet route) takes ninety minutes, two others cover the same areas but add further exhibits of special interest (the three-hour beige tour and the three-and-a-half-hour green), and a final yellow route of five hours combines all three. The basic violet route provides a mix of ancient Graeco-Roman art and works of the fifteenth to nineteenth centuries and includes the gallery of tapestries with work inspired by Raphael, the gallery of maps, and the Sistine Chapel. The beige tour adds the Etruscan exhibits, the Pinacoteca paintings and tapestries of the eleventh to the nineteenth centuries, and the three John XXIII additions, the Gregorian Profane, Pio Christian, and Missionary-Ethnological museums.

The modern religious work brought together by Paul VI is on the green route. So are the Laocoön and the Belvedere Apollo, the Raphael rooms, the Egyptian collection, the Chiaramonti museum, the Barccio Nuovo, the chapel of Nicholas V with the work of Fra Angelico, and the Borgia Apartment.

All four routes offer an embarrassment of riches, with time limitations the problem.

Vatican teleguides in English, French, German, and Spanish explain the wonders of the Raphael rooms and of the Sistine Chapel. They are available for rent at the entrance of the Raphael rooms and are reclaimed at the exit of the Sistine chapel.

Photography with hand-held cameras is permitted, but no flashes can be used during museum hours. Administration permission is needed for the use of tripods.

Freelance guides are on hand at the entrance and are required to abide by the posted schedule of fees.

Elevators are provided for the disabled. Wheelchairs are available but should be reserved by telephoning (06) 698 83333, 698 84466, or 698 84866.

Closed-circuit television and electronic alarm equipment protect exhibits, so visitors are counseled not to cross rope lines or to touch objects.

The museum entrance is three hundred yards from Piazza Risorgimento. Line A on the Metro goes to the Ottaviani station in the Vatican area. Buses that stop near the museums are 19, 23, 30, 32, 49, 51, 64, 81, 492, 901, 913, 950, 991, and 994.

CHAPTER 9

CATACOMBS

AT THE DIRECTION of Pope John Paul II, the ancient Roman catacombs will play an essential role in the year 2000 jubilee.

In no other Holy Year have these early Christian cemeteries and places of worship received so much attention. In fact, in many jubilees, pilgrims had no idea the catacombs existed. Pope John Paul set the tone for the year 2000 role of the catacombs in a 1996 talk.

"Christians," he said with approval, "are returning to prayer in the catacombs. During the jubilee, the Rome catacombs will return to be a privileged place for pilgrimages."

The reason so many of the first Holy Year visitors knew nothing of the catacombs was that memory of them was lost for centuries in the wake of repeated barbarian assaults on the diminished Eternal City. Only at the end of the sixteenth century did an archaeologist, Antonio Bosio, rediscover some of them, and not until the nineteenth century did Giovanni Battista de Rossi begin a scientific investigation. Pope Pius IX took an active interest in the mid-nineteenth century, and now the Vatican has control over the bulk of the underground structures.

The catacombs were the burial places and centers of worship of Rome's Christians from as early as the second century. Cremation was popular among the pagans, but Christians with the expectation of bodily resurrection opposed that practice and burrowed underground for burial places. Martyrs in the recurring persecutions were entombed in the below-ground cemeteries, and their places of burial became centers of veneration. Some of the most ancient Christian paintings appeared on the catacomb walls and, though often faded, are still to be seen: Christ as the Good Shepherd with a lamb across his shoulders; the Madonna; even Jonah and the whale as an Old Testament prefiguration of Christ's own return from the dead.

The loss of memory of the catacombs is especially remarkable because they are so extensive. At least sixty Christian catacombs have been found so far, the most recent fifty years ago. Seven Jewish catacombs have been recovered as well. Sometimes three levels deep, with the most recent additions on the bottom, the catacomb corridors run hundreds of miles under the outer edges of Rome and into the countryside. Even the official American residence, Villa Taverna in Rome's modern Parioli district, has a catacomb, which Clare Boothe Luce, when ambassador, enjoyed showing callers. Even one of the young postwar attachés in the American embassy, Bill McFadden, found, when he rented a villa near the Appian Way, that he and wife, Betsy, had a catacomb of their own.

One problem with the catacombs, pointed out by practical-minded Raymond Flynn, a Clinton ambassador to the Holy See, is that in a preeminently walking city, the open catacombs are out of the way. Even so, the small effort to get to them is worth it.

Five catacombs are easily entered. The depredations of centuries, including earthquakes, floods, and landslides, have made some unsafe, and, at others, such as the one beside the church of Saint Lawrence Outside the Walls, latter-day construction has caused much destruction; Rome built its large modern Verano cemetery atop the catacomb beside Saint Lawrence's.

The five open for visits are these:

• **San Sebastiano.** Inside the catacomb is a pagan mausoleum of the time of Christ. Etched on it is the outline of a fish, the symbol early Christians used, since the initial letters in Greek of "Jesus Christ, God's Son, Savior," spell the word "fish." Many inscriptions on the walls, starting in A.D. 258, call for spiritual help from Saints Peter and Paul, one indication that during the persecutions of Emperor Valerian (253–260) the remains of the apostles may have been hidden there temporarily. A plaque from one of the medieval popes, Damasus, vigorously affirms that indeed the indications are true: "You, whomever you may be, who seek the names of Peter and Paul, should know that the bodies of those two saints, were here at one time. They were sent from the East as disciples. . . . By the shedding of their blood, following Christ through the stars, they attained the gates of Heaven and the reign of the just. Rome more than other cities has the right to hail them as fellow citizens. Damasus here raises their praises."

Giving the catacomb a great early impetus was the burial there of Saint Sebastian, a Roman soldier martyred during the fierce Diocletian attack on the Christians during his 284–305 reign, an assault from which Constantine presently rebounded, legitimatizing the new faith. Burials and tunnels for additional interments quickly accumulated around the soldier's grave, and the catacomb took on its present form.

There is a painting of the Infant Jesus accompanied by the ox and the ass. A basilica at the spot traces to the fourth century but was rebuilt in the seventeenth. Mausoleums of the first structure have been preserved in the new.

An oddity in the basilica is a chapel of relics with a stone bearing a footprint. An ancient Roman legend is that Peter fled from Rome during the early persecutions and was stopped by Christ at the nearby Appian Way chapel of Quo Vadis. "Where are you going, Lord? *Quo vadis?*" Peter asked. Christ replied, "To Rome, to be crucified again!" Shamed, Peter retraced his steps and, in his turn, died on a cross. Skeptics say the stone was, instead, a votive offering.

Long among the most popular catacombs, Saint Sebastian's very attractiveness has been in part its undoing. Most of the original level is in ruins, but parts of the second remain.

There is an explanatory film in several languages. A brother serves as a guide.

• **San Callisto.** These catacombs cover thirty-seven acres and have twelve miles of galleries. They are at 110 Via Appia Antica, not far from Saint Sebastian's. Five hundred thousand persons were buried there. This catacomb was a favorite of John XXIII.

This is where de Rossi began his catacomb excavations in 1849 and is one of the most dramatic. Nine popes from 236 to 283 were buried in a well-preserved crypt. Inscriptions identify five. Two of the markers, for Roman natives Popes Saint Ponzianus (230–235) and Saint Fabianus (236–250), bear in Greek the letters *MTR,* for martyr. The catacomb boasts the remains of fifty martyrs and a total of sixteen popes, among them the Greek pontiff, Sixtus II (257–258), slain by Emperor Valerian; Pope Saint Caius of Dalmatia (283–296); Pope Saint Eusebius, a Greek, whose pontificate lasted only four months; and possibly Pope Saint Melchiades, an African (311–314).

The catacomb includes some of the most ancient Christian paintings—Daniel in the lions' den, from the Old Testament, and the loaves and fishes and a glass of wine, symbols of the miracle of the multiplication and the Eucharist from the New Testament.

• **Santa Domitilla,** Via delle Sette Chiese (Street of the Seven Churches). This is near the other two and was found by Bosio in the sixteenth century and excavated three centuries later by de Rossi. It traces to the first century, when Emperor Diocletian executed the husband of his niece, Domitilla, charging him with being a Christian. Three centuries later, when two of Diocletian's soldiers, Saints Nereus and Achilleus, were put to death for the same reason, a basilica to the two was erected over the site and present development of the catacomb began. Saint Gregory the Great (590–604) preached there about the horrors of the barbarian invasions.

• **Priscilla,** Via Salaria Nuova 430. This dates to the end of the second century and is one of the oldest. Its antiquity is indicated by the hairstyle of one of the women portrayed in a mural. It emulates the style Empress Faustina made popular during the reign of her husband, Antoninus Pius (138–161). Built beneath the first-century residence of the noble Priscilla, the catacomb includes a chapel with an early third-century ceiling painting of the Madonna holding her son on her knees, one of the oldest known images of the Virgin.

Another chapel, dating to the late third century, has a range of pictures from both Testaments—the sacrifice of Abraham; Jonah; the youths in the fiery furnace; and the Good Shepherd. The "Greek chapel," so named from red-lettered inscriptions in that language, has a mural like the one in the Saint Calixtus catacomb, seven people at the table with a chalice, a plate of fish and seven baskets of bread.

• **Sant'Agnese,** Via Nomentana 285. The catacomb is part of the complex of the church of Saint Agnes (Sant'Agnese), a seventh-century basilica that is one of Rome's finest examples of Byzantine architecture. Agnes is remembered as a twelve-year-old who chose virginity over an arranged marriage and was beheaded by Diocletian (284–305). Buried in an already existing cemetery at the site, her grave quickly became a place of veneration, and a catacomb developed, with many wishing to be interred near her. A church in Agnese's honor was erected sometime after 337 A.D. and rebuilt in much of its present form by Pope Honorius of 625–638. Fine fourth-century mosaics remain.

For those wishing to pursue further the examination of the catacombs, there are additional possibilities, both in the immediate Rome area and also a few miles out on the ancient road net.

Priscilla's Catacomb

There is no central entrance to the catacomb at the church of Saint Lawrence Outside the Walls, but there are separate entrances to three parts of it. There are fourth-century frescoes. In addition to the familiar depictions of Jonah and the Good Shepherd, there are paintings of Moses and a Last Judgment.

At the basilica of San Pancrazio outside the gate of the same name there is a much-damaged catacomb with a plaque of the fifteenth century affirming that Pancrazio, a martyr, was buried there. The tradition is that he was a Diocletian victim. It is open daily, but permission must be requested from the Carmelite clergy staffing the basilica overhead.

Seven miles out on the Via Nomentana is the Saint Alessandro catacomb. Three martyrs, Alessandro, Evenzius, and Teodulus, were buried there. A shrine was constructed in the fourth century, fell into ruins, and was replaced by a basilica, of which remnants were rediscovered in 1855. Much interested in the ancient burial places, Pius IX restored the church. To visit these catacombs, application must be made to the Pontifical Commission for Sacred Archaeology, Via Napoleone III, 00185 Rome, telephone 446 56 10 or 446 76 01, fax 446 76 25. Dr. Fabrizio Bisconti is secretary.

Ten miles out on the Via Latina is the Ad Decimum (At Ten Miles) catacomb. It has frescoes of the start of the fifth century showing Peter receiving the code of laws and Saint Paul clutching his sword. The latter is one of the earliest showing Paul in that now-traditional martial way. Permission is needed from the Fathers at the Grottaferrata abbey.

Seven hundred thousand persons visited the catacombs in the typical year of 1995, with five thousand a day at Saint Sebastian's. A doubling of the numbers is expected in 2000. Thought has been given to the opening of a sixth catacomb, while pilgrim groups will be urged to go also to catacombs further away, such as those at Bolsena and Albano.

Christians were not alone in using catacombs. The Jews, too, had them. So far, seven have been found, only two of them available to be seen. Admission is controlled by the Archaeological Superintendance, a subdivision of City Hall. One is at Vigna Randanini. It was found in 1897. The other is under the lawns of the Villa Torlonia. The latter, used in the third and fourth centuries, has the same familiar tunnels and burial places, but the wall decorations have Hebrew motifs. There are many Greek and Latin inscriptions but none in Hebrew.

In addition to the open Christian catacombs, many others are known but remain closed:

On the Appian Way, along with the catacombs of Saint Sebastian and Saint Calixtus, there are those of Santa Croce at Villa Franchetti, Vibia, near a former Trappist monastery, and Pretestato on Via Appia Pignatelli. On Via Ardeatina, in addition to the Domitilla cemetery, there are the sealed catacombs of Nunziatella, Balbina, Basileo, and the unknown martyrs. Near the San Pancrazio cemetery on Via Casal di Pio V, the Calepodio catacomb is closed. Others sealed are San Valentino in Via Flaminia; the Zotico, Saints Marcellino, and Peter cemeteries; the tombs of the Aurelii in the Via Labicana area; and the catacombs of Saints Giodano and Epimaco, of Apronianus and of Dino Compagni in the Via Latina region. Also closed in the Via Nomentana area are the catacombs of Saint Nicomede and the Major Cemetery of Via Asmara.

Other huge underground burial areas out of bounds are those of Commodilla and Saint Tecla on Via Ostiense; of Ponzianus and of Generosa in Via Portuense; of Massimo, the Giordani, and Trasone in Via Salaria Nuova; of Panfilo and Bassilla in Via Salaria Vecchia; of Novaziano in Viale della Regina Margherita; and of Sant'Ippolito in Via Tiburtina.

Practical Information

The five open catacombs charge an entrance fee of 8,000 lire and provide guided tours. Most are open from 8:30 A.M. TO 5:30 P.M., with a lunch and siesta period from noon to 2:30 P.M. They are closed on January 1, Easter, and Christmas. There are some variations.

San Sebastiano. Reached by Metro line A to Colli Albani, then ATAC bus 660. Fare 1,500 lire. Closed Thursday. From October to March, 5:00 P.M. closing. Telephone (06)788 70 35.

San Callisto. Same Metro and bus as to San Sebastiano. 110 Via Appia Antica. Closed Wednesday. October to April closing at 5:00 P.M. Telephone (06)513 67 25.

Santa Domitilla. Buses 93, 94, 319. 280 Via delle Sette Chiese. Closed Tuesday. October to April 5:00 P.M. closing. One-hour tour. Telephone (06)511 03 42.

Priscilla. Buses 56, 57, 319. 430 Via Salaria. Closed Monday and daily at 5:00 P.M. Half-hour tour. Telephone 862 06 272.

Sant'Agnese. Buses 6, 36, 37, 60, 137. 349 Via Nomentana. Closed Monday morning. Open 9:00 A.M.–12:00 P.M., 4:00 P.M.–6:00 P.M. Telephone 861 08 40.

CHAPTER 10

HOLY YEAR CHURCHES

FROM THE FIRST Holy Year of 1300, pilgrims seeking reconciliation with God and the papal indulgence were required to pray at the tombs of Saints Peter and Paul, one on Vatican Hill, the other a mile or so outside the old city walls on the road to the seaport of Ostia. Two basilicas, already by then a thousand years old, marked the place of veneration of the two apostles. Again, in the jubilee of 2000, both churches will be the goal of millions of visitors.

By 1350 a third church was added to the required pilgrim itinerary, the equally ancient Saint John Lateran, and in 1450 a fourth, Saint Mary Major, the greatest among scores of Marian shrines in Rome. At all four of these principal Holy Year churches, holy doors will be opened Christmas Eve with solemn ceremonies, cardinals presiding at three and the pope at Saint Peter's.

For those with sufficient time there are four other venerable churches that have played a part in Holy Year history and merit a visit. They are Saint Mary in Trastevere, which replaced Saint Paul's when the latter was flooded out in 1625 and 1700; Saint Lawrence Outside the Walls; Santa Croce in Gerusalemme (Holy Cross in Jerusalem); and Saint Sebastian above the catacomb on the Appian Way.

The three latter were added to the basic four for just one Holy Year, that of 1575, but they form part of an even older tradition of "the seven churches" of pilgrimage. Toward the end of the first millennium it was pilgrim custom to pray at Rome's five patriarchal basilicas, the four of the later Holy Years plus Saint Lawrence. En route were the additional two, so with time they were added. The road from Saint Paul's to Saint Sebastian, which was part of the route, is still called the Via delle Sette Chiese, the street of the seven churches. Attention in 2000 will focus on the traditional four, but all eight justify a visit.

The Holy Year Four

After Saint Peter's, **Saint Paul's Outside the Walls** is Rome's second largest church, and one of the world's dozen largest Christian places of worship. Like Saint Peter's, it owes its origin to Constantine. The Acts of the Apostles tell of Paul's travel to Rome to stand trial but end abruptly without discussing his beheading in the year 67. A small shrine was constructed over his grave and above that Constantine ordered construction of a basilica, which the emperor's contemporary, Pope Saint Sylvester (314–335), consecrated in 324. Paul's tomb was installed in the apse at a spot now covered by the high altar.

The present basilica dates only from 1854. The first was consumed by a fire in 1823. An investigation indicated that the disastrous loss may have been due to a work force on the roof, a hot coal falling unnoticed, smoldering until midnight, and then bursting into flames. Catholics throughout the world financed the reconstruction. Parts of the original basilica have been preserved, including a Venetian apse mosaic of 1220; a baldachin over Paul's tomb and a ciborium, both of them Gothic masterpieces done in 1285 by

Saint Paul's Outside the Walls

Arnolfo di Cambio; an eighteen-foot-tall Easter candle of 1170 signed "I, Nicholas de Anbelo with Pietro Bassaletto produced this work"; a bronze door cast in Constantinople in 1070; and an outside column inscribed "Siricius Episcopus." Saint Siricius was the bishop of Rome and pope from 384 to 399. A feature pointed out by every guide are mosaic portraits of more than two hundred popes. John Paul II is above the right aisle, near the right transept. Space is getting tight, but there is still room for another twenty-four pontiffs.

Saint Paul's has seen much history. It was sacked by the Lombards in the eighth century and by the Saracens in the ninth. The wall now protecting it dates from the Roman John VIII of 872–882. Another John made history at the basilica. John XXIII used the handsome thirteenth-century cloister of the basilica to announce to a probably startled group of cardinals that he was summoning Vatican Council II, the first such lawmaking assembly of the Church in more than a century and only the second since the Counter-Reformation Council of Trent, Italy, in the sixteenth century.

Saint John Lateran. Although this basilica was omitted from the required two in 1300, it has a special place in Holy Year and papal history. It was from here that Boniface VIII proclaimed the first Holy Year. Just inside the nave on the right is a contemporary fresco, believed to be the work of Giotto of 1267–1337, showing Boniface in the act of launching the 1300 Holy Year. Wearing a cone-shaped headpiece and flanked by two clerics, the pope has his hand raised in a blessing.

For a thousand years the palace, which is part of the Saint John Lateran complex, was the residence of the popes. The church, rather than Saint Peter's, remains the cathedral of Rome, the special church of the pope as the bishop of the city. Momentous church moments took place here. It was at Saint John Lateran that the beloved St. Francis of Assisi in 1210 obtained Pope Innocent III's permission to found the great Franciscan Order. It was here, too, that nearly a quarter of the crucial, lawmaking ecumenical councils of the church took place, those of 1123, 1139, 1179, 1215, and 1512. Niceae, Lyon, and the Vatican had two councils and Constantinople four, but none matched the Lateran in frequency. As late as 1929 the Lateran Palace was back at the center of church activity when the Italian dictator Mussolini and the Holy See secretary of state, Cardinal Pietro Gasparri, met there to end the seven-decade church-state estrangement and to create the Vatican sovereignty, a pact "giving God back to Italy, and Italy back to God."

The odd name of Saint John Lateran stemmed from an eight-century process. Like Saint Peter's and Saint Paul's, the basilica was one of Constantine's creations. The important land-holding family of the Laterans had incurred imperial disfavor, and their holdings had been confiscated. Emperor Maxentius, who Constantine defeated at Rome's Milvian bridge, had been using the Lateran grounds as barracks for his bodyguards. With them suppressed, the convert-to-be erected a basilica to Christ the Savior and provided a papal residence used for the next ten centuries by 162 popes.

"The Lateran" was the name commonly used for the basilica until Pope Sergius III (904–911) renamed it for Saint John the Baptist. A century later, Pope Lucius II (1144–1145) added a second John, the Evangelist. The evolution to Saint John Lateran was complete. Now atop the facade are three figures twenty-two feet tall, Christ flanked by the two Johns. The significance of the basilica is affirmed by a forthright statement retained from the Middle Ages and emblazoned above the front columns identifying it as *Sacrasancta Laterensis Ecclesia Omnium Urbis et Orbis Ecclesiarum Mater at Caput* (The All-Holy Lateran Church, Mother and Head of All the Churches of the City and of the World).

The basilica has undergone repeated vicissitudes—sacked by Alaric in 408 and by Genseric's Vandals in 455, wrecked by an earthquake in 896, and burned out both in 1308 and in 1360, it has been rebuilt each time. The appearance now is essentially what it was in 1700, while preserving much from antiquity and from the medieval period. The central bronze doors date from 29 B.C., when the Emperor Augustus installed them at the Curia in the Forum, the meeting place of the senators. The immense nave, 420 feet long, has a colorful medieval pavement restored in 1425, while overhead is a dramatic coffered ceiling of the Renaissance. Mosaics in the apse date to the thirteenth century. The Gothic altar of 1357 is reserved for the use of the pope. Inside is a wood plank believed to have been used for mass by Pope Sylvester and, according to a legend, by Saint Peter and the thirty-one other pontiffs prior to Sylvester.

Other points of interest include a delightful, peaceful thirteenth-century cloister; an adjoining baptistery of Constantine's time with a door of silver, gold, and bronze that sings when it is moved; Rome's tallest and oldest obelisk, from the time of Pharaoh Thutmose IV (1420–1411 B.C.); and the *Scala Santa*, the holy stairs, which many pilgrims of the millennium Holy Year will mount on their knees, fol-

The Cloisters of Saint John Lateran

lowing a tradition of many centuries. Beside the twenty-nine steps of the *Scala Santa* is a sign reading, "Christ climbed these to the crucifixion on Golgotha."

Saint Mary Major, the fourth of the traditional Holy Year churches, is so named because it is the largest of the dozens of Rome churches dedicated to the Madonna. A legend, depicted in thirteenth-century mosaics in the loggia out front and in others of the fifteenth century in the apse, is that the church was built by Pope Liberius (352–366) after a dream that a snowfall on the Esquiline Hill, not far from Rome's present main railroad station, would instruct him where to erect a shrine. It was August 4, a sizzling time of year in a city that rarely, even in January, sees a snowflake, but next morning the pope did indeed find snow outlining a large area and, accordingly, built.

The story is an old one, but evidence indicates that it was another pontiff, a century later, Sixtus III (432–440) who erected the great basilica to the Virgin, taking his lead from the Council of Ephesus, which in 431 gave Mary the new title of *Theotokos,* Mother of God. The church is one of Rome's most splendid, a fine example of a Roman basilica, with a nave lined with magnificent chapels. The gilded ceiling is said to be leafed with Peruvian gold, the first of the precious metal imported from the Americas and a gift from King Ferdinand and Isabella of Spain to the Spanish pope, Alexander VI, Rodrigo de Borgia (1492–1503.) The mosaic pavement is of the pontificate of Eugenius III (1145–1153). Mosaics in a triumphal arch are from the time of Sixtus III (432–440). Others, especially fine, are in the apse, a contribution of Nicholas V (1288–1292). Among ancient objects of veneration are fragments of what are said to have been part of Christ's crib from Bethlehem. They are conserved in a silver and gold reliquary of 1802 in a confession in front of the main altar.

Nearby in the left transept is the lavishly decorated Borghese family chapel, with a Byzantine Madonna of the twelfth century, much revered as the protector of Rome. Pius XII, a Rome native, said his first mass as a priest in 1899 in front of the painting, returning forty years later as the newly elected pope to commemorate the occasion. To the left of the chapel is the tomb of a predecessor of Pius XII, who, like him, was a Holy Year pontiff, Clement VIII of 1600. Close by, to the right of the main altar, is the tomb of another who left an enduring mark on the ancient city, the creator of the Saint Peter's colonnades. The inscription reads, "Gian Lorenzo Bernini, who brought honor to art and the city, here humbly lies." A floor marker adds, "The noble Bernini family here awaits the resurrection."

In the right transept is the tomb of a five-year pontiff who gave Rome much of its modern look, Sixtus V (1585–1590), carver of new streets such as the fashionable Via Sistina, which bears his name, and mover of obelisks. Just behind Saint Mary Major is one of the obelisks Sixtus V installed in their present locations.

The facade of Saint Mary Major and the organization of the basilica's interior were a Holy Year consequence. To celebrate the 1750 occasion, Pope Benedict XIV (1740–1758) appointed Ferdinando Fugo to make extensive changes, which are now to be seen. Just as Peter and Paul are atop ancient columns in Rome, so is Mary. Since the time of Pope Paul V (1605–1621), the plaza in front of Saint Mary Major has been dominated by the last of eight enormous columns, which were part of the huge Roman Forum basilica of Constantine's foe, Maxentius. The other seven have vanished, but Mary, like the two apostles elsewhere, looks down now from the peak of the shaft.

The Other Pilgrim Churches

Saint Lawrence Outside the Walls traces its origins to Lawrence, a deacon, burned to death on a grill during the persecutions launched by Emperor Valerian (253–260). A shrine was erected over his grave; Constantine created there another of his basilicas; and a succession of popes, Pelagius II (578–590), Honorius III (1216–1227), and Pius IX (1846–1878), made changes.

Saint Lawrence made World War II news in July 1943. At the peak of the struggle for Italy, when the church was struck by Allied bombs, Pius XII drove to the spot the next day; his white cassock was soiled by the debris. Negotiations to declare Rome a noncombatant "open city" presently were successful and further damage was averted. The sedan in which the pope rode that day is now in the Vatican's most recent display of memorabilia, the carriage museum of 1973.

The facade of the old church was shattered and much of the nave damaged, but, by 1949, the basilica was reopened, some frescoes lost, but other damaged areas rebuilt as they had been. The church has sixth-century Byzantine mosaics, a pavement of about the ninth century, and an altar bearing a date inscribed there by its builder, 1148. Relics of several saints, including Lawrence, are in a sarcophagus under the altar.

Saint Lawrence's was a favorite of the last sovereign of the papal states, Pius IX, and, as he willed, he is interred there. A possibility for year 2000 canonization, the entombed pontiff lies in a chapel decorated by mosaics acclaiming the two dogmas of his pontificate, the Virgin's Immaculate Conception, which he proclaimed in 1854, and papal infallibility, an 1870 declaration of Vatican I, the ecumenical council he summoned. Another interred in Saint Lawrence is a post–World War II figure of Italian history, Alcide de Gasperi, the modest Christian Democratic prime minister who led Italy out of the wreckage of Fascism into a flourishing Western-oriented democracy.

Saint Mary in Trastevere. This stand-in Holy Year church of 1625 and 1700 has a rare charm and has some claim to being the site of the first public Christian worship in Rome. There is evidence that Pope Saint Calixtus (217–222) in the time of the emperors Macrinus and Elagabalus constructed an oratory, which Pope Julius (337–352) replaced with a basilica. The latter in its turn was succeeded in the time of Pope Innocent II (1130–1143) by the present structure. The remains of both Calixtus and Julius are interred beneath the main altar.

In addition to its twelfth-century appeal, the church fronts on a quaint plaza in the heart of one of the most down-to-earth quarters of old Rome, a warren of narrow medieval streets chock-a-block with trattorias where both the palate and the purse do well. When imperial Rome shrank from a million inhabitants to a mere fifteen thousand in the Middle Ages, life somehow carried on in humble Trastavere (literally "across the Tiber," a section separated by the river from the elegant and important seven hills). Proud of their modesty, the Trasteveriani have a dialect and even a literature of their own and an annual self-congratulatory festival of *noiantri* ("we others" in the dialect). In the church plaza itself are two outdoor restaurants that long have been enjoyed by such connoisseurs of old Rome as former U.S. Ambassador Clare Boothe Luce.

A point of central interest in the church is the apse, with mosaics of 1140 showing Christ with his arm around his mother and, below that, a 1290 series of episodes of the life of the Madonna. The twenty-one granite columns of the nave originally were in the Baths of Emperor Caracalla (211–217).

Holy Cross in Jerusalem. One of the ancient "seven" and one required in the Holy Year of 1575, Santa Croce in Gerusalemme is a half-mile along the Aurelian city walls away from Saint John Lateran. While not as picturesque as some of the other jubilee shrines, it has an unusual history and houses relics that have been venerated for more than a thousand years.

The story of the church is that Saint Helen, mother of Constantine, made a pilgrimage to the Holy Land about 326, returning with a fragment of Christ's cross and some of the earth of Calvary. Helena came back to her residence in the imperial Sessorian palace and a hall was converted into a chapel to house the relic. The Calvary soil served as flooring.

Pope Lucius II (1144–1145) reconstructed the edifice, raising much of the pavement except in the area of the earth from the mount of the

Crucifixion. His Romanesque eight-story bell tower survives. Benedict XV (1740–1758), the pope of the 1750 jubilee, undertook a thorough rebuilding, giving the church its present shape. Helena's relics and others are in a chapel reached by a staircase to the right of the left aisle. There also venerated are several other articles traditionally believed to have been part of Christ's Passion: an arm of the cross of the Good Thief; fragments of the mocking inscription about "the king of the Jews"; two thorns from the crown of suffering; a fragment of the post of the flogging; and even a finger joint of Doubting Thomas.

Saint Sebastian. Another of the "seven," Saint Sebastian seems to have been added to the first-millennium pilgrim route merely because it was en route from Saint Paul's to Saint John Lateran. Even so, it has a claim to interest of its own. Not only is it above the celebrated catacomb of the same name, but there are indications that at one time it was the resting place of the remains of Saints Peter and Paul. An old tradition is that, when Emperor Valerian of 253–259 banned Christian religious meetings, the remains of the apostles were taken temporarily to this less public spot where prayer services might continue. Excavations in 1915 uncovered many third-century graffiti imploring the prayerful help of the two Church leaders.

In mid-fourth century a church was erected at the site and called the Basilica Apostolorum, the apostles' basilica. Several centuries later it had an adjusted name, the Basilica of the Apostles and Saint Sebastian. The latter was a victim of the final assault on Christianity waged by Diocletian (284–305). An officer in the emperor's Praetorian Guard, he was denounced as a Christian, shot by a firing squad of archers, and clubbed to death. An altar to the left inside the nave contains Sebastian's relics. Invoked in the Rome plague of 680, the saint became the object of so popular a cult that, by the ninth century, his name alone was used for the structure. Reconstructed in the thirteenth century and again in the sixteenth, the church preserves in its facade six granite columns of the edifice of the 1200s. A chapel of 1625 includes an arrow said to have wounded Sebastian and a column to which he reportedly was bound.

Practical Information

Saint Paul's Outside the Walls. Open daily, 7:30 A.M. to 6:30 P.M. In addition to masses in Italian there is one in Latin on Sunday at

9:00 A.M. Telephone (06) 54 10 341. Cloisters closed at midday from 1:00 P.M. to 3:00 P.M.

Saint John Lateran. Open Monday through Saturday, 7:00 A.M. to 6:00 P.M., and Sunday, 1:00 P.M. to 5:00 P.M. In addition to masses in Italian there is one in Latin Sunday at 10:00 A.M. Telephone (06) 69 88 64 33. Cloister and museum admission charge 2,000 lire. Baptistery open 9:00 A.M. to 1:00 P.M. and 3:00 P.M. to 5:00 P.M. in winter, 4:00 P.M. to 6:00 P.M. in summer. Lateran Palace historical museum open every first Sunday of the month, 8:45 A.M. to 1:45 P.M. One-hour guided tour Tuesday, Thursday, and Saturday at 9:30 A.M., 10:45 A.M., and noon. Admission charge, 5,000 lire. Holy Stairs open 6:30 A.M. to noon, and 3:30 P.M. to 6:30 P.M. in summer. In winter the afternoon reopening is at 3 P.M.

Saint Mary Major. Open 7:00 A.M. to 6:45 P.M. In addition to masses in Italian, there is one in Latin at 10:00 A.M. Sunday. Admission to the loggia with thirteenth-century mosaics, 4,000 lire. Telephone (06) 48 81 094.

Saint Lawrence Outside the Walls. Open daily, 7:30 A.M. to 6:30 P.M. Telephone (06) 54 10 341. Cloisters closed at midday from 1:00 P.M. to 3:00 P.M.

CHAPTER II

OTHER GREAT SHRINES

WHILE MANY Holy Year pilgrims will limit themselves to prayers at
Saint Peter's and perhaps also at the other Holy Year basilicas and the
pilgrimage seven, those with more time will do well to pay a call at
other shrines in which the history of all twenty Christian centuries is
reflected.

San Clemente in Piazza di San Clemente. This extraordinary
place of worship two blocks east of the Colosseum records every moment back to the very first years when another religion from the east,
Mithraism, posed an important challenge to newborn Christianity.
Saint Clement's is dedicated to Peter's third successor as bishop of
Rome. He is recalled as the pontiff of A.D. 88 to 97, the time when
the last of the Gospels were being written. Until the middle of the
nineteenth century all that was known of the church was that Pope
Paschal II (1099–1118) erected it; that it had fifteenth-century frescoes and a Gothic chapel to Saint Catherine of Alexandria; that there
was a *schola cantorum,* an enclosure for the choir, dating to the time
of Pope John II (533–535); and that Irish Dominicans had been in
charge since 1677.

Much else was mystery until archaeologists in 1857 broke through
the floor to find what was below. What they discovered permits the
millennium visitor to stroll on the same pavements Romans used at
the time of Nero's infamous first-century assault on the newborn
Christian community.

Just below the present church the excavators found almost intact
one of the earliest Christian basilicas, the work of Pope Saint Siricius
(384–399), built less than a century after the legalization of the faith.
Below that they uncovered residences of the first century A.D. with
clear indications that they had been damaged in the notorious fire of
A.D. 64. Still to be seen are reconstructions the local residents made
after the flames. Alongside the rebuilt structures there is still a per-

fectly preserved shrine to Mithra, complete with a statue of the god performing the cult's bloody sacrifice, the slashing of a bull's throat to release life-giving forces. Next to the god in impotent rage are the cult's symbols of evil, a dog, a snake, and a scorpion.

When Siricius built his church he installed it above the temple of the by-then vanquished pagan cult and over the old brick houses without paying them heed, thus sparing them for the third millennium. For the next eight centuries the basilica was in service. In it, still to be seen, are frescoes of the ninth to the twelfth centuries, including a series about a Roman prefect, Sisinius, which has been called the first comic strip. According to the Sisinius series, the prefect suspected that his wife attended Clement's clandestine masses. The official and his aides trailed her, were all struck blind, and then wandered away in befuddlement, shouldering a stone column they mistook for the prayerful spouse. Also on the walls, fascinating to students of language, are writings in a degenerating Latin, the beginnings of Italian. What is most dramatic about Saint Clement's is that there was enough damage wreaked by the Normans in 1084 that Pope Paschal decided to build from scratch. He rescued the *schola cantorum* but used rubble to fill up much of the rest of the old basilica and the Roman remains below. Soon memory was lost of what had gone before and of what was still there under foot.

Saint Clement's is one of the parish churches given to cardinals as their own special charge in Rome, a reflection of earlier centuries, when Rome's pastors clustered around the city's bishop served as a primitive forerunner of the five-continent College of Cardinals to come. The assigned cardinal often serves as a financial angel for his church, and so it was that when seepage in the excavated Mithraeum below rose to a depth of six feet early in the twentieth century, William Cardinal O'Connell of Boston, then Saint Clement's titular, put in a proper pumping system.

Interred in the upper basilica is a later titular, Amleto Giovanni Cardinal Cicognani, the Vatican's representative in Washington in mid-twentieth century and later the Holy See's chief executive officer, the Vatican secretary of state. Back home in Italy, the cardinal never forgot the states. On his desk as chief of papal affairs, resting at his elbow, was a baseball.

Santa Pudenziana. Among the oldest churches of Rome is that of Saint Pudenziana in via Urbana near Saint Mary Major. There is a tradition that Saint Peter lived at the site in the home of a Senator

Pudens. Saint Paul's second letter to Timothy, written from Rome, speaks of a Pudens, although it is not clear that he was the same person. In a message apparently directed to the Ephesians, Paul wrote: "Get here before winter if you can. Eubulus, Pudens, Linus, Claudia and all the brothers send greetings. The Lord be with your spirit. Grace be with you" (4 : 21–22).

The tradition is that the senator had two daughters, Pudenziana and Prassede, both of whom helped Christians during the Nero reign of terror, both of them remembered as saints. Pope Saint Pius (140–155) is said to have converted the Pudens home into a church. By the fourth century, Pope Saint Siricius coupled his work at Saint Clement's with construction of a basilica at the Pudens site, and Pope Saint Innocent (401–417) continued construction. The church has a fourth-century apse mosaic with no sign yet of the approaching Byzantine period of the Middle Ages. There is some flooring from ancient times, but much of the structure's present appearance dates from a 1588 renovation. The bell tower is twelfth century.

Santa Prassede. This church of Saint Praxedes is dedicated to another of Senator Pudens's daughters. It is on a street of the same name and is another near Saint Mary Major. According to tradition, Praxedes and Pudenziana preserved the blood of martyrs in a well under a large porphyry disk just inside the main door of the present church. There is evidence that a private home on the site was used for Christian worship in the first centuries and that a church was erected no later than 489. The present structure dates in great part to Pope Paschal of 817–824, who is depicted in an apse mosaic wearing a square halo, showing that he was then alive. The rest of the mosaic portrays Saint Peter with an arm around Pudenziana and Saint Paul in a similar pose with Praxedes, the two apostles presenting the heroic sisters to Christ. Pope Paschal thought so well of the church that he moved to it the remains of 2,300 believed martyrs from the catacombs of Saint Alessandro.

Santi Giovanni e Paolo. This church of Saints John and Paul is near the Colosseum on a plaza of the same name. It was the titular church of New York's Francis Cardinal Spellman and owed to him that visitors can now explore the ancient housing beneath the church, where, it is believed, the two saints lived and were martyred. Needed substantial financing was provided by the cardinal. A church was erected at the site in the fourth century, sacked by Alaric in 410, shaken by an earthquake in 442, wrecked again by Robert Guiscard's

Normans in 1084, rebuilt in the twelfth century, and, finally, given its present internal appearance in the eighteenth century. The bell tower is from the twelfth century.

Traditionally John and Paul were thought to be brothers, both officers in the service of Emperor Julian the Apostate, the sovereign of 361–363 who attempted unsuccessfully to roll back the clock by restoring the ancient paganism. The two brothers are said to have insisted on remaining Christian and thus were martyred inside their home on this site. A cleric on the church staff in 1887, curious to verify the ancient story, obtained permission to dig below and made discoveries now available for all to see. An ancient Roman residence was indeed there, one of three buildings, with a total of more than twenty rooms. On one wall there is a fresco of a woman with her arms outstretched in the sign of the cross, an *orante*, a person in prayer, her posture the same as that used now by priests in the celebration of the mass. Whitewash covered one wall, concealing a pagan painting evidently considered nineteen centuries ago as no longer an appropriate decoration. That covering coat is off now, revealing a perfectly preserved second-century fresco appearing to show Persephone, the queen of the pagan underworld, on one of her annual springtime return visits from Hades.

Fulton Sheen, the television preacher, was consecrated a bishop in Saints John and Paul. Since the time of Clement XIV (1769–1774), Passionist priests have administered the premises.

Santa Sabina. This fourth-century church atop the Aventine Hill was redone in the sixteenth century and in following generations in baroque style but now, happily, has been restored to the form of sixteen centuries ago, a type of basilica early Christians knew. Bright and airy, yet sober, the church has fifth-century doors of cypress wood with one of the earliest depictions of the Crucifixion. The church dates from 425, when it was built above the home of Saint Sabina. She is remembered as a woman converted by her Syrian servant, Serapia, both of them martyred under Emperor Hadrian in 119. Excavations have uncovered a third-century house.

An attractive feature of the church is its intimate association with the Dominican Order. Three years after Pope Honorius III (1216–1227) allowed the Spaniard Dominic to found his order, the pontiff confided Santa Sabina to the care of the new religious society. Saint Dominic made it his headquarters. He established the flower-filled Romanesque cloister and monastery next door. The room he used is preserved as a chapel. So is another room, that of the Dominican pope Saint Pius V of 1566–1572. Faculty members in the monastery included the great thirteenth-century theologian Saint Thomas Aquinas of 1225–1274. Munoz de Zamora, the eighth general of the Dominicans, who died in the initial Holy Year of 1300, is commemorated by a mosaic tombstone in the center of the nave.

Santa Prisca sits near Santa Sabina on the crest of the Aventine, with a fine view of Saint Peter's, on the far side of the Tiber. This church, reconstructed in the seventeenth and eighteenth centuries, seems rather recent in appearance but was one of the first places of Christian worship in Rome, dating from the second century. As in the case of San Clemente, there is a Mithraeum beneath it. Saint Prisca is said to have been baptized by Peter; decapitated, she became the first woman martyr. She has been described as either the wife or daughter of the Aquila to whom Paul referred in chapter sixteen of his Epistle to the Romans: "Give my greetings to Prisca and Aquila; they were my fellow workers in the service of Christ Jesus, and even risked their lives for the sake of mine."

The Aventine from the fifth century B.C. was a center of original thinking and rebellion and perhaps provided a sympathetic environment for the wholly new thoughts and beliefs of the Christians. Near Saint Prisca and Saint Sabina in Piazza dei Cavalieri di Malta is the Priory of the Knights of Malta, with a sight no visitor should miss.

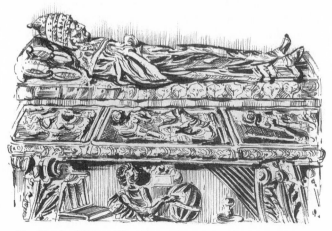

The Tomb of Sixtus IV

Peeking through the front-door keyhole—and that is not considered poor taste—one sees Saint Peter's on the horizon framed beautifully by trees.

Sant'Agnese Outside the Walls is one of the finest examples of the Byzantine period of the Middle Ages, although its origins go back much further. Saint Agnes, whose symbol is a lamb (*Agnus* in Latin), is remembered as a Christian maiden in her early teens who refused to offer incense to pagan gods and was decapitated under Diocletian (284–305). She was buried in the catacombs beside this church. Lending credence to the memories of Agnes is that Saint Ambrose, the bishop of Milan (340–397), one of his century's strongest church leaders, spoke of her in his writings only a few decades after her time.

Saint Constantia, a daughter or granddaughter of Constantine, was so taken with Agnes that she erected a church to her on this site in 324 and a mausoleum for herself next door. Pope Saint Symmachus (498–514) restored Constantia's edifice, and Pope Honorius (626–636) rebuilt it as it has largely remained. The apse mosaic of Honorius's time is one of the finest Byzantine art works in Rome. It shows God's hand reaching down to crown Agnes, who is clad anachronistically as a Byzantine empress. On either side of the saint are the two papal builders of the church, Symmacus and Honorius, the latter holding a model of the church as he redesigned it.

Relics of Saint Agnes are now at the altar. Beside it is an alabaster sculpture of the Egyptian goddess Isis, reworked in about 1600 with gilded bronze head and hands added to represent Agnes. The saint is shown holding a lamb, a reference to a custom of the church that now touches every metropolitan archbishop throughout the world. On January 21, 2000, the Feast of Saint Agnes, as on every recurrence of that date, two lambs will be blessed at Agnes's altar. From there the two will be taken to a Trastevere convent to be raised. On Holy Thursday the lambs will be shorn and their soft wool woven into long slim bands known as *pallia*. These will be taken to Saint Peter's Basilica to be stored in the confession near the tomb until June 29, the feast of Saints Peter and Paul. On that day the pope will forward them to newly named metropolitan archbishops to be worn with other vestments as their indicator of office.

The most recent significant restoration work at the church of Saint Agnes was in 1855–1856, when Pope Pius IX, the sovereign of the papal state, and accompanying cardinals and prelates narrowly escaped disaster. They were in the building beside the church. The floor collapsed into the room below. The members of the party suffered no serious injuries; an 1858 fresco by Domenico Toietti now preserves the memory of the near-tragic event.

Santa Costanza. The mausoleum St. Constantia erected along with the church to Agnes began merely as the burial place Constantia had in mind. Later it became a baptistery and, finally in the time of Pope Alexander IV (1254–1261), a church dedicated to Constantia. Round like the Pantheon, with a cupola seventy-four feet in diameter, the structure is a magnificently preserved ancient Roman building with green and white fourth-century depictions of winemaking. These latter are among the earliest Roman mosaics.

Santi Cosma e Damiano. As Pope John Paul II pointed out, in calling for a jubilee commemoration of the martyrs of the twentieth century, one after the other of the first Christian places of worship trace their origins to those who gave their lives in defense of the faith. This church dedicated to two physician brothers, Cosmas and Damian, is another such example. The two are recalled as victims of Diocletian.

The church, on the Via dei Fori Imperiali, which Mussolini carved out to link his Piazza Venezia headquarters to the Colosseum, is an illustration of how the young Christian community made use of the remnants of antiquity. Pope Saint Felix IV (526–530) received permission from Queen Amalasuntha (498–535) to honor the two martyrs with a church erected inside the remains of two old structures, those of the library of the Forum of Peace, built by Emperor Vespasian (69–79), and of the temple that Emperor Maxentius, the last of the pagan rulers, erected in the Forum to the worship of his deified son Romulus, a youth prematurely dead in 307. Preserved are much of Romulus's temple and also marble pavements of the Forum of Peace.

The church as it appears now is largely in the form given to it by the pope of the 1625 Holy Year, Urban VIII. From Felix's time there is a handsome Byzantine apse mosaic of Christ in a golden toga welcoming the two martyrs to Paradise. Also notable is a seventh-century mosaic of the Lamb of God. A feature of the church much loved in Rome was an eighteenth-century Neapolitan crèche with hand-made terra-cotta, wood, and porcelain figures in period costumes. In November 1988 thieves made off with many of the precious figures causing an indefinite closing off of what remained.

San Lorenzo in Miranda. An even more spectacular example of Christian worship sprouting from pagan origin is close to Saints Cosmas and Damian, on the same street, at the intersection of the Via in Miranda. The best view is from below, on the Sacred Way in the Forum. Rising high overhead are the columns and porch of the temple that the Senate erected to the goddess Faustina, the deceased wife of Emperor Antoninus (138–161), later renaming it for both of the divinized pair. Their two names are still to be seen across the front of the temple but now soaring triumphally from the porch, rising from the heart of the structure, is the seventeenth-century baroque church of Saint Lawrence. Just when the conversion of the structure occurred is not clear, but there are estimates that it was in the seventh or eighth century. There are records of it by 1192.

Santa Maria in Cosmedin. This church with a twelfth-century appearance is best known for a feature of its front porch, the *bocca della verita* (the mouth of truth).

The legend connected with the "mouth" was exploited for a high-spirited scene in *Roman Holiday,* starring Gregory Peck and Audrey Hepburn. A staring face with a wide-open mouth is a standing challenge to reach inside. As the medieval story went, any liar who was brazen enough to do that would find his arm terminated at the wrist. The broad disk formerly was in another wall of the church, but since 1632 the disk has been in its present place. The best guess is that the object is an ancient manhole cover with the face of the god Oceanus.

The church goes back to an early work of Christian charity. In ancient times, many centuries before Christ, the area was the Forum Boarium, Rome's grain market. In the third century B.C. a temple was erected to Ceres, the goddess of agriculture, from whom we have the word cereal. By the sixth century A.D. there was an oratory on the site and a deaconry distributing food to the poor. With Ceres' temple tottering, Pope Hadrian (772–795) pulled down what remained and built a church, which Popes Gelasius II (1118–1119) and Calixtus II (1119–1124) reworked into the edifice's present appearance. A stairway to the right of the Gothic baldachin of 1294 leads down to a crypt dug into the foundations of Ceres' temple. Noteworthy at the site is a splendid Romanesque bell tower of Gelasius's time.

Santa Maria in Aracoeli. This church of Holy Mary at the Altar of Heaven is on most of the once-over-lightly bus tours of Rome. Its brick facade, never completed with the usual covering of marble, sits dramatically atop a sheer flight of 124 steps just behind Piazza Venezia's glaring turn-of-the-century white marble monument to Italy's King Victor Emmanuel II. The steps up to the church were a votive offering from the Roman people in 1348 for their survival during a plague.

The church is at the peak of the Capitoline, one of the seven ancient hills dedicated to worship. A temple of Jupiter's wife, Juno, was on the site. According to a legend, it was there that Emperor Augustus was told by an oracle, *"Haec est ara primogeniti Dei"* (Here is the altar of God's firstborn), a pronouncement that so impressed him that he erected an altar there. Greek monks set up a monastery in the sixth century. They were followed by Benedictines in the ninth. The present structure dates from 1285–1287, when members of the newborn Franciscan order erected it. In 1250, Franciscans were granted the site by Pope Innocent IV (1243–1254), just twenty-two years after the canonization of their founder, Saint Francis of Assisi, and only twenty-four years after the great saint's death.

The church has fine frescoes by Pinturicchio and Benozzo Guozzoli. The mosaic pavement is from the thirteenth century. The coffered ceiling of the sixteenth century celebrates a 1571 Christian naval victory over the Turks at Lepanto, Greece. The Christmas season is a special one at the church. There is a crèche in a chapel just to the left of the main door. It is open for view only in the Christmas period, when the statue of the Infant is placed in his crib. It is a tradition for the children of Rome to come to the crèche at that time to recite to the Infant some bits of memorized poesy. Not to be missed before leaving the church area is the handsome plaza beside it, the work of Michelangelo.

San Stefano Rotondo. With martyrdom a Jubilee 2000 theme, there will be interest in this fifth-century church of Saint Stephen. The Rotondo in the name refers to the rotund shape, the oldest of the type among the churches of the city. Encircling the interior are thirty-four sixteenth- and seventeenth-century renditions of torture and martyrdom, nothing for the squeamish to enjoy. This is another of the churches built over a Mithraeum.

San Pietro in Vincoli. Located in a plaza of the same name near the Colosseum, this church of Saint Peter in Chains traces to third-century Roman housing beneath it but has been far better known by generations of visitors for Michelangelo's contribution to the never finished grand funerary monument of Giuliano della Rovere, Pope Julius II (1503–1513), the successor of Rodrigo de Borgia, Pope Alexander VI of 1492–1503.

Julius ordered a three-story-high, forty-statue memorial for himself to be placed in Saint Peter's and commissioned Michelangelo to carve a dramatic, muscular figure of Moses as part of it. One of the few items ever completed for the project and placed here rather than in the Vatican basilica, the statue nonetheless is appreciated as another of the masterworks of the sixteenth-century genius. Preserved at the main altar are chains believed since the fourth century to have shackled Saint Peter in Jerusalem.

Santissimi Apostoli. This church of the Most Holy Apostles in the plaza of the same name had Michelangelo as a parishioner. In one of the two Renaissance cloisters beside the building is the sarcophagus in which the sculptor-painter lay for seventeen days after his death on February 18, 1564, prior to interment in Florence in the church of Santa Croce.

The church dates to the time of Pope Pelagius (556–561) but underwent extensive changes in the eighteenth century. On the right is a monument to Maria Clementina Sobieska (1702–1735), wife of James Stuart of 1688–1766, the "Great Pretender," who insisted to no avail that it was his birthright to be recognized as King James III of England. The couple lived nearby. A recent addition to the church is the portrait of Saint Maximilian Kolbe (1894–1941), the priest who volunteered to take the place of a married man when ten prisoners at Auschwitz were chosen by the Gestapo to be executed in retaliation for another inmate's escape. The priest's offer was accepted, and he was killed by an injection of carbolic acid. As a seminarian from 1912 to 1919, Maximilian Kolbe had lived in the monastery next door.

Santi Quattro Coronati. This church on the Caelian slopes near the Colosseum on a street of the same name looks like a fortress, and, indeed, it did serve that purpose as a Middle Ages protection for Saint John Lateran farther uphill. To enter, one passes through the outer defense walls into two courtyards and finally into a church dedicated to "four crowned saints," Roman soldiers executed by Diocletian for refusing homage to Aesculapius, the god of medicine. Also revered in the church are relics of five Hungarian sculptors, martyred at the same time for disobeying orders to carve a statue to the healing god.

Dating possibly to the time of Pope Melchiades (311–314) and, with more certainty, to that of Leo IV (847–855), the church was burned so badly by the Normans in 1084 that Paschal II (1099–1118) did a complete reconstruction, creating an architectural curiosity. He kept Leo's apse but shrank the width of the nave so that the apse is now as broad as the whole church.

A fascinating feature is the outside chapel of Pope Saint Sylvester (314–335). It has naive frescoes of 1246 showing a procession through Rome with Sylvester as the newly legalized bishop of the capital, riding a white horse in the position of honor to the rear of the sovereign.

Santa Maria Sopra Minerva. Out front of this church, across the street from the Pantheon, is a Renaissance oddity that catches the eye, an obelisk rising from the saddle of an elephant. The obelisk was carved in Egypt in the sixth century B.C., found in Roman excavations in 1665, and mounted on a carved marble elephant two years later by suggestion of Gian Lorenzo Bernini. Known as the church of Holy Mary above Minerva, the edifice gets its name from the belief that the ruins beneath it are those of a temple to Minerva, the goddess of wisdom, arts, and war. Pompey the Great (106–48 B.C.) constructed the temple in thanks for victories in Asia.

Erected by Dominicans in 1280, this is the oldest Gothic church in Rome. Much history of the Middle Ages and the Renaissance is associated with it. Interred under the main altar is the Dominican nun Saint Catherine of Siena (1347–1380), who pleaded successfully for the return of the papacy from Avignon to Rome. The saint died nearby at 14 Via Santa Chiara. Along with Saint Francis of Assisi, Catherine is considered a special patron of Italy. Also entombed here are the eminent Dominican painter Fra Angelico (1387–1455) and two Medici popes, Clement VII of the 1525 Holy Year and Leo X (1513–1521). Two other popes were elected in conclaves held in the church, Eugenius III of 1431–1447 and the pope of the 1450 Holy Year, Nicholas V.

Santa Cecilia in Trastevere. This church in the heart of the Trastevere quarter has been known as one of the city's important shrines at least since 499, when an accounting was made in connection with a synod. Saint Cecilia is remembered as a married woman who was martyred in the third century with her husband, Valerian; her brother-in-law Tiburius; and an instantly converted onlooker,

Maximus. A place of worship was set up inside Cecilia's house by the fifth century, a basilica was erected by Pope Paschal (817–824), and much of the present appearance dates from 1599.

The tradition is that Cecilia was sentenced to die by asphyxiation inside her own family *caldarium,* a steamroom. After surviving the ordeal for three days, she was stabbed to death. Her sarcophagus was opened for inspection in 1599 with the sculptor Carlo Maderno (1556–1629) an onlooker. He carved a statue exactly reproducing the posture he had observed. It is now beneath the main altar. The *caldarium* is preserved as a chapel. Still to be seen are the vents through which heated air came. On view in the crypt are sarcophagi containing the remains of Cecilia and her three fellow martyrs, all now venerated as saints. Beside them are the tombs of two early popes, Saints Urban (222–239) and Lucius (253–254), both of them Romans.

Saint Cecilia has been the patroness of music and musicians since the fifth century. Accounts of her martyrdom speak of the way she "sang within heart to God alone" during her marriage festivities, seemingly oblivious to the *cantantibus organis,* the "singing" of the musical instruments. A curious misreading of the Latin caused a widespread belief in the fifteenth century that the word *organis* (of the instruments) meant that she played the organ. Sebastiano Conca's ceiling painting of Cecilia in Glory reflects that misunderstanding by including an organ.

Of interest in the apse is a ninth-century Byzantine mosaic of Christ, Cecilia, Valerian, and others, including Pope Paschal, who is shown with a square halo indicating that he was the artist's contemporary. In the nun's choir in the adjoining convent is a Last Judgment by Pietro Cavallini, a masterpiece of 1293 that has been called one of Rome's great hidden wonders.

Santa Maria della Pace. This church to the Madonna of Peace, two blocks west of the north end of Piazza Navona, was erected by Pope Sixtus IV in 1480 in thanksgiving for the Turkish withdrawal from the Otranto area of southern Italy and also for the end of combat between Florence and the Pope's dominion. The church is considered by some to be one of Rome's loveliest. Renaissance masters contributed to it. The first chapel on the right has four sibyls painted in 1514 by Raphael. They show how much the painter was influenced by Michelangelo's similar contemporary depictions in the Sistine Chapel. The simple but elegant two-story cloister to the left of the church was the first of Donato Bramante's many works in Rome and is just the way he created it in 1504.

The design of the church is unusual, a short nave flowering into a broad octagonal cupola-topped central area in front of the main altar. Above the altar is a fifteenth-century painting of the Madonna of Peace that is considered miraculous. Originally in the portico of a twelfth-century church in the same location, it is said to have bled when it was struck in 1480 by some flying object, a stone or a ball.

Santa Maria dell'Anima. Next door to Santa Maria della Pace is Holy Mary of the Soul, one of the two national or ethnic churches in the immediate Piazza Navona area. It is the church of the old German empire and includes many Dutch and German tombs, including that of the last non-Italian to serve as pope from the early Renaissance until the 1967 election of John Paul II. Interred to the right of the choir is Adriano Florensz, Pope Adrian VI, of Utrecht, Holland, whose brief pontificate was from March 1522 to September 1523.

The origins of the church trace to 1386 on the eve of the third Holy Year when a hospice was set up on the site to care for German, Dutch, and Flemish pilgrims. The hospice chapel was replaced with the present church. Begun in 1500, the church was completed under Adrian VI. The church is modeled after the German *Hallenkirchen,* with a "hall" design, the aisles the same height as the nave.

San Luigi dei Francesi. Across Piazza Navona from Santa Maria dell'Anima, on the east, is "Saint Louis of the French," the national church of France. It is a dramatic example of the merging of faith and patriotism. Much of France's history is mirrored on the walls. The church is dedicated to King Louis IX of France (1214–1270), who was canonized by the pope of the first Holy Year, Boniface VII, in 1297, only twenty-seven years after his death in Tunis in the course of his second crusade. He was a sovereign known for justice, ability, charity, and piety. France's royalty as supporters of the church are not only honored throughout the building but were important in financing it. Cardinal Giulio de' Medici, later pope Clement VII (1523–1534), laid the cornerstone in 1518, but the opening of the church was not until 1589, after Catherine de' Medici, wife of Francis I, and Kings Henry II and Henry III aided with funds.

Four of France's kings and queens adorn the late Renaissance facade. On the first level are Saint Louis IX on the right and, on the other side, Charlemagne (742–814), the king of the Franks, who gave the popes their thousand-year sovereignty over central Italy. Above are two queens, Saint Clotilde of 474–545, who made a convert of her husband, Clovis, the founder of the French kingdom, and Saint Joan of Valois (1464–1505), the daughter of King Louis XI and briefly the queen of King Louis XII. In the nave there are chapels to Saint Louis IX, Saint Clotilde, and Saint John of Valois, and also to Saint Remigius, the bishop of Rheims (437–530), who baptized Clovis and thousands of his troops.

Saint Louis's chapel is in the middle of the nave on the left, with a painting by Ludovico Gemignani showing the monarch giving Christ's crown of thorns to the archbishop of Paris. Louis received the reputed relic from the Latin Emperor of Constantinople, Baldwin II (1217–1273), and to house it built the magnificent Saint-Chapelle near the Cathedral of Notre Dame in Paris. A ceiling fresco by Charles-Joseph Natoire portrays the death and glorification of Louis in Tunisia: A figure representing the French nation kneels at the royal bier, while a knight weeps in the foreground.

Across the nave from Louis's chapel is that of Joan of Valois, who, in her later years, founded a Franciscan contemplative order of nuns, the Annonciades of Bourges. Just beyond Saint Joan's chapel is the chapel to Saint Remigius. Jacopone Del Conte's altarpiece shows Remigius baptizing while Clovis smashes pagan idols. Near the entrance on the left is a statue of Saint Joan of Arc (1412–1431), the Maid of Orleans, the battlefield defender of King Charles VIII; she was burned at the stake as a heretic, exonerated twenty-five years later, and canonized in 1920 as a patron of France. A chapel to Saint Cecilia, the second on the right, has fine frescoes by Domenichino (1581–1641), and another chapel to the left of the high altar displays three acclaimed works of Caravaggio (1573–1610) depicting the life of Saint Matthew.

Santa Maria del Popolo. This church of Holy Mary of the People is one of three on the Piazza del Popolo, the people's plaza, the dramatic entranceway to Rome for pilgrims descending from the north through the Via Flaminia. The site and the church are rich in the history of Rome's past two thousand years. Nero was buried here after committing suicide in the first century, and as late as the first years after World War II, the plaza was a favorite of Palmiro Togliatti, Communist leader, who used a platform on the river side to harangue threadbare throngs in an unsuccessful effort to move Italy into the Soviet bloc.

By the time of Pope Paschal II (1099–1118), superstition was so strong that the ghost of Nero was haunting the location that the pontiff exorcised the belief by erecting an oratory on the spot. Rebuilt several times, the present church dates from 1472–1477. An Augustinian monastery next door, destroyed in the 1527 sack of Rome, had as one of its final guests in 1511 a German monk of that order, Martin Luther.

Giants of the Renaissance created the church as we see it now. Donato Bramante extended the apse. Gian Lorenzo Bernini provided baroque decorations for the interior and carved statues of the Old Testament prophets Daniel and Habakkuk. Pinturicchio did a fresco of the Madonna and Child in the first chapel on the right and the Coronation of the Virgin for the vault of the choir area. Raphael provided the sketches for the dome mosaic of the Chigi chapel, God the Creator with the planets of the solar system. Caravaggio's masterful contribution was frescoes of Peter's crucifixion and Paul's conversion. They are in the chapel immediately to the left of the choir.

In a long history anything is possible, and the length of the ongoing Roman epic is suggested by the obelisk in the plaza's center. Soaring 118 feet high, second in height only to the one at Saint John Lateran, the single shaft of granite was erected originally in 1200 B.C. in Heliopolis, Egypt, by Ramses II and his son Mineptah. It was brought to Rome by the all-powerful Emperor Augustus for display in the Circus Maximus and was moved to its present site sixteen centuries later, in 1589, by the Rome-reorganizing Pope Sixtus V.

Completing the scene, which pilgrims from the north have observed since the seventeenth century, are twin churches on either side of the Via del Corso, the street that runs south through Piazza Venezia, past the Forum to the Colosseum. The two are Santa Maria di Montesanto, Holy Mary of the Sacred Mount, of 1679, and Santa Maria dei Miracoli, Holy Mary of Miracles, of 1681.

Santa Maria della Vittoria. This church of Holy Mary of Victory shares the intersection of Via Venti Settembre and Via Barberini with the church for Americans, Santa Susanna. Its main interest is Gian Lorenzo Bernini's superb 1649 marble of Saint Teresa of Ávila in ecstasy, an extraordinary artistic achievement in which the stone figure in rapture appears to be weightless. Saint Teresa (1515–1582), founder of sixteen reformed convents of the Carmelite nuns and the first reformed monastery for Carmelite monks, wrote in her autobiography that she had a vision of an angel piercing her heart with an intense yet sweet pain "that one never wants to lose nor will anyone be satisfied with anything less than God." It was that which Bernini successfully portrayed.

Built by Carlo Maderno in 1608–1620, the edifice commemorates a Catholic victory over the Protestants on November 8, 1620, in the Battle of White Mountain near Prague, an episode of the fratricidal inter-Christian Thirty Years' War. A Carmelite chaplain, Dominic of Jesus and Mary (1559–1630), found an image of the Madonna in the rubbish of the Castle of Pilsen and wore it at his neck during the fighting. Taken as a token of victory, the small Bohemian image was brought to Pope Gregory XV (1621–1623), who gave it to the newly built church as its symbol. Destroyed by an apse fire in 1833, a replica of the image is in place now at the main altar. Four paintings of the Battle of White Mountain are in the sacristy.

San Pietro in Montorio. This church atop the Janiculum Hill affords a sweeping view of Rome from Castel Sant'Angelo to the bright white monument to King Victor Emmanuel II, to the ancient arches of the Basilica of Maxentius in the Forum, and to Saint John Lateran on its hill.

Of special interest is a small circular *"tempietto,"* little temple, honoring the crucified Peter. It was designed by Antonio Bramante in 1508–1512 in a successful early Renaissance experiment in round form construction. Of interest to Irish in the main church of 1481 are the tombstones of three of their patriots who sought refuge in Rome after a failed 1598 uprising against England's Queen Elizabeth: Earl Hugh O'Neill of Tyrone, who died in 1616; his son, Baron Hugh of Dungannon, deceased in 1609; and Earl Roderick O'Donnell of Tyrconnel, who died in 1608.

Gesù. Just behind the Palazzo di Venezia on the Corso Vittorio Emmanuele is the Church of the Most Holy Name of Jesus, commonly known as the Gesù, the church of Jesus. For the hundreds of thousands who have studied in the schools and colleges, worshiped in the parishes, or prayed in the missions conducted by the tens of thousands of members of the order of the Jesuits, this deserves a high ranking on the list of places to see.

This is the site of the church of the Madonna della Strada (Mary of the streetside), which Saint Ignatius Loyola and his small band of former students of the University of Paris took over as their place of worship shortly after their Society of Jesus was born. It was from here that thirty-four-year-old Father Francis Xavier, S.J., with all the enthusiasm, confidence, and daring of the infant order, set off to convert Asia. Not all Asians were Christians when he died twelve years later off the Chinese coast, but the saint's piety and preaching had led to so many thousands of baptisms in India, New Guinea, the Philippines, and Japan that many of his Christian communities still flourish. Next to Saint Paul, Xavier is remembered as the Church's greatest missionary. Since the time of Pope Saint Pius X (1903–1914), Xavier has been the Church's patron of foreign missions. December 3 is his feast day.

The Gesù complex consists of a church and four rooms beside it at 45 Piazza del Gesù. The latter is where Saint Ignatius established his residence and the headquarters of the Society of Jesus in 1544 ten years after he, Xavier, and five other original Jesuits bound themselves together as a new religious society, and four years after Pope Paul III, Alessandro Farnese, 1534–1549, granted formal approval.

The Jesuit Order grew so rapidly that the little church of the Madonna della Strada had to be replaced within a few years. The cornerstone for the new church of the Gesù was laid in 1551, three years before Saint Ignatius's death, but was not finished until thirty-three years later. For some, the facade may be disappointing, too commonplace, too familiar, lacking some of the charm and variety of the earlier Imperial, Byzantine, Romanesque, and Gothic structures, but the fact is that the Gesù's transition from Renaissance to Baroque seems so ordinary for the very fact that hundreds of other churches in Rome, Europe, the Americas, and even Asia have adopted it as a model.

In the extraordinarily ornate interior, the two transept altars facing one another are those of Francis Xavier and Ignatius Loyola. Each was canonized within seven decades of his death. Ignatius is interred beneath his altar. Xavier is buried in India, but his right forearm, brought here in 1614, sixty-two years after his death, is revered as a relic below his altar.

The statue of Saint Ignatius above his altar has had a history of its own. Modeled by Pierre Legros and cast by Federico Ludovici, it has a body of bronze and silver and originally had a head, hands, and feet of pure silver. When Napoleon exacted tribute from Pope Pius VI in 1798, the solid silver was melted down to give to him, and it has been replaced now by silver-coated stucco.

Saint Ignatius's celebrated *Spiritual Exercises* were published while he resided next to the church, although they had been written earlier. His Constitution for the Jesuits, on the other hand, was composed in his next-door four-room suite: a reception area, his private room and study, an oratory, and a room for an attendant. Converted into chapels in 1605, the area was restored to its original state in 1991, the five hundredth anniversary of Ignatius's birth. The Ignatius rooms are open to be visited.

The Madonna della Strada is not forgotten. The chapel to the left of the apse is dedicated to the memory of the first church and includes a fifteenth-century fresco of the Virgin and Child preserved from the first edifice.

Sant'Ignazio. Two blocks north of the Gesù across the Corso Vittorio Emmanuele is another huge Jesuit church, this one named for Ignatius. It is on a square that is a rare sight of its own, an early eighteenth-century rococo space designed to look like an opera setting and succeeding eminently in the attempt. Two streets enter from either side of a building and look like the wings from which a troupe of singers could emerge at any moment. Off to the right is a sidewalk pizzeria rarely found by tourists and a favorite of such postwar Italian film stars as Vittorio de Sica.

Saint Ignatius stands on the site of a smaller place of worship that served the students of the Roman College founded in 1551 by Saint Ignatius for new Jesuits, a school modeled after his alma mater in Paris. By the time of Pope Gregory XV (1621–1623) the college had grown so large that the pontiff urged the creation of a much bigger place of worship to be named for the newly canonized founder of the Jesuits.

A striking feature of the church is a trompe-l'oeil. Perhaps because funds were running low and a cupola was part of the plan, a Jesuit Brother, Andrea Pozzo, painted on the flat ceiling an extraordinarily convincing impression of a cupola. Fifty-six feet across and 112 feet above the floor, the mock dome shows Christ flashing a ray of light to the heart of Ignatius and from there out to Africa, the Americas, Asia, and Europe, where Jesuit missionaries were already at work.

In chapels in the transepts are the tombs of two Jesuit boy saints, Aloysius Gonzaga, a twenty-three-year-old student at the Roman College who died of the plague in 1591 while tending other victims of the epidemic, and John Berchmans, 22, another student at the college in the early seventeenth century. Both died before they could be ordained as priests.

Near Saint Aloysius's altar is the tomb of another Jesuit saint, Saint Robert Bellarmine (1542–1621), a theologian who had Aloysius as a student at the Roman College and asked to be interred near him. Little remains of the Roman College, which was succeeded by the vast Gregorian University a fifteen-minute walk away, but next to the church one may visit the rooms used by the two boy saints.

All three saints have a prominent place in the Church calendar. Saint Aloysius Gonzaga was proclaimed the protector of young students by Pope Benedict XIII (1724–1730) and patron of Catholic youth by Pope Pius XI (1922–1939), with June 21 as his feast day. Saint John Berchmans is the patron of altar boys, his feast on November 26. Saint Robert Bellarmine was acclaimed a Doctor of the Church by Pius XI. His feast day is September 17.

Sant'Andrea al Quirinale. This church of Saint Andrew at 51 Via del Quirinale is across the street from the thousand-room Quirinal presidential palace and is another of the great Jesuit shrines of Rome. Designed by Gian Lorenzo Bernini, it was reopened for service in the time of Clement X, the pontiff of the 1675 Holy Year. Elliptical in shape and rich in many-colored marbles, the church was said to be Bernini's favorite among his many additions to Rome and his own place of retreat for prayer.

The church was built as a shrine for the Jesuit novitiate of 1566, which stood next door. Prominent in the church is an altar to another of the Jesuit boy saints, Stanislaus Kostka (1550–1568). His dramatic story is recounted in part in a photocopy of a letter on display in a nearby reconstruction of the room in which the young saint died. It is from Peter Canisius, the provincial of the Jesuits in Germany, recommending this "fine young man" to the Jesuit general, Francis Borgia. The youth walked the six hundred miles from Vienna to Rome, was enrolled as a Jesuit at seventeen, and died nine months later. All three of those involved in the exchange have been canonized, Francis Borgia in 1671 with a feast day of October 10, Stanislaus Kostka in 1726 (November 13 feast day), and Peter Canisius in 1925 (December 21 feast day). Stanislaus Kostka is a Patron of Poland and Peter Canisius a Doctor of the Church.

The novitiate alumni included others now honored on the altars, Jesuit Fathers Robert Southwell, Henry Walpole, and Thomas Garnet, all three of whom were hanged, drawn and quartered in England between 1595 and 1608, and thirty-three-year-old Blessed Rudolph Acquaviva, a missionary, killed by Hindus in 1583.

Practical Information

The lower excavated areas beneath San Clemente's are open from 9:00 A.M. to 12:00 P.M. and 3:30 P.M. to 6:00 P.M., with a delayed morning opening (10:00 A.M.) on Sundays and public holidays. There is a 2,000-lire charge.

Santa Pudenziana is open from 8:00 A.M. to noon and from 3:00 P.M. to 6:00 P.M., with a morning delay (9:00 A.M.) on Sundays and holidays. The doorbell is on the left.

Santa Prassede. Hours are 7:00 A.M. to noon, 4:00 P.M. to 6:30 P.M.

Santi Giovanni e Paolo. The upper church is open from 8:00 A.M. to 11:30 and 3:30 to 6. Closed during 1997, the underground access will be open from 8:30 A.M. to 11:30 A.M. and from 4:00 P.M. to 6:00 P.M. when reopening resumes. The winter season afternoon hours are 3:30 P.M. to 5:00 P.M. Offerings are accepted.

Santa Sabina. Access to the garden is through the sacristan.

Sant'Agnese Outside the Walls. Open 7:00 A.M. to noon, 4:00 P.M. to 7:30 P.M.

Santa Costanza. For admittance, apply at Sant'Agnese next door.

Santa Maria in Cosmedin. Open 9:00 A.M. to 1:00 P.M., 3:00 P.M. to 5:00 P.M.

Santa Maria in Aracoeli. There are guided tours. The hours are 9:00 A.M. to noon, 3:30 P.M. to 5:30 P.M.

San Stefano Rotondo. Open Monday through Friday, 8:30 A.M. to noon.

San Pietro in Vincoli. 7:00 A.M. to 12:30 P.M., 3:30 P.M. to 6:00 P.M. Mornings only on Sunday.

Santissimi Apostoli. Open 10:00 A.M. to noon, 4:00 P.M. to 6:00 P.M.

Santi Quattro Coronati. To see the Saint Sylvester chapel, request the key at the convent off the inner courtyard.

Santa Cecilia. Open 10:00 A.M. to 11:45 A.M., 4:00 P.M. to 5:00 P.M.

Santa Maria della Pace. The church and cloisters are open Tuesday, Wednesday, and Friday, 10:00 A.M. to noon, 4:00 P.M. to 6:00 P.M. On Sundays and holidays, 9:00 A.M. to 11:00 A.M. only. Cloister entrance is at 5 Vicolo Arco della Pace.

Santa Maria dell'Anima. Entrance is by the side door on Via della Pace.

San Luigi dei Francesi. Open every day except Thursday afternoons. 7:30 A.M. to 12:30 P.M., 3:30 P.M. to 7:00 P.M.

Santa Maria della Vittoria. Open 6:30 A.M. to noon, 4:30 P.M. to 7:30 P.M.

Gesù. To see Saint Ignatius's rooms, enter through 45 Piazza del Gesù. Open 4:00 P.M. to 6:00 P.M., and Sundays 10:00 A.M. to noon. Summer schedule may vary.

Sant'Andrea al Quirinale. Open 10:00 A.M. to noon and 4:00 P.M. to 7:00 P.M.

CHAPTER 12

ENGLISH-SPEAKING CHURCHES

A SCORE OF Rome's churches have special interest for American, English, Irish, Scottish, Canadian, and other speakers of the English language. Among them are the following.

American

Santa Susanna. There was no national church for people of the United States until the six-decade-old Paulist Order, a group founded to convert America, set out to get one in 1922, not just any one but specifically an edifice near the American embassy, the handsome Grand Hotel and the main railroad station, the Stazione Termini. The seldom-open Santa Susanna on Via Venti Settembre not only filled the bill but also traced to the first Christian decades. Except for occasional colorful vicissitudes, Santa Susanna has been a home away from home for people of the United States ever since.

Beneath the sanctuary visitors can see remnants of the city wall of 387 B.C., now serving as a support for the graceful facade of 1603. Also in view is a patch of mosaic flooring of an ancient residence over which successive churches were built or restored in the fourth, ninth, and sixteenth centuries. The house below is believed to have been that of Saint Susanna, the martyred niece of Pope Saint Caius (292–296).

The church is little changed from the way Carlo Maderno reconstructed the edifice, which was erected by Pope Saint Leo III (795–816). Brilliant frescoes tell the story of two Susannas, a maiden falsely accused by lecherous elders as described in the thirteenth chapter of the Book of Daniel and, from New Testament times, a third-century martyr of Diocletian.

Of special interest on the right side is a chapel honoring the relics of Saint Genesius, the patron saint of actors. He is remembered as a third-century comedian who was converted on stage in the presence of the emperor while in the very act of mocking baptism, a reversal that cost him his life. Actors have a special tie to the church. A group of them, including Loretta Young, Helen Hayes, Ed Sullivan, and Jane Wyman, are recorded on a plaque as contributors to a refurbishing of the Genesius shrine. During the filming of *Cleopatra*, Carroll Hayes, famous since for his Archie Bunker, adopted his son, Hugh, through the parish.

Santa Susanna still remembers a stormy start when Rumanian diplomats tried physically to evict the Paulists so that Catholics of their own country could have the ancient church. Even more troublesome was an eight-year period when parishioners were ousted, ostensibly because of a need for ceiling repairs but clearly to the satisfaction of a three-century-old Cistercian convent that is a co-tenant of the site. Pope John Paul II ended the dispute in 1993, inviting the Americans back.

The North American College. The seminary for American priests has two locations, each of them equipped with handsome chapels. The original one, at 30 Via dell'Umilta, around the corner from the Trevi Fountain, is also the American Bishops' Center for Visitors to the Vatican. Beginning in 1598 the site was used successively for convents for Dominican nuns and for those of Saint Francis de Sales's Visitation Order, each ousted in turn by revolutionaries. In 1859, with a grant from Pius IX, the bishops of the United States opened the country's first Rome seminary for an initial class of twelve. By the time of the 1959 centennial celebration, the ranks of the alumni included 6 cardinals and 117 archbishops and bishops.

The thousands of Holy Year visitors who make their way to the Via dell'Umilta premises will walk in the footsteps of many celebrities who have preceded them—Mark Twain; Buffalo Bill's Wild West touring company, who paid a call in 1890; Will Rogers in 1926; and Al Smith in 1937. G. K. Chesterton lectured in 1929.

The Via dell'Umilta premises are a residence now for graduate students, while those studying for ordination are in huge modern premises on the Janiculum Hill, a structure for which ground was broken in 1948 on extraterritorial land of the Vatican state. A generous contributor, who inspected the progress of construction on each of his annual Rome visits, was New York's Cardinal Spellman. Celebrity visits continued there, with callers including General Dwight Eisenhower and Presidents Truman, Kennedy, and Nixon.

Nearby on the same hill is the church of Sant'Onofrio, which still has the aura of a hermitage imparted to it in 1434 by the monks of the order of Hermits of Saint Jerome. Since 1947 it has been in the care of the Franciscan Friars of the Atonement, the 1898 Garrison, New York, order of Anglican priests that became Roman Catholic in 1909.

English

Numerous places of veneration in Rome are associated with the people of England.

San Silvestro. This church, in Piazza San Silvestro, next door to the main post office, has been the national church for English Catholics since 1887. The building itself sits on Roman walls of twenty-five centuries ago and dates from Pope Saint Paul, of 757–767, who converted his family residence into a monastery for exiled Greek monks and into a church. He dedicated the latter to Saint Stephen of A.D. 35, the first martyr, and to Pope Saint Sylvester of 314–335.

Seven popes, and relics of Pope Saint Sylvester, are entombed in the church. The Romanesque bell tower was added by the monastery's Benedictine monks in the twelfth century, while the Franciscan nuns who succeeded them in 1285 restored the church. The present form dates from 1601. The altar is atop seven steps, an idea of Michelangelo's. The church's most venerated object is what is said to be the head of Saint John the Baptist. In the church since the twelfth century, it is encased in a silver reliquary made by order of Martin IV (1281–1285).

The genesis of Saint Sylvester's as a special center for English Catholics traces indirectly to Pius VII (1800–1823). With Napoleon's troops withdrawn from Rome and the British Catholic Relief Bill ending England's anti-Catholic penal code, Pius decided that there should be enhanced religious opportunities for the English-speaking. He arranged for preaching and religious instruction in English at three churches, Sant'Andrea delle Fratte near Piazza di Spagna, Holy Trinity in Via Condotti, and San Salvador in Onda near the Sisto bridge. From that beginning evolved the idea of the San Silvestro parish. Monsignor Giovanni Montini of the Vatican Secretariat of State, before he became Paul VI, added to the parish facilities in 1949, dedicating a conference center and meeting place.

The Church of Santo Spirito in Sassia. This church, at the corner of Borgo Santo Spirito and the Via de' Penitenzieri, two blocks east of Saint Peter's Plaza, dates from a few score years after Saint Augustine arrived in England in 597 as a missionary and as the first archbishop of Canterbury. With kings and commoners soon coming as pilgrims to Saint Peter's, the area between the Vatican and the river became so popular as a place to house the British that it became known as the Burgus Saxonum, the Saxons' burg, with a hospice set up in the seventh century. From that the church emerged. The nearby section of the riverbank highway is still known as the Lungotevere in Sassia, literally the road along the Tiber in the Saxon neighborhood.

Built in the eighth century and reconstructed in the twelfth and sixteenth, the church is now Renaissance in appearance. England's King Ine and Queen Ethelburga of the eighth century are among many English interred in the church.

The Venerable English College. The eighth-century hospice in the Burgus Saxonum passed out of English hands and became the Santo Spirito (Holy Spirit) Hospital in 1204. It still continues as Rome's oldest medical center and as a first aid station for injured Vatican pilgrims. No longer with a hospice of their own, the English community was so impressed with the number of medical emergencies during the Holy Year of 1350 that they decided to try again. This time, with the approval of Pope Gregory XII, it was in the Via di Monserrato near the Campo dei Fiori on the Tiber's left bank. An eighth-century church at the spot, originally named for the Most Holy Trinity of the Scots, was rededicated to the Trinity and to two English martyrs, King Saint Edmond of East Anglia (841–870) and Canterbury's archbishop, Saint Thomas Becket (1118–1170). By 1579 the hospice had evolved into what is now known as the Venerable English College, with the church at its heart and the training of priests for England and Wales rather than the care of pilgrims as its purpose.

Frescoes in the church honor priests, including graduates of the college who were executed in England for violating the sixteenth- and seventeenth-century law against the practice of the Catholic religion. In the school's first century, 40 of the 410 graduates sent to England were executed. Paul VI conducted a mass canonization for them in 1970. With later efforts to reconcile the Catholic and Anglican churches, many faithful of the latter have been guests at the college, among them the poet John Milton.

Saint George and the English Saints. The Church of St. George and the English Saints is on Via Sebastianello, at the north end of Piazza di Spagna. A late addition to Rome, opened in 1887, it has as a mission the reunion of the Anglicans and Catholics. The origin of the church dates to the Crimean war, when one of Florence Nightingale's nurses, the English Protestant Magdalen Taylor, was so moved by the piety of dying Irish soldiers that she became a Catholic and in 1870 founded an order of nuns, the Poor Servants of the Mater Dei, the Mother of God. Taking the name of Sister Magdalen of the Sacred Heart, she opened her Rome convent in 1880 and within a decade added the present church. In the church is a reproduction of the oldest known painting of the Madonna and Child, the fresco in the catacomb of Priscilla. It is honored as a pledge of Anglican-Catholic reconciliation.

Santa Maria in Campitelli. This church, in Piazza Campitelli, to the rear of the Capitoline Hill, has a close association with the Stuarts, the last Catholic royalty of England. When James II's grandson, Duke Henry Stuart of York, a claimant to the vanished throne, was made a cardinal in 1747, he chose this church as the center of his titular parish and provided a fund for perpetual masses and benedictions. The benedictions continue every Saturday evening, with a prayer for "the return of English brethren separated from the unity of the Faith."

Cardinal Stuart revered a five-by-ten-inch Syrian-style gilded enamel copper icon of the Madonna called the Santa Maria in Portico. It is on display atop a spiral staircase at the rear of the altar. It has been the object of centuries of devotion as a protector of Rome. The story is that it appeared miraculously in the time of the first Pope John (523–526) coincidental with the end of an epidemic. The church to house it was consecrated in 1073 by Pope Saint Gregory VII (Hildebrand) and rebuilt in much the present form by Alexander VII (1655–1667).

Saint Gregory on the Caelian Hill. It was from this church not far from the Colosseum that Pope Saint Gregory the Great (590–604) dispatched Saint Augustine on his mission to evangelize England and to become the first archbishop of Canterbury. In the atrium are listed other monks of the adjacent Benedictine monastery who followed in Augustine's wake, Saint Lawrence and Saint Mellitus, two other archbishops of Canterbury; Saint Paulinus, the bishop of York; Saint Justus, the bishop of Rochester; and Saint Peter, the first abbot of Saints Peter and Paul at Canterbury. All were priests of the first decades of the seventh century. Entombed in a courtyard is Sir Edward Carne, who was sent by Queen Mary Tudor in 1555 to restore English obedience to Rome. With reversed fortunes in London, the ambassador never returned there, staying on instead in Rome, a warden of the English College.

Also interred at the church is Robert Peckham, who asked as his epitaph that he be remembered as an "Englishman and Catholic," one who could not live in England "without the Faith," and who died "because he could not live apart from his country."

The church is believed to have been erected over Gregory's home. It was rebuilt in the twelfth century, dedicated to him, and restored in the seventeenth and eighteenth centuries. In a chapel next to the fifteenth-century altar is a stone throne said to have been Gregory's. A painting shows King Richard II endowing the Madonna with the English nation. On the church grounds are three other chapels, one to Saint Andrew, with paintings by Domenichino and Guido Reni, of 1608. Near them is a stone table Gregory is said to have used in feeding the poor.

Close by Saint Gregory's is another missionary starting point that had England as its goal. Blessed Dominic Barberi, a Passionist priest, left his monastery at the Church of Saint John and Paul in 1840, became the Passionist provincial in England, had a role in the conversion of Cardinal Newman, and then had as his successor in the provincialate his friend, the former Anglican Hon. George Spencer, grand-uncle of Winston Churchill and great-great-grand-uncle of this century's Princess Diana. As a priest, Father Spencer founded a Crusade of Prayer for England's return to Catholicism.

Irish

The Irish have four centers in Rome, the Pontifical Irish College and Chapel, dedicated to All the Saints of Ireland, Saint Isidore's College and Church of the Irish Franciscans, the college of the Irish Dominicans at Saint Clement's basilica, and St. Patrick's College and Church of the Augustinians. All four were founded in the seventeenth century in a flight from English control of Ireland, and each of them, by the changing tides of history, became beneficiaries of English protection in the eighteenth century. When Italian nationalists abolished the papal states in 1870, it was England that stepped in successfully to protect the Irish centers. Each of the four has a dramatic story.

The Pontifical Irish College and Chapel. The college structure on the Coelian Hill near Saint John Lateran dates only from 1926, when Pius XI (1922–1939) and Catholics of Ireland, the United States, and Australia provided funds, although Irish establishments in Rome had begun centuries earlier. Monks from Ireland were at the abbey of the Holy Trinity at least by the eleventh century, and the first Irish college was opened in 1625. It was on the Pincian Hill at the church and monastery of the Spanish Saint Isidore.

The 140 years at Saint Isidore's were followed by a peripatetic existence at the Via degli Ibernese (The street of the Hibernians), on the slopes of the Quirinal Hill; the Via delle Botteghe Oscure, behind the Gesù; and the Via Mazzarino, near Saint Mary Major. One move was provoked by Napoleon's suppression of the seminary in 1798 and another was motivated by a search for larger premises. In the meantime, class after class graduated priests and bishops for Ireland, the United States, Australia, New Zealand, and South Africa.

Just to the right on entering the college's Chapel of All the Saints of Ireland is an 1855 monument to William O'Connell (1755–1847), the member of London's House of Commons who fought successfully for the religious freedom of Ireland's Catholic majority. An inscription says: "This monument contains the heart of O'Connell who, dying at Genova on his way to the Eternal City, bequeathed his soul to God, his body to Ireland and his heart to Rome." Added is this: "At the bar of the British House of Commons in 1829 . . . he refused to take the anti-Catholic declaration in these remarkable words: 'I at once reject this declaration: part of it I believe to be untrue, and the rest I know to be false.' "

Above the main altar is a fresco, commissioned in 1953, showing episodes of Irish Catholic history. Depicted are Saint Patrick (389–461) baptizing Prince Aengus of Munster; Saint Brendan the Navigator (484–577), thought by some to have discovered America; Saint Brigid (450–525), the "Mary of the Gael," foundress of Ireland's first convent; and Saint Oliver Plunkett (1629–1681), a graduate of the Irish College, Primate of All Ireland, and, in 1681, the last of the priests hanged, drawn and quartered at London's Tyburn gallows.

Saint Isidore's. When a seminary for secular priests was set up at Saint Isidore's in 1625, a college was also established for Irish Franciscans. They have remained there ever since. The church is a good example of seventeenth-century architecture. Never forgetting that Saint Isidore (1070–1130), a Madrid native, was a farmhand, and is the agriculturists' patron saint, the church each November offers a Sunday harvest mass of thanksgiving. Farmers in country costume attend bringing baskets of corn, wine, and fruit. The college alumni include the first bishop of Adelaide, Australia, and martyr missionaries to Ireland.

Saint Clement's. While a church of interest to all visitors because of the layers of construction going back to the time of Nero, Saint Clement's has special meaning for the Irish. The property has been in the hands of Irish Dominicans since 1667, when it was assigned to them to help compensate for what they had suffered under Oliver Cromwell (1599–1658)—all their monasteries confiscated and one hundred fifty of their members killed or exiled. The Irish language as well as English was used in ministry at the church in the seventeenth and eighteen centuries, and the Community Council Book records awards given for good preaching, an extra dish at dinner for an oration in English and two for a good one in Irish.

Many footnotes to history have been written at Saint Clement's during the Irish Dominicans' three-century tenure. When Pius IX in mid-nineteenth century had to flee from Rome during a popular uprising, first he slipped in disguise into Saint Clement's to pray. In 1776, when the papal states accepted the fact that the Stuarts no longer could be considered the legitimate royalty of England, San Clemente's prior lost his position by insisting nonetheless on extending royal honors to the Young Pretender, Prince Charles Edward.

England's Kind Edward VII, as Prince of Wales, visited the Dominicans and their church in 1859, 1862, 1863, 1865, and 1867, fascinated by what was found when 130,000 cartloads of rubble were removed exposing the long-lost church below.

Amid all this, the little community of Irish Dominicans exported members to take up church leadership positions across the world. Prior Luke Concanen was assigned in 1807 as the first bishop of New York, and Father Raymond Griffith was named the Vatican's first Vicar Apostolic at the Cape of Good Hope.

Saint Patrick's College and the Irish Augustinians. Like the

Pontifical Irish College, the Augustinians' college and church of Saint Patrick has had a rocky history across three centuries but is now well established. It is on Via Buoncompagni, a couple of blocks east of the American embassy compound. The community's history began in 1656, when Augustinian survivors of the Cromwell assault were given the Priory of San Matteo on Via Merulana, a peaceful haven after the slaying of eleven of their society in Ireland. The respite was short-lived, as the better-financed Italian Friars of Perugia replaced them within five years. Seven decades later, Pope Clement XII (1730–1740) gave the friary back to the Irish, but their Jobian troubles were not over; within three or four generations, Napoleon's troops decided that Rome had too many religious centers and razed San Matteo.

Ever resilient, the Augustinians from the Emerald Isle obtained the Priory of Santa Maria in Posterula from Gregory XVI (1831–1846). It was comfortably near the Vatican, but that too soon met an end; it was demolished to make way for a new Tiber bridge.

Since 1913 there has been a happier ending. Erected over earth from Downpatrick, the believed place of burial of Saint Patrick, there is now both an Irish seminary and a church. The church has a shrine to Saint Oliver Plunkett, the first erected to him. The courtyard is Tara Hall, with a name famous among filmgoers through *Gone With the Wind*. World War II made fresh history for the church. Wehrmacht officers were billeted there, subsequently yielding place to Irish-descended worshipers from the armed forces of England, America, Canada, Australia, New Zealand, and South Africa.

Scottish

The Scots College and Church. The present Scottish College and church on the Via Cassia dates only from 1964, but, as twenty stained glass windows in its Church of Saint Andrew and Saint Margaret emphasize, the Scottish history in Rome goes back many centuries. The first window shows Saint Ninian, a Scot consecrated a bishop in Rome in the time of Pope Siricius (384–399) and, after that, an evangelizer in his home country. Further on are King Malcolm III and his queen, Saint Margaret. They are believed to have created a core of Scottish settlement in the eleventh century by erecting a Scots Hospice near Piazza di Spagna and the present eight-century-old basilica of Saint Andrea delle Fratte (Saint Andrew of the Countryside). The latter is on Via Capo le Case. Early Scottish independence victories over England followed by the changes and the execution of Mary Queen of Scots pave the way in the series of windows for Clement VIII's creation of a Scots College at the time of the Holy Year of 1600. It was then one of only five national colleges in the Eternal City, a pioneer among the present eighty.

Except for interruptions caused by Napoleon and World War II, the Scots College in Via Quattro Fontane, near Piazza Barberini, continued to educate Scotsmen for the priesthood and to maintain a chapel for Scottish Catholics until 1962, when repair costs on the old college became so high that wholly new construction on Via Cassia was chosen as the wiser course. The chapel on Via Quattro Fontane has continued to serve Scottish worshipers.

Canadian

Church of the Canadian Martyrs. Among the postwar churches of Rome is the Church of Our Lady of the Blessed Sacrament and of the Canadian Martyrs. It is on the grounds of the Villa Massimo on Via G. B. De Rossi and serves two purposes, veneration of the Blessed Sacrament and the cult of seventeenth-century Jesuit missionaries martyred by Indians in Canada and New York.

A chapel in the church honors the slain Jesuits. John de Brebeuf (1593–1649) and four companions were put to death in Canada, and Isaac Jogues (1607–1646) and three others lost their lives in New York. Brebeuf joined the Jesuits in Rouen, France, in 1617. He volunteered for the dangerous Canadian mission and worked for more than two decades among the Huron Indians, converting some seven thousand. He compiled a dictionary and catechism for the Hurons, and then fell into the hands of their enemies, the Iroquois, who tortured and killed him.

Isaac Jogues studied with the Jesuits in his native Orleans in France, enrolled among them in 1624, asked for assignment among the Hurons, and, like Brebeuf, was captured by Iroquois, who killed his comrade Rene Goupil and tortured and mutilated him for a year. He escaped, returned briefly to France, volunteered again for work among the Indians, and, this time, accompanied by Jean de Lalande, was seized, tomahawked, and beheaded by Mohawks near Albany,

New York. Lalande was slain the next day. Pius XI beatified Brebeuf and Jogues in the 1925 Holy Year and in 1930 canonized them as Patrons of Canada and North America.

The church is headquarters of the Congregation of the Most Blessed Sacrament, which Saint Peter Julian Eymard (1811–1868) founded for the adoration of the Eucharist. Father Eymard was one of the first proponents of eucharistic congresses, one of which will be a major event of the Jubilee 2000.

The church combines both themes, Canadian and Eucharistic. Tall concrete arches through the nave suggest the soaring trees of the primeval Canadian forests, and a six-foot-in-diameter monstrance dominates the high altar, a gift from Catholics of Australia.

Religious Worship Information

CATHOLIC SERVICES IN ENGLISH

Santa Susanna, Piazza San Bernardo, 15 Via Venti Settembre, 00187 Rome. Weekday masses including Saturday at 6:00 P.M., Sunday at 9:00 A.M. and 10:30 A.M. in the church and 11:00 A.M. at Marymount International School. Telephone 482 7510 at the church and 488 2748 at the Paulists' residence. Telefax 474 036, Confessions before all masses. Lending library Sunday 10:00 A.M. to 12:30 P.M., Tuesday and Thursday 10 A.M. to 1 P.M., Wednesday 3:00 P.M. to 6:00 P.M., Friday 1:00 P.M. to 4:00 P.M. Summer hours reduced. Buses 60, 61, 62, and 492 stop in Largo Santa Susanna; 16, 37, 136, and 137 stop on Via XX Settembre; 57, 64, 65, 75, and 170 stop on Via Nazionale in front of the Hotel Quirinale.

Saint Patrick. Sunday mass, 10:00 A.M. Telephone 488 5716.

San Silvestro. Sunday masses 10:30 A.M., 6:00 P.M. Telephone 679 7775.

OTHER FAITHS IN ENGLISH: SUNDAY SERVICES

Anglican and Episcopal
All Saints Anglican Church, 153 Via del Babuino. Telephone 3600 2171. Rev. Geoffrey B. Evans. Eucharist Tuesday, Wednesday, and Thursday at 6:00 P.M., Saturday at 6:30 P.M., Sunday at 8:30 A.M. and Sung Eucharist at 10:30 A.M. Organ Vespers at 5:30 P.M. Wednesdays. Evening Prayer, Sunday at 6:30 P.M.

Saint Paul's American Episcopal Church, 58 Via Napoli at Via Nazionale. Telephone 488 3339. Rev. Dr. Michael L. Vono, 58 Via Napoli at Via Nazionale. Holy Eucharist 8:30 A.M., Choral Eucharist and church school (nursery provided), 10:30 A.M.

Assemblies of God
International Christian Fellowship, c/o Saint Paul's Church, 58 Via Napoli. Telephone 8689 0882. Pastor Terry Peretti. Sunday worship, 2:30 P.M.

Baptist
Rome Baptist Church, 35 Piazza San Lorenzo in Lucina. Telephone 687 6652. Rev. Kenneth D. Lawson. Sunday 10:00 A.M. worship.

Methodist
Ponte Sant'Angelo Methodist Church, 3 Via del Banco di Santo Spirito. Telephone 656 83 1. Rev. Richard Grocott. Sunday service and Sunday School, 10:30 A.M.

Presbyterian
Saint Andrew of Scotland, Church of Scotland, 7 Via Venti Settembre. Telephone 482 7627. Rev. David Huie. Sunday service and Sunday School, 11 A.M.

Jewish
Temple is at Lungotevere dei Cenci. Telephone 687 5051.

AMONG NATIONAL CATHOLIC CHURCHES

The United States.
Santa Susanna, 15 Via Venti Settembre, telephone 482 7510, 488 2748.

Canada
Church of the Canadian Martyrs, Via G. B. de Rossi, 862 115.

England
San Silvestro in Capite, Piazza San Silvestro, 687 775.

France
Saint Louis of the French, Piazza San Luigi dei Francesi, 653 629.

Germany
Santa Maria dell'Anima, 651 130.

Greece

Sant'Anastasio, 46 Via dei Greci (Byzantine in Greek language), 687 025.

Ireland

Saint Patrick, Via Buoncompagni, 465 716.

Russia

Sant'Antonio Abate, 40 Via F. Clementi (Byzantine-Paleoslav Rite), 684 0014.

Spain

Iglesia Española de Montserrat, Via Giulia, 565 861.

CHAPTER 13

THE MANY ROMES

AMONG THE MANY wonders awaiting the year 2000 visitor, whether he be pilgrim or tourist, will be the opportunity to step back into the past, back to the year one, which began the two thousand years we are celebrating, back, indeed, even a half-millennium before that. The same streets are there to be walked, the same monuments of Gospel times still present to be enjoyed. The Rome that has thrilled generations of poets is still there to intrigue those who come at the start of the third Christian millennium.

The living record, sometimes glorious, sometimes profoundly shameful, of the whole of Western civilization will be spread before the visitor, the Rome of Anno Domini One, the city of 200 subsequent decades, and the even more ancient community, the Rome that claims a history of 750 earlier years, while archaeologists credit it with much more, at least another millennium and perhaps a few more centuries as well.

Spread before the visitor will be the Rome of pagan antiquity, then the city of transition as Christianity conquered, next papal Rome, and finally a traffic-glutted but beguilingly charming modern city of three million.

In a myriad of ways, the Roman tourist and pilgrim at the millennium will find the roots of his civilization burrowed into the seven hills and across the Tiber at the Vatican. A word like "palace" traces to one of the seven hills, the Mons Palatinus, the Palatine, atop which the emperors built magnificent residences, fabulous "palaces," which are still there in good part, available to be visited. "Propaganda," a word now with negative overtones, found benign birth in downtown Rome three and a half centuries ago as the name for the still surviving Holy See institute for missionaries, the congregation for *"propaganda fidei,"* the propagation of the faith. Obstetrics and its Cesarean sections reminds us that Caesar was removed from his mother's ab-

Santa Maria in Trastevere

domen by surgery. In matters of attire, the cassocks and mass vestments of priests recall the skirtlike togas of Rome's earlier residents.
The Roman influence ripples ever further—into concepts of law and
in language, mangled and reborn as Italian, French, Sard, Silician,
and Rumanian, and surfacing in sesquipedalian phrases in English.

The list knows no end. For every visitor, his own Rome and Italy
await.

Poets and painters, writers and historians will recall the excite-
ment so many of their predecessors experienced amid the golden
sunshine of a Roman evening, in the mysterious sense of "home" a
foreigner feels in a land that he would expect to be alien, in a place
where so many human dreams expanded and collapsed, only to be
replaced by others that flourished. The tributes from those earlier
visitors are legion.

Percy Bysshe Shelley (1792–1822), in "Julian and Mattel" in 1819:

> How beautiful is sunset when the glow
> Of Heaven descends upon land like thee,
> The paradise of exiles, Italy.

Or as the same English poet put it in a note about entering the peninsula: "No sooner had we arrived in Italy than the loveliness of the earth and the serenity of the sky made the greatest difference in my sensations."

George Gordon, Lord Byron (1788–1824), reacted similarly. In *Childe Harold's Pilgrimage* (1818), he exulted:

> O Rome! My country! City of the soul.

And again:

> Italie! O Italie: Thou who hast
> The fatal gift of beauty.

Robert Browning (1812–1889) was no less enthusiastic in "De Gustibus" (1855):

> Open my heart, and you will see
> Graved inside of it, Italy.

Nikolay Gogol (1809–1852), the Russian dramatist and novelist, found the land of the ancient Romans a revelation: "Who has been in Italy can forget all other regions. Who has been in Heaven does not desire the Earth. Europe compared to Italy is like a gloomy day compared to a day of sunshine."

Henry James (1843–1916), the American novelist who chose England as his place to reside, gave no second rating to the land of the Italians: "At last, for the first time, I live."

He was agreeing with Stendhal (1783–1842), the French novelist: "The charm of Italy is akin to that of being in love."

Painters for many generations have flocked to the Roman sun. A favorite corner for them at the start of the twentieth century was the Piazza di Spagna, where peasant girls in their then still widely used picturesque costumes, sat through the day on the great sweep of the Spanish Steps, waiting to be hired as models. With the models gone now, hundreds of sightseers use the same marble benches to rest tired feet.

Camille Corot (1796–1875), the Impressionist, was one artist who found the bounteous radiance of the Roman air an abundance too much. The land of the Tiber, he found, was not that of his northern Seine. "The sun," he said, "spreads a light that makes me despair. . . . I perceive the helplessness of my palette."

For some, the contemplation of Rome, the fallen military master of the known world, has been melancholic. The Forum at the foot of the seven hills was such for Shelley as he wrote in 1818 to Thomas Love Peacock: "The Forum is a plain in the midst of Rome, a kind of desert full of heaps of stones and pits; and, though so near the habitations of men, is the most desolate place you can conceive."

Charles Dickens (1812–1870), in *Pictures of Italy* (1846), was of like mind at the Colosseum: "To see it crumbling there, an inch a year; its walls and arches overgrown with greens; its corridors open to the day, . . . to climb its upper halls, and look down on ruins, ruins, ruins, all about it, . . . the temples of the old religion fallen down and gone; is to see the ghost of old Rome."

Edward Gibbon (1737–1794) was so moved by the abundant remains of ancient Rome that he gave much of his life to writing the classic *Decline and Fall of the Roman Empire*. In his memoirs, published in 1796, he told how his Herculean task was undertaken: "It was at Rome, on the fifteenth of October, 1764, as I sat musing amidst the ruins of the Capitol, while the barefoot friars were singing vespers in the temple of Jupiter, that the idea of writing the decline and fall of the city first started to my mind. . . .

"My temper is not very susceptible of enthusiasm, and the enthusiasm I do not feel I have ever scorned to affect. But at the distance of twenty-five years I can neither forget nor express the strong emotions which agitated my mind as I first approached and entered the eternal city. After a sleepless night, I trod with a lofty step the ruins of the Forum; each memorable spot where Romulus stood, or Tully spoke, or Caesar fell, was at once present to my eye; and several days of intoxication were lost or enjoyed before I could descend to a cool and minute investigation."

Recent decades, with easy transportation, have been even more generous in sending and satisfying callers, whatever their quest. The physical loveliness enjoyed by a Shelley, a Byron, or a Gogol was still there to thrill the octogenarian Bernard Berenson, collector and chronicler of the art of Italy, when in the 1960s he invited an American journalist to join him on the roof of the Hassler Hotel to observe the soft, cinnamon glow of sunset behind Michelangelo's cupola on

Saint Peter's Basilica. Frail and shivering under a blanket, the aged connoisseur of things beautiful was lost in the savoring of the vision before him.

Orson Welles (1915–1985), the ironic movie maker and unsparing critic of newspaper tycoon William Randolph Hearst, a corpulently ballooning man, guffawed at a streetside restaurant table over private jokes with journalist-author John Gunther. Whatever the quips, they were not darts flipped at Rome and the Italians, for it was Welles who inserted these words into Graham Greene's script for the movie *The Third Man*: "In Italy for thirty years under the Borgias they had warfare, terror, murder, bloodshed, but they also produced Michelangelo, Leonardo da Vinci, and the Renaissance. In Switzerland they had brotherly love, they had five hundred years of democracy and peace. And what did they produce? The cuckoo clock."

For the movie stars Tyrone Power and Linda Christian the Forum was a good place to marry. Throngs of cameramen, newsmen, and sightseers crammed the elegant tenth-century church of Santa Francesca Romana at the Palatine's foot to watch the actors pledge fealty.

For seminarians from scores of countries, including many young blacks from Africa, Rome showed the way to a life of prayer.

For whatever the start-of-millennium visitor seeks, Rome has an answer.

CHAPTER 14

ALL ROADS TO ROME

THE ALREADY ANCIENT Rome of Caesar, Augustus, and Tiberius sprawled far beyond the original heartland of the Roman Forum and is still to be seen piecemeal scattered across the modern city and into the countryside. Highways, aqueducts, city walls, bridges, and monuments tell their mute story.

Among the most dramatic are the remains of the **Appian Way**, which starts from the valley between the Palatine and Coelian hills. Inaugurated in 312 B.C. by the censor Appius Claudius, sections of the road in the original form still are visible outside the Aurelian city walls. The smooth, many-sided basalt stones of the pavement continue to carry traffic. The old road is thirteen and one-half feet wide, broad enough for two-way chariot movements. Sidewalks of hard-packed earth were on either side, many still there.

At first, going only 132 miles to Terracina, a four- or five-day trip, the Appian road by the second century before Christ reached 365 miles to Brindisi, the seaport opening the way to Greece and the East. A marvel of engineering across marshes and through mountain passes, the thoroughfare still impresses highway constructors, who note that it drove straight toward distant objectives, bypassing villages just as superhighways do now. Side roads tied in the communities en route.

The network of ancient roads bringing visitors from all points of the compass still serves modern travelers: the Via Latina, along which General Mark Clark marched north from the Anzio beachhead in 1944 for a bloodless occupation of Rome; the Via Salaria, through which beardless teenaged German soldiers withdrew Northeast away from the oncoming Allies; the Via Flaminia, also northbound, beside which a few war-ravaged families were still living in two-room caves in the heart of the modern city as late as 1946;

the Via Aurelia, passing Saint Peter's toward the northwest; and the Ostian Way, swinging southwest to the sea.

Even before the Romans built their roads across modern Europe and into the Middle East they gave thought to unwelcome callers who might, and did, arrive with or without a highway system. Two sets of protective walls were built, one already centuries old by Tiberius's time, another constructed in the centuries just after him. Ample sections of both remain.

Those arriving by train at the main station, the Stazione Termini can see a few dozen feet of the first **Roman walls** just to the right as they exit into a plaza crowded with buses outbound to all corners of the city. Made of huge gray blocks of stone, the wall was the work of Servius Tullius, the Etruscan who was Rome's fifth king. Appalled by the Celts who burnt and sacked the young city in 390 B.C., the king surrounded the seven hills and a two-square-mile area with a wall seven miles long, punctuated by twenty-three gates.

Offense is the best defense, so the militaristic Romans, busy conquering other peoples, felt no need for new walls until the first centuries of the new era, when the thousand-year empire, self-indulgent and weak, tumbled toward collapse. Aurelian, the emperor of A.D. 270 to 275, erected the new barriers, and they continue to be a striking sight. Twelve miles long, made of concrete faced with red brick, the walls were, and in many stretches are, twenty-one feet high and thirteen feet thick at the base. The Vatican and its neighbor, the community of Trastevere, both of them on the opposite side of the Tiber, had been left out by Servius Tullius but, in the second round, were included. Strengthened by Emperors Maxentius (306–312) and Honorius (395–423), the walls proved to be of no avail, however, as waves of barbarians swept over Italy, sacked Rome, and inaugurated the Middle Ages.

Two blocks from the United States embassy on the sophisticated Via Veneto, a favored tourist center, is one of the best-preserved sections of the Aurelian walls. Their sole function now, unintended but inevitable, is to snarl traffic as cars weave through the occasional gates. For some Romans the walls just to the right of Via Veneto even serve as narrow but fashionable homes hollowed out inside. Electric buzzers beside doorways are there to announce callers. A most impressive section of the walls is at the Porta Sebastiana, where the Appian Way heads South. There the walls soar five stories high.

One way to thwart the defenders of Rome, the barbarians discovered, was to cut the extraordinary system of **aqueducts** that the Romans had built across the centuries, immense arched structures soaring above the surrounding fields. By Augustus's time there were four of them, the Appia of 312 B.C., the Vetus of 272, the Marcia of 144, and the Tepula of 125. By the approach of the year one, there were two more, the Virgo of 19 and the Ansietina of 2 B.C.

Romans continue to fill containers at public fountains from which gush the particular aqueduct water they prefer. For many Romans, after World War II the countryside arches of the water supply system served an additional purpose that never ceased to astonish writer John Gunther on his repeated visits to the ancient city. Families huddled below them as their place of residence. A ride out the Appian Way offers excellent views of the still magnificent aqueduct structures.

Rome grew on its seven hills on the Tiber's left bank, but the crossing of the river posed a challenge from the start. It is said that a wooden bridge was put in place as early as the second half of the seventh century B.C., but it was not until 179 to 142 B.C., a few generations before Julius Caesar, that a stone structure crossed the river waters. It is the **Pons Amelius**, just downstream from the island in the Tiber, and is one of the city's most startling ruins. Frequently repaired, it finally succumbed in the fifteenth century A.D., losing both ends, leaving in place the central section, the piers of 179 B.C. and the arches of 142. The Romans now know it as the *"ponte rotto"*, the useless midstream broken bridge.

A few yards upstream, however, two bridges used by the Romans of the year one are still hard at work. Using the island as the middle section of the crossing, the **Pons Caestius** goes out from one bank and the **Pons Fabricius** from the other. Both were constructed in the first century B.C.

Across the city there are many other remains from the time of the first Caesars. Midway on the Corso Vittorio Emanuele, one of the main east-west thoroughfares of the city, there is an open block uncovered by Benito Mussolini. Determined to identify modern Italy with the Caesars, the Duce demolished medieval neighborhoods in several parts of the city in an archaeological quest for antiquity. The **Largo Argentina** alongside the Corso is one of the results. The site is two blocks west of the Gesù on the Corso Vittorio Emanuele. Ten feet below the level of the modern city, excavators found the black-

and-white mosaic floors and the tall columns of four temples from 101 B.C., the youngest, to as early as the third century B.C. Mindful of all needs, the ancients did not neglect to include a marble latrine off to the side. All is now in plain view.

A few blocks west of the Largo Argentina, at the edge of the Campo de' Fiori, a busy marketplace, are a few remains of the **theater of Pompey**, where Julius Caesar was stabbed to death. Built in 55 B.C., Rome's first stone entertainment place, the theater was a sensation in its time, with an auditorium for forty thousand. Four hundred lions and eighteen elephants were killed in the spectacular opening ceremonies. Now only foundations remain and can best be seen in the underground restaurant of San Pancrazio, a favored tourist eating place. Pompey, the builder, born in 106 B.C. and one of the great Roman conquerors, ruled temporarily in a triumvirate with Caesar but in 48 B.C. lost to him in battle and was killed.

A good place to start in the quest for the city of the first Christian years is the **Roman Forum**, snuggled at the feet of the seven hills. It can be seen from 9:00 A.M. to 7:00 P.M. except in winter, when the closing is at 3:00 P.M. The admission charge includes access to the Palatine Hill overhead.

Another place of major historical and Christian interest, now only in vestigial form, is the **Circus Maximus** at the south side of the Palatine Hill. Built in 326 B.C. and reconstructed in 174 B.C., it is now just a broad, grassy valley dominated by the tall brick walls of the imperial palaces atop the Palatine. The emperor's viewing platform is still there. The elongated shape of the stadium, with its long chariot racetrack, can still be made out, but there is little else. This is where many Christian martyrs are believed to have died. It was a place of savage entertainment, with thousands of animals among the slaughtered.

More extensive is what is left of two monuments to the Emperor Augustus, his **mausoleum** from 28 B.C. and the **Ara Pacis Augustae**, the Augustan altar of peace, of 9 B.C. The two are next to the Tiber at the Via di Ripetta and the Lungotevere in Augusta, a few blocks west of the Piazza di Spagna.

The mausoleum is a huge mass, 131 feet high and 295 feet across. An unimposing brick pile now, the structure was built of concrete sheathed in *opus reticulatum,* small triangular blocks of tufa stone, and then encased in brilliant while marble. Originally, a fifty-foot bronze statue of Augustus loomed above. The interior is now stripped, but, for a century, this was the favored imperial burial place. Entombed there were Augustus and his third wife, Livia Drusilla, the mother of Tiberius, then Tiberius himself, followed by Emperor Claudius (A.D. 41 to 54). The last interred was Nerva, in A.D. 98, just about the time John wrote the fourth and last Gospel.

Opposite the mausoleum is the Ara Pacis, the Altar of Peace, a tribute to the brief respite Augustus accomplished in a millennial history of Roman wars. The Altar of Peace, encased now in glass, can be visited from Tuesday to Saturday from 9:00 A.M. to 1:30 P.M. and 9:00 A.M. to 2:00 P.M. on Sunday. From April to December it is also open from 4:00 P.M. to 7:00 P.M. The altar has had an odd history. With Rome often sacked, sinking from a population of one million in the time of the emperors to fifteen thousand in the heart of the Middle Ages, the memory of the shrine vanished. During the Renaissance, the papal rulers of Rome began reacquiring bits and pieces of it. Some parts came back from the Louvre in Paris, some from Vienna. In 1930, it was reassembled. Depicted in the carvings are scenes of the first imperial times, with Augustus impressively represented as taller than anyone else. With him is Tiberius, who built the altar. Alongside are the *flamen*, the lighters of the ceremonial flames. Reflected in the altar is a high point of the pagan civilization at its then unrealized turning point. The tumultuous final imperial years, the disastrous invasions, and the emergence of the new Christian era lay just ahead.

CHAPTER 15

FALLEN ROME

AMONG THE MANY dramatic sights awaiting the year 2000 visitor to Rome is the tangible record of how an immensely powerful society peaked and then plunged into a chaos from which a new vision of life emerged. With the world at their feet paying tribute in the yet unrecognized new era of the Gospels, the Romans lost the will to struggle for the national defense and hegemony. They gave themselves up to indolence and frivolity, including the depraved enjoyment of others' suffering. For a while they outdid their forebears in the construction of astonishing monuments, but, beneath the surface, a revulsion was setting in. The Christians, with their beatitudes, their concept of chastity extending to the whole society and not merely to a few symbolic vestal virgins, their sympathy for the poor, their belief in the value of every individual, and their extraordinary acceptance of martyrdom, slowly were undermining the foundations of the pagan regime.

Will Durant (1885–1981) gave his opinion of what befell Rome when he wrote in an epilogue to his 1944 *Caesar and Christ*: "A great civilization is not conquered from without until it has destroyed itself within. The essential causes of Rome's decline lay in her people, her morals, her class struggle, her failing trade, her bureaucratic despotism, her stifling taxes, her consuming wars."

The first three centuries of the modern era saw pagan Rome on its highest plateau of architectural achievement while morally tumbling forward toward dissolution. All this is still to be seen in the sites and structures of the old city. The two centuries on either side of the start of the first millennium were a period of great achievements in the literary arts, with Cicero (106–43 B.C.) orating, Horace (65–8 B.C.) and Ovid (43 B.C.–A.D. 17) writing poetry, and Tacitus (55 B.C.–A.D. 120) recording history, but it was also a time of domestic cruelty, ushering in new horrors. In 73 B.C., the gladiator

Spartacus, a man from Thrace, rebelled against servitude, raising an anti-Roman army of seventy thousand, only to suffer defeat two years later. He died in battle, but six thousand of his followers were subjected to the torture of crucifixion. Cicero was decapitated when Octavian (later Augustus) took Rome; his head was placed on view on the orators' rostrum in the Forum.

Emperors were no more fortunate. In A.D. 69, the year after Nero's suicide, Rome had four successive emperors: Galba, who was slain in the Forum by Otho, who took over only to be replaced by

Constantine's Arch and the Colosseum

Vitellius, who in his turn was killed in the Forum, and, finally, Vespasian, who ruled for ten years.

Despite the violence, ever more impressive construction continued for generations and is still to be seen. Just twelve years old at the start of the initial Christian millennium was an odd creation, a pyramid, no stranger to Egypt in that era but a novelty for Rome then and now. Cestius, a well-to-do politician, built it as his tomb at the start of the Ostian Way. Soaring eighty-eight feet, it took a year to build. It is still standing. It is Christian tradition that Saint Paul was taken a mile out on the Ostian Way to be beheaded. Cestius's pyramid would have been one of his last views of the city.

One of the most spectacular imperial residences was that of Nero, who reigned from A.D. 54 to 68, dead at age thirty-one. Rome had been suffering disastrous fires, one in A.D. 27, another in 36, then the furious blaze in 64. The area just east of the Forum was gutted. It is a Christian memory that Nero blamed some of Rome's first Christians as the arsonists, executing them as human candles and as food for beasts.

Nero's immediate predecessor, Claudius, emperor from 41 to 54, had been declared a god, in accordance with the then century-old practice, and a temple in his honor was under construction, but Nero tore down parts of it to make way for a gigantic structure sprawling across the Palatine and Coelian Hills and part of the Forum. To adorn it Nero raised a colossus, a 120-foot gilded bronze image of himself. A section of Nero's palace, with rooms decorated with grotesque designs, still exists but has been closed in recent years to all but students of the arts.

It was under Nero in Rome in either A.D. 64 or 67, according to ancient Christian tradition, that Peter was put to death, crucified upside down. Seen as the first pope, it is to him that the popes of the Catholic Church trace their origin and their authority as bishops of the ancient city and as vicars of Christ. With the account of Peter's death, Christianity, then no more than a generation or two old, made its first Roman appearance.

When Peter reached Rome is not known for certain, but the official Vatican account listed in the *Annuario Pontificio*, the official Holy See yearbook, cites a commentary of the year 354 suggesting that Peter served twenty-five years as Rome's bishop. That would have placed his arrival at either 39 or 42, during the reigns of the mad Gaius Caesar Caligula (37–41) or of Claudius (41–54).

Nero had shown little regard for Claudius's shrine, and Vespasian, in his turn, treated Nero's palatial area with similar disregard. He used much of the site to put up Europe's most spectacular relic of antiquity, a building that drew its name from Nero's colossus, the **Colosseum,** an object along with Saint Peter's Basilica that is on every visitor's short list.

Begun by Vespasian in A.D. 72, the Colosseum was inaugurated in 80 by his son and heir, Titus, and finally finished by Domitian, the emperor of 81–96. Two-thirds of a mile in circumference, the structure is 490 feet wide and 620 feet long, twice the length of a football field. It rises in four tiers to a height of 159 feet, the equivalent of a fifteen-story building. Designed for spectacular, blood-spilling entertainment, it had seventy-six entrances, each labeled with Roman numerals carved into the stone and still to be seen. Each entrance led to a particular part of the stadium, good seats for senators and other important people below and poorer areas above for women, the plebes, and others of lesser status. Fifty-five thousand spectators could enter and leave through the exits, the *"vomitoria,"* in little more than ten minutes.

The interior now has the pocked and broken aspect of a honeycomb, exposing the dens for wild animals that were below the original surface. During the time of its use, up to the year 523, a wooden platform served as the fighting surface for gladiators and wild animals. Sand, called *arena* in Latin, covered the flooring, thus providing us a word for our sports vocabulary.

Just east of the Colosseum, at the juncture of the Vias Labicana and San Giovanni in Laterano, is the surviving training area for the gladiators. In a city that never ceases to uncover new remnants of ancient times, the gladiator school was not discovered until the 1960s. Like much of the rest of central Rome, it is ten feet lower than the present street level. Millennia of debris and erosion had piled a thick earthen blanket over the site and over the rest of the central city.

For more than three centuries, as the empire declined, the Colosseum provided degraded, death-dealing entertainment, with hundreds of gladiators losing their lives and thousands of lions, tigers, leopards, elephants, giraffes, ostriches, and hippopotamuses slashed out of existence.

There is debate over whether Christians were put to death in the Colosseum rather than in the nearby Circus Maximus, but popes took steps in the seventeenth century to preserve what was left of the vast structure as a monument to the early martyrs of the faith. A cross was erected inside the stadium, and the fourteen Stations of the Cross, devotional reminders of Christ's progress toward Calvary, were installed. Princely families, many of whom gave popes to the Church during the Middle Ages and Renaissance, had made use of the Colosseum for generations as a quarry for building palaces; that was stopped. A feature of Holy Week observances in the 1990s has been Pope John Paul II's visit to the Colosseum to shoulder a cross and to take part in the Stations of the Cross ceremony.

From the Forum the Colosseum appears complete, but a walk around to the right reveals the ravages of the millennia. In addition to the looting of building materials, a lightning strike in 217 and an earthquake in 847 have permitted only two-fifths of the mass to survive.

Just across the street from the Colosseum, inside the **Roman Forum**, is the **Arch of Titus**. Remarkably preserved, it commemorates a calamitous event of the first-century Holy Land. Jews rebelled against the Roman occupation in 66 and Nero sent General Vespasian to put down the revolt. Midway, Nero's suicide intervened and the troops of Vespasian installed their general as emperor. He left his son Titus to lay siege to Jerusalem for seven months and then to destroy the Jewish capital. Succeeding to the empire in his turn, Titus ruled from 79 to 81. Like his father, he was hailed at death as a god. Emperor Domitian, who followed, in one of his first acts erected the arch. Still emblazoned across it is the inscription "The Senate and the People of Rome: To the Divine Titus Vespasian Augustus, son of the Divine Vespasian." Helping the arch endure was the fact that the princely Frangipani family used it as part of a fortress, employed sometimes during later tumultuous centuries as a papal refuge. Restoration to its present form was in 1821. Rome's oldest surviving arch of triumph, the structure gloats over the crushing of the Jews. Bas-reliefs tell the story. Titus is shown riding in a triumphal procession. Depicted are the victory trophies, the looted silver trumpets, and the seven-branched golden candelabra of the Jerusalem temple. Titus is depicted ascending into heaven on an eagle's back.

Trajan seems to have ignored the growing Christian community, but his successor, Domitian, is remembered as one who took as murderous note of them as Nero had; a reprobate who bedded his niece as his mistress; and a harsh master who condemned at least one unchaste vestal virgin to be buried alive. Domitian's imprint is seen especially atop the Palatine, a favored place of residence from as far back as the bronze age of the fourteenth to the eleventh centuries. He was neither the first nor the last of the emperors to covet the spot. Before him were Augustus, Tiberius of 14–37, Caligula, Claudius, and Nero and, after him, Hadrian (117–138), Antoninus Pius (138–161), Commodus (180–192), Septimius Severus (193–211) and finally Elagabalus in 218–222. Domitian leveled the hilltop, leaving much that remains, but each of the other emperors contributed to massive surviving walls and foundations, Corinthian columns, marble pavements, and an aqueduct.

A stadium in Domitian's palace has been identified as possibly the *"hippodromus palatii,"* the Palatine hippodrome, where the Acts of the Martyrs says Saint Sebastian in 288 was put to death. With its cypresses, above the city sounds, the Palatine now is a peaceful place of retreat.

Among other dramatic survivals from the era are the **market, forum**, and **victory column of Trajan**, the emperor of 98 to 117. Trajan's victory column of the year 113 tells us an immense amount about the man who, as sovereign of the Roman state, styled himself Imperator Caesar Nerva Traianus Augustus. The shaft is one of the most perfect remains of antiquity, providing detailed insights into ancient life, and especially into that of the military.

The column is in its original position just east of the Piazza Venezia between the Via delle Fori Imperiali and the Via Alessandrina. It stands 125 feet high, as lofty as a twelve-story building. One long strip of bas-reliefs winds around it for a length of 656 feet and describes the way General Trajan expanded the Roman empire across the Danube River, conquering the Dacian tribes in what is now Romania and bringing the empire to its broadest expanse, reaching from Britain to Morocco to upper Egypt and to Armenia. The column portrays one hundred episodes: Trajan haranguing his troops, forts constructed, armored soldiers crossing the Danube on pontoon boats, the long-haired, bearded enemy in long-sleeved jackets and pantaloons, Dacian women torturing Romans and, finally, stacks of Dacian heads presented to the victor. Made of Carrara marble, the same material Michelangelo used for his sculptures fourteen centuries later, the column is hollow inside, with a 185-step staircase leading to the top and forty-five loopholes illuminating the interior. Trajan was interred in the column, but, since the Middle Ages, there has been no trace of his remains. Beside the column are huge Trajan constructions, a forum, and a market place, the latter boasting a six-story-high brick complex of shops snuggled against the Quirinal Hill.

Where the persecution of Christians was concerned, Trajan had what he must have considered a moderate policy. He sent instructions to the Middle East to punish the followers of Christ but to ignore anonymous denunciations and to grant forgiveness to those who renounced their faith and prayed to "our gods." At death a temple was erected to Trajan and his wife, Plotina, and they were incorporated in the ranks of those to whom the apostates were required to pray. A statue to Trajan was placed atop his column, remaining there for a millennium until December 4, 1587, when Pope Sixtus V replaced it with Giacomo della Porta's bronze image of Peter the fisherman.

While Trajan left so much, his successor, Hadrian, outdid him. The Pantheon, the Castel Sant'Angelo, the Forum temple of Venus and Rome, and the astonishing three hundred-acre residence known as Hadrian's villa outside Rome on the Tiburtine hills are all his works. Inside the small Christian community, by the Vatican count, two Greeks were pope, Telesforus (125–136) and Iginus (136–140).

The **Pantheon**, a few blocks northeast of Piazza Venezia, in a tightly crowded section of old Rome, is an incomparable survival from ancient times. For the emperors it was the *pan-theon,* the shrine of all the gods. It was built originally as a small rectangular structure in 27 B.C. by Marcus Vipsanius Agrippa of 63 to 12 B.C., Emperor Augustus's son-in-law, a battle-tested fleet commander. His name can still be seen above the entranceway columns. Gutted by fire, the interior was rebuilt from 117 to 136 in the present dome-covered rotund form. Surviving from Agrippa's time are thirteen of the sixteen huge granite columns of the portico.

A triumph of Roman architecture unmatched until recent times, the structure has a dome 143 feet across, larger even than Michelangelo's imitative one on Saint Peter's Basilica. Lighting is an oculus, a thirty-foot "eye" and peephole in the roof through which rain falls to a catch basin and drain below. A scraping of a foot at the drain below the oculus sends echoes back from every point of the ceiling. The stucco and marble veneer of the interior is Hadrian's, a rare glimpse of the furnishing of an ancient construction. The marble Corinthian columns are of a type known as antique yellow, a material hard to find even in ancient times.

The immense bronze doors are of Hadrian's time, but the gilded bronze coverings of the roof were plundered by the Byzantine emperor Constans II in 655 and replaced with the present lead by a Syrian pope, Saint Gregory III (731–741). Marble once covered the outside, but only a few patches of it remain; the rest was stripped away for other purposes across the centuries. The underlying brick now is exposed.

Interred in the Pantheon are the painter Raphael (1483–1520), two kings of Italy, Victor Emmanuel II (1878), and Umberto I (1900) and the latter's queen, Marguerita (1926), for whom, rather inelegantly, the basic tomato and cheese pizza is named. Helping preserve the Pantheon was the fact that Pope Saint Boniface IV (608–615) consecrated it as a church, reburying inside it many cartloads of remains from the catacombs.

Dramatic as the Pantheon is, even more imposing is **Hadrian's tomb**, which he built for himself just upstream from the Vatican Hill on the banks of the Tiber. He started it in 123, six years into his rule, building the Pons Aelius across the river to the site in 133, but not quite completing the great funerary structure by the time of his death. His successor, Antoninus Pius, finished the work in 139.

An immense round mass, modeled in part on the tomb of Augustus of a century and a half earlier, the structure served as the burial place of a succession of emperors, Antoninus Pius, Marcus Aurelius (161–180), Commodus, Septimius Severus, and Caracalla (211–217), all of them well known to history at a time when the papal succession quietly, all but invisibly, was continuing, with Popes Pius of Aquilea, Italy (140–155), a Syrian; Anicetus (155–166), Soterus of Campania, Italy (166–175); Eleutherius of Epirus (175–189); Victor, an African (189–199); and Zeferinus, a Roman (199–217).

Dominating the east end of the Via della Conciliazione, the great tomb is now a dramatic counterpoint to the even more immense basilica of Saint Peter. The building has had an extraordinary history. When Caracalla died, the tomb was converted into the fortress of Rome. In 590, with Rome suffering from one of a recurrence of plagues, Pope Saint Gregory the Great, then beginning a fourteen-year pontificate, reported seeing an angel atop the fortress, sheathing a sword. It was taken as a celestial sign of mercy, for the epidemic ended. Nearly a millennium later, during the Renaissance pontificate of the Roman Alessandro Farnese, Pope Paul III, a marble statue of a sword-wielding Saint Michael the Archangel was raised above the mass as a conspicuous feature of the Roman skyline. Now in a courtyard of the castle, the image has been replaced aloft since the pontificate of Benedict XIV (1740–1758) by the present one of bronze. What had begun as an imperial mausoleum assumed its present name, the **Castel Sant'Angelo** (the Castle of the Holy Angel).

The tomb-castle has served both as a Renaissance prison and as a place of residence and refuge for popes during times of tumult. Pope

Saint Leo IV, a Roman (847–855), built a barrier around the immediate neighborhood of the Vatican, the tall brick Leonine Wall, using Castel Sant'Angelo as the main strongpoint. Another Roman, Giovanni Gaetano Orsini, Nicholas III (1227–1280), topped the wall with a covered passageway, allowing besieged popes to flee through it to the castle. The Spanish Rodrigo de Borgia, Alexander VI (1492–1503), updated the escape route. That was in the nick of time, for a generation later, in 1527, Pope Clement VII, the Florentine Giulio de' Medici (1523–1534), had to make his way through it when the troops of Emperor Charles V sacked Rome.

It has been many generations since the walkway has been used, but it is still to be seen leaving the Vatican over an archway just to the left of the colonnades of Saint Peter's plaza and proceeding East on the Via dei Corridori just north of the Via della Conciliazione. That stretch of the Leonine Wall serves now merely to bedevil drivers as they twist their cars through its arches.

Of the Pons Aelius with which Hadrian spanned the Tiber, just the three central arches remain. Clement IX, Guilio Rospigliosi (1667–1669), added the two riverbank arches. Known now as the Ponte Sant'Angelo, the bridge is adorned with baroque statuary of the sixteenth century, with Peter and Paul at either end and huge angels bearing the symbols of the Crucifixion, the cross, the scourge, the crown of thorns, the nails, the soldier's lance, the garment, and the sponge of bitter wine.

In addition to the Pantheon and his tomb, Hadrian, in 135, made another addition to the city, the **twin temples of Rome and Venus**. Their fifty columns and broad platform, 361 by 174 feet, are at the edge of the Forum opposite the Colosseum. The section of the Rome deity faces the Forum, and Venus's the Colosseum. Nero's thirteen-story-tall statue to himself was still in the way at the time of construction, so Hadrian harnessed twenty-four elephants to move it. Making a city a god was something new for Rome, although there had been Greek precedents.

Hadrian in his turn joined the divinities. Antoninus Pius dedicated a structure to him as Divus Hadrianus, the god Hadrian. Three blocks northeast of the Pantheon and near the Church of Saint Ignatius, it was put to tax-collecting use in 1695. In recent years, it has served as the Italian stock exchange. Clear to be seen in the outside wall are eleven of the temple's forty-five-foot-tall Corinthian columns.

Commemorating the late-second-century time of **Emperor Marcus Aurelius**, there is another startling **victory column**. Erected by Commodus, the son and heir of Marcus Aurelius, the ninety-six-foot-tall marble column imitates the shaft of Trajan, describing in a long spiral frieze how the late emperor defeated Germans in the Danube valley. For centuries the emperor's statue topped the column, until Pope Sixtus V in the sixteenth century paired Peter on Trajan's column with Paul on that of Marcus Aurelius. The column shares its area now with the Palazzo Chigi of 1580, the headquarters of the Italian prime minister, and is catercorner with Rinascente of 1885, the city's first department store, boasting Rome's original shopping center escalator.

Septimius Severus, the first emperor of the third century, is remembered with a massive, handsomely preserved, seventy-foot-high **triumphal arch** in the heart of the Forum. With him the Roman invasion of Britain reached a high-water mark, stopping short of a conquest of all of Scotland, but the structure celebrates his sanguinary achievements in the valley of the Tigris and Euphrates in the Middle East. It is said that Septimius Severus killed all the men in northern Mesopotamia, taking one hundred thousand women and children as slaves. The arch depicts the two rivers supine in defeat. It hails Septimius Severus as Caesar, Augustus, and *pater patriae,* father of the country. It also honored sons Caracalla and Geta until such time as Emperor Caracalla slew his sibling; still to be seen are the marks where Geta's name was chipped away.

Known as Caracalla from the hooded Celtic cloak he wore, the new emperor preferred a longer name identifying him with greats who had preceded him, Imperator Caesar Marcus Aurelius Severus Antoninus Pius Augustus. A murderer, he was killed in his turn after a five-year rule but not before he added to Rome an enormous monument whose remains served after World War II as a popular center for summer outdoor opera performances, the **Baths of Caracalla**.

The baths' twenty-seven-acre space is near where the Appian Way departs from the city. It attracted world television attention in the late 1990s when three great tenors, Luciano Pavarotti, Jose Carreras, and Placido Domingo, sang in concert there. Built as a bathhouse to serve 1,600 persons, the complex included hot, tepid, and cold bathing areas, a library, a stadium, lecture rooms, and gardens. Much has fallen, but a great part of the domed circular brick and concrete *caldarium* still stands. The bathhouse fulfilled its assigned purpose for three centuries until the invading Goths in the sixth century cut the necessary aqueduct.

The Vatican chronology lists fifteen popes in the third century. None were of great historic renown. They served only briefly, averaging six or seven years, but the reigns of the faltering emperors were even more truncated. With constant violence and repeated assassinations, there were twenty-seven third-century emperors, six of them in the single year of 238.

With religious speculation increasing and both Mithraism and Christianity from the East winning converts, the emperor Elagabalus toward the end of the first quarter of the third century made his own attack on the old state religion, trying to replace Jupiter with a sun god, a deity of another Eastern cult. The platform of the temple the emperor built, 230 feet by 130, still occupies the northeast corner of the Palatine Hill, but it served its assigned purpose only briefly. A monstrous personality and a transvestite, the youthful emperor was beheaded by his troops and thrown into the Tiber, and the sun god's temple was rededicated to Jupiter the Avenger.

With Christianity continuing to grow in the third century despite repeated imperial efforts to suppress it, two final builders of the old regime remained, Diocletian of 284–305 and Maxentius of 307–312. Their creations are still large on the Roman scene. **Diocletian** built a **bathhouse** even greater than Caracalla's. With a three-thousand-person capacity, it covered thirty-two acres, much of the space between Stazione Termini, the Grand Hotel, and the church of Santa Susanna. By one account, forty thousand Christians were forced to do the construction work, and every kiln in Rome produced bricks.

Much of the bathhouse remains. Pope Pius IV, the Milanese Giovan Angelo de' Medici (1559–1565), hired Michelangelo to convert the central hall of the *frigidarium,* the cold bath, into the **Church of Santa Maria degli Angeli**, Saint Mary of the Angels. The Renaissance genius treated the ancient structure with respect, preserving eight huge red granite columns and the original vault. Since then, a reworking in the eighteenth century has given the church its present form; Michelangelo's area is used as a transept, the main door placed in the *caldarium,* and the *tepidarium,* the warm baths, also incorporated.

Opposite Santa Susanna's, a long block from Santa Maria degli Angeli, is another church, the rotund **San Bernardo delle Terme**. It was created inside one of the bath's four corner towers during the time of the Florentine Pope Clement VIII, Ippolito Aldorbrandini (1592–1605).

Pagan Rome achieved an extant climax at the very moment it met its end, the **basilica of Maxentius** on the Via dei Fori Imperiali, on the north side of the Forum. Emperor Maxentius (307–312) was the general who faced his rival emperor Constantine at the Milvian Bridge over the Tiber at the city's north side. The bridge is still there but has often been reworked and is closed to vehicular traffic. It was while confronting Maxentius that Constantine is said to have seen a cross in the sky with the legend *"in hoc signo vincis,"* "In this sign shall you conquer." Maxentius drowned; Constantine won and soon legalized Christianity.

Maxentius's basilica, an immense hall of brick-faced concrete soaring 113 feet high, was the largest vaulted building ever attempted by the ancient architects. Much has collapsed, possibly due to the earthquake of 1349, which damaged the Colosseum, but a vast section remains.

The basilica covered 65,000 square feet. Incomplete at Maxentius's overthrow, the finishing touches were provided by Constantine, including a mammoth statue of himself. Broken up over the centuries, two pieces of it are now on museum display, the head more than six feet tall and a foot of equal length. Without eliminating the great deal of grandeur that still remains, parts of the basilica were scattered across Rome. One of the marble Corinthian columns, forty-four feet high, now dominates the plaza in front of Saint Mary Major. Handsome gilded bronze roofing tiles were carted across the Tiber to increase the adornments of Saint Peter's.

It was on the streetside wall of the proud basilica that the dictator Mussolini tried to identify himself with the conquerors of the distant past by posting there the images of his grandiloquent dream, four maps showing the tiny original Rome of the legendary Romulus and Remus and the early Sabine kings, then the Roman empire at its greatest expanse, next modern Italy, and, finally, Mussolini's own ill-fated and short-lived revival of imperialism—the aggressive incorporation of Libya and Ethiopia under the Fascist insignia. One of the first acts of the postwar democratic coalition of Prime Minister Alcide de Gasperi was to efface map number four.

Even the still-vast brick ruins of **Maxentius's circus** three miles out beside the Appian Way eventually paid tribute to the arriving

Christian order. Pope Innocent X took the circus's obelisk in 1650 to serve as the present centerpiece in Piazza Navona.

Three centuries after Tiberius, the once mysterious and obscure Christians were on the verge of triumph. The nightmare of their early beginnings was ending. Constantine in 313 granted full freedom to the Christians, restoring to them their confiscated properties. Although he still had the title of Pontifex Maximus, head of the old state religion, and although the state by established custom deified him at death, Constantine is said to have accepted baptism on his deathbed in 337. What is sure is that he took a paternal, even intrusive, interest in the Christians. He went so far as to summon the first of the twenty ecumenical councils of history, that of Nicaea, where delegates drafted the Nicene Creed, the basic statement of Christian beliefs and a formula recited at all Catholic masses. The last of the great triumphal arches was dedicated to him in 315. It stands beside the Colosseum, suffering now from the erosive fumes of automobile engines.

A second spike was driven into the fate of ancient Rome when Constantine abandoned the old seven hills to establish his residence further east on the banks of the Bosphorus in modern Turkey. He did it in a community named for him as the city of Constantine, Constantinople, now called Istanbul. The emperor's move had an immense impact on the Christian future, for the Byzantine, or Orthodox Church took form there, eventually separating itself from Rome and the papacy.

If Constantine's role, from a Western view, thus had some elements of the equivocal, no doubt there are good reasons why his equestrian statue will greet Holy Year visitors at the entranceway to Saint Peter's. In addition to giving the popes their residence at Saint John Lateran for the next thousand years and erecting enormous Christian basilicas there and at the Vatican, the emperor set an irreversible force in motion, ending the pagan era. By 324 pagan sacrifice was banned and gladiatorial combat was outlawed. In 380 Emperor Theodosius (370–395) went further, ordering all of his subjects to embrace Christianity as defined at the Council of Nicaea.

The Christian victory was complete, although the travails of the tottering empire were only beginning. In 390, the barbarians of Gaul from the land of Caesar's conquest sacked and burned the city, the first of many invasions to come.

Practical Information

Colosseum. Open daily from 9:00 A.M. to two hours before sunset except Wednesday, Sunday, and holidays, when the closing is at 1:00 P.M. Closed January 1, May 1, and Christmas. 8,000-lire admittance. Telephone (06) 70 04 261.

Roman Forum. Via dei Fori Imperiali. Open 9:00 A.M. to two hours before sunset. On Sunday and holidays, closing is at 1:00 P.M. Some evening openings with illumination are planned for 2000. Closed January 1, May 1, and Christmas. 12,000-lire admittance. Telephone (06) 69 90 110.

Trajan's Forum. Via dei Fori Imperiali. Open every day except Monday, 9:00 A.M.–1:00 P.M., 3:00 P.M.–6:00 P.M.

Pantheon. Piazza della Rotonda. Open 9:00 A.M.–6:00 P.M. Closing is at 4:00 P.M. in winter and 1:00 P.M. on Sunday and holidays. Closed January 1 and May 1.

Castel Sant'Angelo. Normally it has been open 9:00 A.M. to 7:00 P.M. and, in winter, to sunset, with the last admission an hour before closing and with no access on January 1, May 1, and Christmas. For 2000, with rare exceptions, the monument will be open from 9:00 A.M. to 10:00 P.M. 8,000-lire admittance. Free for those under eighteen and over sixty. Telephone (06) 68 75 036.

Baths of Caracalla. Passeggiata Archaeologica. Open 9:00 A.M. to two hours before sunset. Closing is at 1:00 P.M. on Sunday, Monday, and holidays. Closed January 1, May 1, and Christmas. 8,000-lire admittance. Telephone (06) 57 58 626.

Santa Maria degli Angeli. Open 9:00 A.M. to noon and 4:00 P.M.–6:00 P.M. Telephone (06) 48 80 812.

CHAPTER 16

ROME NOW

THE LIKELIEST first impression of the year 2000 visitor will be that traffic is chaotic. Tourist buses, taxis, private cars, and, especially the feisty little motorbikes, rush chockablock through the narrow streets, yielding no hope to those seeking to cross. It is not something new—sleepless ancients complained so bitterly in the time of the Caesars about chariot wheels crashing at night over cobblestones that ordinances against them had to be adopted.

The motorbikes now are particularly spectacular. Women in the latest high fashions flash by astride them. Men properly outfitted in jacket and tie, some of them chatting on portable telephones, dart in and out among the cars. The cyclists seem to live by an intrepid code of their own, treating red lights as if they were yellow cautions. They use sidewalks both as highways and as parking spaces. Not all the cyclists, however, are as fearless as they seem. Automobiles entering traffic from the right have precedence, and occupants of parked vehicles may at any moment swing open left-side doors, either one potentially lethal for passing cyclists.

What seems like hapless confusion does have explanations and some solutions. To the astonishment of strangers, Romans will step into the traffic flow, bringing it to an instant stop. For generations pedestrians have had that right and rarely have regretted exercising it. A tragic exception was in the waning months of World War II, when American army trucks rolled through the city. Battle-weary drivers assumed, unfortunately, that they had the right of way, and walkers died.

Modernizing would mean an attack on the rich accumulation of millennia, ancient walls through which buses and cars must wriggle their way, seven venerable hills rumpling the topography, squares like Piazza Navona that once were a chariot racetrack, all of it a wealth of peerless antiquity, and all of it in the way. Not to let negative well enough alone, the muddy Tiber, father of the venerable community, adds to the confusion by twisting twenty-one and-a-half miles through the capital.

To cope with the challenge, Rome's city hall has divided the city into pedestrian-only areas like Piazza di Spagna, while converting some streets to one-way traffic and limiting others to public transportation. The tangled pattern is so baffling that some taxicabs have a sign at the driver's back: "If you have a route you prefer, please indicate it before we start." The sign serves an important purpose. Passengers startled to see the cab drive off in the opposite direction need not suspect the cabby of running up the bill. If challenged, and if there is a common language, the driver can explain that he has memorized all the route combinations and that there is no more direct path to follow.

The hills, which add their bit to chauffeurs' problems, are not immediately apparent under the sprawl of modern Rome, though visitors will find themselves always rising or dipping downward. Actually, the inner city has eight hills, not seven. The tallest is next to the Vatican, the Janiculum, on the river's right bank. It boasts the best view of the city and is topped by the heroic century-old equestrian statue of Giuseppe Garibaldi (1807–1882), the general who unified modern Italy in 1870. The legendary seven hills are on the Tiber's left bank clustered around the Forum, the premier meeting place of antiquity. They are, going clockwise from the palace hill, the Palatine, a bluff a few dozen feet high, the place of the first settlement; the Capitoline Hill, with the finest view of the Forum; the Aventine to the South behind it; along the north far side, the Quirinal; the Viminal; the Esquiline; and, in the southeast, below the Colosseum, the Caelian. Each hill is alive with a tirelessly ongoing history.

With the tourists' favorite, the Trevi Fountain, at its foot, the Quirinal is dominated by the thousand-room, eighteenth-century palace of the president of Italy. Built as a cool summer residence for the popes when they were the temporal as well as spiritual sovereigns of central Italy, the structure was commandeered in 1870 for the kings of modern Italy and then passed on to the presidents of the post–World War II republic.

The memory of the changeover from royalty to republicanism is still vivid among Rome's senior citizens. Compromised with the fallen Fascist regime, King Victor Emmanuel in May 1948 abdicated in favor of his son, Umberto. The latter, in what proved to be roy-

Traffic in Via della Conciliazione

alty's last days, appeared on the Quirinal balcony with his attractive queen and their small children, hoping that a youthful change at the top might save the regime, but, though a few hundred royalists cheered in the plaza below, Umberto survived only as the "king of the May," a one-month sovereign swept into exile by a plebiscite.

To the right of the Quirinal, with very little valley in between, is the Viminal, whose palace serves as the Ministry of the Interior. Across a dip in the road is the Esquiline Hill, topped by the Stazione Termini and the huge basilica of Saint Mary Major. Swinging left to Saint John Lateran on the Coelian completes the circle of the seven ancient hills.

CHAPTER 17

WALKS

ROME IS A WALKING CITY, much of it concentrated on the seven hills and the valley of the Forum. Wear sturdy shoes, a hat, and remember the modest dress code of the many churches. Bare arms and shorts, fine for the beaches, may see you turned back at such places as Saint Peter's. With that in mind, a feast of experiences for both pilgrim and tourist awaits. There are many possible itineraries. These are some:

On the Esquiline Hill

Begin at the church of Saint Mary Major, the largest of Rome's many shrines to the Madonna. Nearby are two churches associated with the memory of Saint Peter, those of two sister saints, Pudenziana and Praxedes. The Christian church Pudenziana is said to have established inside the family home is among Rome's oldest.

To reach the Church of Santa Pudenziana, go to the rear of the basilica of Santa Maria Maggiore, crossing the Piazza dell'Esquilino and, straight ahead, entering the Via Agosto De Pretis. Turn left after one block into the Via Urbana. The church is close by on the right. It is open weekdays from 8:00 A.M. to noon and 3:00 P.M. to 5:00 P.M., and from 9:00 A.M. on Sunday and holidays. If closed, ring the bell to the left of the entrance.

The church dates from the final years of the fourth century and includes mosaics of that time that are among the city's earliest. The bright colors and lively figures still have ancient Roman characteristics, uninfluenced by the later, more rigid Byzantine fashion. Diggings under the church have exposed an ancient Roman dwelling, including baths of the second century.

Saint Praxedes' basilica is reached from the front plaza of Saint Mary Major. With your back to the entrance of the basilica, cross the

Piazza Santa Maria Maggiore, going out at the far right corner, where you enter the Via di Santa Prassede. The church is on the second block, on the right. Hours are 7:00 A.M. to noon, 4:00 P.M. to 6:30 P.M.

This, too, is a church above an ancient residence. It dates at least from 489 and was reconstructed in 822 by the Roman native Saint Pasquale (817–824). Pasquale thought so highly of the church as a place of special reverence that he transferred to it from catacombs the remains of two thousand persons believed to have been martyrs.

On the Caelian Hill

Starting from Saint John Lateran, with its basilica, palace, baptistery, and Holy Stairs, walk across the Piazza di San Giovanni in Lateran to the Viale Carlo Felice. With the city walls of Emperor Aurelianus (270–275) off to your right, walk six blocks to the Piazza di Santa Croce in Gerusalemme (Holy Cross in Jerusalem). The Holy Year basilica is on the right.

Return to Saint John Lateran, going to the right of the palace and baptistery, descending the Caelian on the Via dei Santissimi Quattro. On the left is the Church of the Four Crowned Saints, looking like the fortress it was in the Middle Ages. It did double duty as a place of prayer and an early defense of the Saint John Lateran papal palace against assaults from bellicose princely families based in the Colosseum and on the Palatine just ahead.

After this church, go right on Via dei Querceti to the Piazza San Clemente and its extraordinary multilayered basilica. From San Clemente walk two blocks downhill on Via di San Giovanni in Laterano to an open-air area on the right, the training ground for the gladiators. Towering above you at this point is the nineteen-century-old Colosseum, still solid on its foundations.

The Colosseum can be visited from 9:00 A.M. to two hours before sunset. It closes at 1:00 P.M. on Wednesday, Sunday, and public holidays. Like many of Rome's sites, it is closed January 1, May 1, and Christmas. The charge is 8,000 lire.

To see Michelangelo's masterful sculpture of Moses, go two blocks north from the Colosseum on the Via di Terme di Tito, turning left through the Largo di Polviera to the Via Eudossiana and the Piazza di San Pietro in Vincoli. The great statue is at the piazza in the church of the same name.

Returning to the Colosseum, continue to its far side and the triumphal Arch of Constantine of A.D. 315, a structure from the era of the legalization of Christianity. Continuing around the Colosseum, go up Via Claudia to the Via di San Stefano Rotondo and the circular fourth-century church of that name. The church is open Monday through Friday, 8:30 A.M. to noon.

Return to Via Claudia. Cross it and bear right to the Via San Paolo della Croce, named for Saint Paul of the Cross, Paul Francis Danei of Ovada, Italy (1694–1775), founder of the Passionist Order. At the far end of the street are two ancient churches with special interest for the English-speaking, those of Saints John and Paul and of Pope Saint Gregory the Great.

Administered by the Passionists since 1773, the sixteen-century-old church of Saints John and Paul was the starting point in 1840 of a Passionist mission in England that contributed to the conversion of the future cardinal, John Henry Newman. It is also remarkable for the discoveries beneath it, five dwelling places of the first to the fourth centuries, including one of the second century clearly identifiable as a place of Christian occupancy.

To reach the sixth-century Church of Pope Saint Gregory the Great, descend the picturesque Clivo di Scauro to the left of the Church of Saints John and Paul. It was from the church just ahead that the monks of Saint Gregory, led by Saint Augustine, the first archbishop of Canterbury, set out in 596 to evangelize England.

In the Forum and on the Palatine

A starting point is Piazza Venezia, with the monument of King Victor Emmanuel II ahead and Palazzo Venezia, the old embassy of Venice and Mussolini's headquarters, to the rear on the right.

At the far left corner of the plaza, go west past the church of Santa Maria di Loreto to the 125-foot-high victory column of Emperor Trajan (98–117), an excellently preserved monument of antiquity, with 2,500 skillfully carved figures recording the emperor's battlefield achievements. Once topped by Trajan's statue, Saint Peter's has surmounted it since 1587. A short distance up the Via Magnanapoli to the Via IV Novembre are the extensive remains of Trajan's marketplace, where 150 shops in tiers climb the side of the Quirinal Hill.

Returning downhill to the Via dei Fori Imperiali, cross it and enter the Via di San Pietro in Carcere (Saint Peter in Prison). Beneath

Saints Cosmas and Damian in the Forum of Augustus

the 1597 church of San Giuseppe dei Falegnami (Saint Joseph of the Carpenters) is the infamous ancient Roman Mamertine Prison, consecrated in 1726 as a place of incarceration of Peter. While the saint's incarceration there is challenged, there is little question that such a foe of Rome as King Jugurtha of Numidia (112–104 B.C.) was starved to death there and that Vercingetorix, the Gallic chieftain conquered by Caesar, was beheaded there in 46 B.C. The prison can be visited from 9:00 A.M. to noon and 2:30 P.M. to 6:00 P.M. (in wintertime, 2:30 P.M. to 5:00 P.M). A donation is requested.

Take the Via Curia back toward the Via dei Fori Iimperiali and go right along the Via della Salaria Vecchia to the entranceway to the Forum and the Palatine Hill, and to two churches springing from the remains of antiquity. Especially astonishing, in Via Miranda, is the Church of San Lorenzo, sprouting from inside the temple to Emperor Antoninus and his queen, Faustina, both of whom were deified in the second century. Seen from the Forum, the colonnades of the temple still bear the inscription, *Divo Antonino et Diva Faustina* (To the God Antoninus and the Goddess Faustina). Rising from within is the church of the eleventh century.

A few steps further on is the Church of Saints Cosmas and Damian of A.D. 526, this one athwart the temple of Romulus, the deified son of Constantine's conqueror Maxentius, and also above the library of the forum of Vespasian (69–79). This was the first of the Christian churches erected inside the Forum. The Forum and Palatine are open from 9:00 A.M. until two hours before sunset, except in winter, when the opening is at 1:00 P.M. There is no access January 1, May 1, and Christmas. The charge is 12,000 lire.

An astonishing walk back into the time of the Emperors and of the Gospels awaits the visitor. At the foot of the entrance slope is the Via Sacra, the sacred way, through which triumphant generals rode in their chariots. Going counterclockwise around the Forum, the visitor passes the underpinnings of the Basilica Aemelia of 179 B.C. and, next, the Senators' Curia of Julius Caesar's time. Missing from the latter now is the bronze door, taken three centuries ago to adorn Saint John Lateran. Near the Curia is the Arch of Emperor Septimius Severus, still showing where the name of his son Geta was chipped away.

Next is the rostrum from which silver-tongued Romans orated, and beside it the circular *umbilicus orbis,* the "belly button of the city," and the milestone column from which all distances from Rome were calculated. Ahead, covering the east side of the Capitoline Hill, are the huge gray blocks of the Tabularium of 78 B.C., the hall of records, and in front of it a collection of columns and foundations of structures to pagan divinities: the temple of Concord of 367 B.C., the temple of the Emperor God Vespasian of the time of the Gospels, the temple of Saturn of 497 B.C. In the extreme left corner is the Portico of the Dei Consenti, Jupiter and his council of eleven gods and goddesses, his wife, Juno, Neptune and Minerva, Mars and Venus, Apollo and Diana, Vulcan and Vesta, and Mercury and Ceres.

Turning east along the base of the Palatine, there are remains of the 358-foot-long basilica built by Julius Caesar. Next are the haunting columns of the fifth-century B.C. temple of Castor and Pollux, a vision as symbolic of ancient Rome as the Eiffel Tower and the Statue of Liberty are of Paris and New York.

The sixth-century B.C. temple of the vestal virgins, the arch of Titus with its grim souvenirs of the first-century savaging of Jerusalem, and the second-century A.D. temples of Venus and Rome are just ahead, while to the left are the soaring arches of the basilica Maxentius started and his vanquisher Constantine finished.

Rising from part of the temples of Venus and Rome is the eighth-century church of Santa Francesca Romana. A curiosity of the church are stones said to have the imprints of Saint Peter's knees. The legend is that the encounter Saint Peter had in Samaria with the evil magician Simon, as reported in Acts 8 : 9–25, was duplicated in the Forum. The magician, according to the story, attempted to deceive people by flying into the air, while Peter prayed that the ploy would fail and that Simon would crash.

To the right of the Arch of Titus is the Clivus Palatinus, the climb up to the Palatine. A peaceful oasis now, the plateau was the place where Romulus, the boy raised by a wolf, is said to have founded Rome in the middle of the eighth century B.C. With its sharp slopes and its strategic location just above the island in the Tiber, a natural stepping stone to the river's north bank, the hill lent itself to the uses the Romulus legend suggests, and, in fact, structures of the early Iron Age have been found.

At the approach of the New Testament era the Palatine was a popular residential area. Cicero lived here. So did Augustus. After the first emperor, one after another of his successors erected palaces here. What is to be seen now is a mass of foundations, walls, columns, murals, temple remains, and a sports stadium.

To the left at the top of the hill is the Domus Flavia, the palace of the Flavian emperors, Vespasian (69–79), Titus (79–81) and Domitian (81–96), with a 131-foot-long throne room and beyond it the basilica where the emperor passed judgments in cases at law. Further ahead is the palace's courtyard, where, it is said, Domitian was so hated that he arranged for shiny walls so that he could see the reflections of potential attackers behind him.

Bearing to the left after the Domus Flavia, the path leads to Domitian's 159-yard-long stadium. East of it is a bathhouse called that of Septimius Severus (193–211) but possibly dating rather to Maxentius a century later.

Turning left and north, the path leads to the remnants of the Domus Augustana, Augustus's official palace. Further north is what is left of the temple of the sun erected by Elagabalus (218–222) in his short-lived attempt to replace the traditional deities with a different, Eastern god.

Following the path back west halfway cross the hilltop, the House of Livia is on the left. Many murals survive. This is where Augustus is believed to have lived with Livia, his wife. Nearby, just to the south, are cisterns of the sixth century B.C. A few steps beyond them are the so-called cabins of Romulus' village, huts of twenty-seven centuries ago. Close beside them are the remnants of the 191 B.C. temple of Cybele, the Magna Mater, mother of the gods. From here the path curves north through the scant remains of the vast Domus Tiberiana, the palace of Tiberius (A.D. 14–37), leading to the Clivus Palatinus and descent from the hill.

On the Capitoline and Aventine Hills

The walk starts from the Capitoline, the tiniest of the seven hills, but the most sacred, and the one that gave us the word for money. In the time of the Etruscan kings of Rome, more than half a millennium B.C., a temple, of which foundations remain, was erected to Jupiter, with spaces on either side for shrines to Minerva and Juno. The city treasury and mint were there and, according to legend, so were a flock of geese who honked a warning to the Romans when Gauls descended on the capitol in 390–388 B.C. Juno Moneta (Juno, the warner) was the shrine's name after that, and the product of her mint became money.

Without going further, the Capitoline, reached from Piazza Venezia by the Cortonata ramp, has much to offer. On the north spur is the Church of Santa Maria d'Aracoeli (Holy Mary of the Altar of Heaven), open daily from 9:00 A.M. to noon and 3:30 P.M. to 7:30 P.M. A place of Christian devotion at least since 552, the present church of the Franciscans dates from 1250. Below the church, in a saddle of the hilltop, is the Campidoglio square, which Michelangelo designed. On its west side are Rome municipal offices tracing to the twelfth century. Behind them, reached from the right of the structure, is a magnificent view of the Forum below.

On either side of the plaza are two of the finest museums of antiquity. Both date from the fifteenth century. The museum of the Palazzo dei Conservatori houses in its courtyard a few startling pieces of the thirty-three-foot-high seated statue of Constantine that once adorned the Basilica of Maxentius. The head, with a serene expression of command, is almost as tall as a man. A hand with an upraised forefinger is tall as a child. An arm has a bicep bulkier than a barrel.

Inside, among thousands of items from Rome's earlier centuries, is a fifth-century B.C. bronze of a she-wolf, a fine work of Greek or Etruscan origin. During the Renaissance Antonio del Pollaiuolo added two suckling infants to represent the mythical founders, Romulus and Remus, abandoned tots raised by a maternally minded wolf.

Also in the museum is the *spinario,* an exquisitely graceful first-century B.C. bronze of a youth fully absorbed in removing a thorn from the pad of his left foot.

Across the plaza is the Capitoline Museum. Among its marvels is the equestrian statue of Emperor Marcus Aurelius, the model for later statues of heroes on horseback. For centuries it stood at Saint John Lateran, apparently mistaken for an image of Constantine, an error that may have saved this souvenir of one of Christianity's persecutors. Michelangelo moved the statue to the center of the plaza, but in 1990 it was carried indoors to save it from the corrosive outdoor environment. Bits of the original gilding survive on the ruler's face and mantle and on the horse's head and back. A Roman legend is that when the final shreds of gilding are lost the Last Judgment will occur. Another of the museum's special possessions is the bronze of the Dying Gaul, a Roman imitation of a Middle Eastern statue of two centuries B.C. It reflects the courage and pride of an expiring warrior and is a masterpiece of antiquity.

Descend the broad staircase, turning left on Via del Teatro di Marcello. On the right is the first-century B.C. Theater of Marcellus, which was dedicated by Augustus to his nephew. Built to provide for an audience of 13,500, the structure's lower-tier arches are still a prominent feature. Parts of the building served as models for the Colosseum. Heaped incongruously overhead are palatial apartments put there in the sixteenth century.

To the right of the theater is what is left of the Jewish ghetto of 1555–1870, a walled area where members of the ancient Jewish community of 100 B.C. were confined each night from evening to dawn. Much of the densely crowded quarter was demolished in 1888, but there are still narrow, twisting streets, a Hebrew Museum, a riverbank synagogue of 1904, and restaurants like Piperno's, where the exquisite flattened and fried artichokes called *carciofi alla Giudea* (Jewish-style artichokes) are well worth savoring. Pope John Paul II, pursuing his policy of rapprochement with the Jews, made an historic, prayerful visit to the synagogue.

To the right after the Theater of Marcellus is the Church of Saint Nicholas in Prison, an edifice of possibly as early as the seventh century, built above three temples believed to have honored Janus, Juno, and the principle of hope, the earliest dating to the second century B.C. The "Janus" temple was used as a Byzantine jail in the seventh century, hence the church name. There are guided tours daily except Sunday, 9:00 A.M. to noon.

With the street changing its name to Via Petroselli, continue straight ahead in the direction of the Piazza Bocca della Verita. On the right is the modern building of the Anagrafe, where foreign residents must join Italians in registering births and where the outlanders learn that there are to be no juniors. The son of Giuseppe may not be another Giuseppe.

At the next corner, exit briefly to the right on Via del Ponte Rotto to see the island in the Tiber and the *ponte rotto,* the broken bridge. The island, just upstream, was a convenient stepping stone across the river in antiquity and is still served by bridges on either side from the first century B.C. The broken bridge is the oddest of monuments, sitting calmly in midstream minus the arches to either shore. Both of the side spans were lost to the river's fury in 1598.

Back at Via Petroselli, turn right to the Piazza Bocca della Verita and the bevy of architectural riches around it. Immediately on the left is the Via Velabro with the Arch of Janus and the church of Saint George in Velabro.

The heavy arch, a city gateway, dates to the fourth century and was dedicated to Janus, an ideal guardian for a street intersection. Beyond the arch is the sixth-century Church of Saint George. It was the church assigned to Cardinal John Henry Newman as his titular parish, and it is of special interest for the English-speaking. It honors George, the legendary dragon slayer, the patron saint of England and also of its highest knightly honor, the Order of the Garter. George is also the patron of Portugal, Germany, Aragon, Genoa, and Venice, and of the Boy Scout movement.

Back in Piazza Bocca della Verita a vision of ancient Rome is provided by two temples of the second century B.C., the rectangular Fortuna Virile (human fortune) and the round Vesta. The latter was dedicated to Catholic worship in the sixteenth century as the church of Saint Mary of the Sun. Opposite the two is the sixth-century Saint Mary in Cosmedin atop a second-century B.C. temple.

To climb the Aventine Hill, go along the right side of Santa Maria in Cosmedin into the Via della Greca and on into the Via del Circo Massimo, the street of the Circus Maximus. Halfway along it, on the right, is the Piazzale Ugo La Malta, named for one of Italy's post–World War II democratic politicians. It offers a fine view of the space of the ancient stadium and of the Palatine Hill opposite.

The outlines of the stadium are still visible. Dating back possibly to the Etruscan kings of half a millennium B.C. and steadily improved by Caesar and an array of emperors, the racing area is 656 yards long, with accommodations for an audience of 300,000. The biga, triga, and quadriga chariots flashed around the track, those drawn respectively by two horses, three, or four. Still to be seen is Augustus's box atop the Palatine. The last time the stadium was used was in 549.

To ascend the Aventine, go west on Via di Valle Murcia. In May, the rose garden is one of the city's sights. Go left through the Clivo dei Publici to the church of Santa Prisca, another of Rome's earliest Christian places of prayer, dating from the second century. As in the case of San Clemente and some others, there is a Mithraeum, with statuary and frescoes of the cult. Prisca is said to have been baptized by Peter and to have been the first woman martyr, executed like Paul on the road to Ostia.

In the Piazza di Santa Prisca, turn sharp right into the Via del Tempio di Diana, then right again into the Via Eufemiano and left into the Via San Alberto Magno. Ahead, slightly to the right, is the Savello Park, with a sweeping view of Rome from the Janiculum and Saint Peter's to the Monument of Victor Emmanuel II. To the left is the fifth-century church of Santa Sabina, whose monastery next door was the residence of Saint Dominic, the founder of the Dominicans, and a place where Saint Thomas Aquinas, the theological genius of the thirteenth century, lectured to fellow Dominicans. Thanks to the removal of Renaissance additions, the church appears now as it was fifteen centuries ago, a fine example of an early Christian basilica.

Leaving the church of Santa Sabina, turn right along Via di Santa Sabina two blocks to the church of Sant'Alessio. Dating at least from the eighth century, the church was at the center of a popular fourteenth-century legend about the fifth-century Alexis. According to the unverified story, Alexis, known as the "man of God," grew up in a wealthy home on the site. He went east for seventeen years, living in evangelical poverty and piety. Returning home as an unrecognizable beggar, he passed the rest of his life as a tolerated but never identified occupant of a cramped space under his father's staircase. On the left just inside the nave is a descent into the ancient house below. Much of the present church dates to the time of Pope Honorius III (1216–1227), with renovations of 1750.

Directly ahead is the Piazza Cavalieri di Malta, with the Priory of the Knights of Malta, a property that began as a Benedictine monastery in 939, passing permanently in the twelfth century into the hands of successive crusader knightly orders. Peak through the keyhole of the knights' gate for a unique tree-framed view of Saint Peter's cupola.

Turn south on Via Porta Lavernale to the century-old church of San Anselmo, built in an attractive Romanesque style. At 9:30 A.M. on Sunday there is Gregorian chant at a mass in Italian. The telephone is 575 0073.

Piazza di Spagna

A good starting place is the office the American Catholic bishops have set up at 30 Via dell'Umilta to assist American visitors. The genial Monsignor Roger Roensch of Washington, D.C., is in charge.

Before heading north to the Trevi Fountain and Piazza di Spagna, there is a Sunday alternative. Go east on Via dell'Umilta to its extension, the Via della Dataria. Climb it up the slopes of the Quirinal Hill to the palace of the same name, the thousand-room sixteenth-century summer residence of the popes, which became Italy's royal residence in 1870 and home of the presidents of the Italian republic since 1947. The uniformed guards are all, at a minimum, an awe-inspiring six feet and three inches tall. The palace is open for visits Sunday from 9:00 A.M. to noon. The phone is (06) 46 991.

Returning downhill through the Via della Dataria, turn right into Via di San Vincenzo to the celebrated Trevi Fountain just ahead. John Secondari, a war correspondent from New York, helped add to its fame with a post–World War II novel, film, and song, *Three Coins in the Fountain*, emphasizing the legend that coins tossed backward over your shoulder into the waters can assure you a return visit to the Eternal City. Inveterate travelers imbued with the charms of Rome have found it to be true.

Agrippa, the builder of the Pantheon, constructed a water conduit to this spot and Pope Clement XIII, the pontiff of the 1575 Holy Year, took advantage of the flow to commission the present baroque masterpiece topped by the papal coat of arms. The central figure is that of Ocean riding a chariot drawn by two sea horses. Throngs of jubilant picture-taking tourists can be expected at all times, but, sad to say, so can the pickpockets. Watch your valuables.

Go left of the fountain on Via Poli to the heavily traveled Via del Tritone. Cross it, bearing left to Piazza San Claudio. Cross that plaza to Piazza San Silvestro, with its flock of buses fanning out to all corners of Rome. Ahead is the main post office and the church of the English Catholics, San Silvestro.

Bear right into Via della Mercede. At 54 is the center for the news correspondents of forty nations who cover Italy and the Vatican, often ranging afield to report also on the news of North Africa, the Middle East, and Eastern Europe. The journalists' building was the work of Mussolini, who staffed it free of charge with his own people, presumably to keep tabs on the alien news seekers.

Continue two blocks to Via Capo le Case and the twelfth-century church of Sant'Andrea della Fratte, in the heart of what was the Scottish quarter during the Middle Ages. Turn north in Via Propaganda to the Piazza Mignanelli and, beyond it, the Piazza di Spagna, for generations a favored center for foreigners.

In the first plaza is the Palace of the Propaganda Fide, the Propagation of the Faith. Founded in 1622 by Pope Gregory XV, it is the center of the church's missionary activities and since 1988 has been known as the Congregation for the Evangelization of the Peoples.

In the center is a column erected to the Madonna in 1856 to celebrate Pius IX's proclamation of the dogma of the Immaculate Conception. It is a papal custom to pray at the column on the feast day of the dogma, December 8. Mary's statue in bronze is at the summit of the shaft and Old Testament figures, Moses, Isaiah, Ezekiel, and David, cluster at the base.

On the left is an embassy of 1647 that gives the area its name, that of the still functioning embassy of Spain to the Holy See. On the right is American Express, a swarming center of American tourist activity.

The Piazza di Spagna still has the form that evolved from 1500 to 1900. The love foreigners have lavished upon it for centuries is evident not just in the continuing throngs resting on the right on the broad Pincian hill staircase of 1723–1726, the Spanish Steps, but also in structures. At the foot of the stairs, on the right, is the house where the young English poet John Keats died of tuberculosis in 1821. A museum now, it is open Monday through Friday, 9:00 A.M. to 1:00 P.M. and 3:00 P.M. to 8:00 P.M. (in October to April, 9:00 A.M. to 1:00 P.M. and 2:30 P.M. to 5:30 P.M). It is closed on public holidays and on June 29, the middle two weeks of August, and Christmas. At the bottom on the north side is Rome's most eminent tea house, Babington's, long a port of call for the English and venerable enough now to find a place in guidebooks.

The Spanish Steps are especially brilliant in springtime, when a blanket of azaleas covers the lower reaches. A joyful place, it is another spot where warnings are appropriate. Girls not yet in their teens have been known to grab an arm with one hand, using the other to slip off a wristwatch.

Several choices await the walker in Piazza di Spagna. One is to go forward on the Via del Babuino, created by Pope Clement VII for the 1525 Holy Year. It opened a direct way into the heart of the city for northern pilgrims descending the Via Flaminia and entering through the Aurelian Walls at Piazza del Popolo. The street is lined now by antique shops in palaces of the seventeenth and eighteenth centuries.

Seven blocks ahead is the Piazza del Popolo, laid out in its present form by Giuseppe Valadier (1762–1839). With twin churches on the near side, a more interesting third one is across the plaza adjacent to the Aurelian Wall. It is the fifteenth-century Santa Maria del Popolo, with a trove of Pinturicchios and Caravaggios. One of Rome's broadest plazas, this place was used by Napoleon's occupying force in 1813 as a location for resolving problems of street disorders. To do so, they set up a guillotine.

To return to Piazza di Spagna, go back one block on Via del Babuino and turn left on Via della Fontanella to Via Margutta. Go right on that street to its end. Ever since the seventeenth century this has been the charming street of artists, Italians and foreigners alike, one studio after another. At the end turn right on Via d'Alibert to get back to Via del Babuino.

Another major choice in Piazza di Spagna is to go west into the luxurious Via Condotti or the parallel shopping street of Via Frattina. A few steps into Via Condotti on the right at 86 is a coffee shop which should not be missed for an espresso or an ice cream. It is the Caffè Greco of 1760. Since 1953 it has been designated by the government as "a place of historical and national interest." When models in native costumes waited on the Spanish Steps in the nineteenth century hoping to be hired for the day by the artists who crowded the area, many of the latter took moments off to meet their fellows over a coffee at the Greek's. A roster of Europe's artistic greats and notorious and a smattering of America's tasted the cafe's wares.

From the north end of the plaza, the Via della Croce, paralleling Via Condotti, leads to the Tiber and to two great survivals from antiquity, the mausoleum of Augustus, burial place of emperors, and the Ara Pacis, the altar of peace, the 9 B.C. salute to the Pax Romana, the temporary calm near the peak of the imperial power.

Pantheon

Starting from the Gesù and the rooms of Saint Ignatius Loyola in the Piazza del Gesù on Corso Vittorio Emanuele II, go north across the busy Corso through the Via del Gesù to the Via Pie de Marmo. Turn right and immediately left into the Via Sant'Ignazio and the church of that name. In the church enjoy the trompe-l'oeil in the flat ceiling of the church, the cupola that is not there. Also observe the piazza out front, everyone's idea of an operatic stage. If it is lunchtime consider a pizza and a fresh salad at the sidewalk restaurant on the right.

Go out through the opera wings straight ahead to the Via di Pietra. Turn left into the Piazza di Pietra and observe the massive remains of the A.D. 145 temple to Hadrian. Used by the pope of the 1700 Holy Year, Innocent XII, as a customs house, it has been the Italian Chamber of Commerce and stock exchange since 1879. The fifty-foot-tall white marble Corinthian columns of Hadrian's temple adorn the outer wall.

At the southwest side of Piazza di Pietra, take Via dei Pastini to the Piazza della Rotonda. Dominating it is the Pantheon, once the temple of all the gods of paganism and, since the seventh century, the church of the Madonna and all the martyrs, an extraordinary intact monument from the time of Christ. A sidewalk cafe on the north side of the plaza is a good place for another coffee and a fine view of the huge round edifice and, in front of it, the fountain of 1578 and the obelisk of 1711.

Bear left of the Pantheon to Santa Maria Sopra Minerva, the eighth-century church of Mary sitting above the temple Domitian built for the goddess Minerva at the very time Saint John was writing the final gospel. Known as a museum church for its many works of art, it is also the burial place of Saint Catherine of Siena, who persuaded the papacy to return from Avignon to Rome. At the far end of the Plaza of Minerva turn right into Via di Santa Chiara, passing at 14 the convent where Saint Catherine died on April 23, 1380.

At the far end of Via di Santa Chiara, cross Piazza Caprettari to Piazza Sant'Eustacchio. Curve sharp left into Via Teatro Valle and take the first right two blocks across Corso del Rinascimento to Piazza Navona, a place of relaxation and entertainment for Romans and foreigners alike ever since Caesar, Augustus, Domitian, and Nero first developed it as a 300-yard-long sports stadium.

The track is gone but the shape remains. Always cheerfully alive, the plaza reaches a special peak in December when the north end is converted into an open-air market for crèche figures. Many families already have the Holy Family and perhaps the three Wise Men and an ox and an ass, but it is the custom to add a few new anachronistic pieces each year, a butcher, a baker, a candlestick maker. The idea of the Italian crèche is that Palestine might have been like an Abruzzi mountain village, so that there is no problem adding figures of this and other centuries to those of the Middle East of two millennia ago.

If it is lunch time, or even if it is not, the sidewalk restaurants are a joy.

Not to be missed is Gian Lorenzo Bernini's 1651 fountain of the rivers in the plaza's center. The great water flows of the world are represented by giant human figures, one each for Europe's Danube, Asia's Ganges, Africa's Nile, and the Rio de la Plata of Argentina and Uruguay. Opposite the fountain is the thousand-year-old church of Saint Agnes in Agony, with a facade by Francesco Borromini. Roman wags have long joked that the Nile has his head under a veil and another "river" has an upraised arm and a turned back because both feared that Saint Agnes's top-heavy facade was about to fall on them, a Bernini jab at his rival Borromini. None of that, however, is true. The Nile's veil meant that no one of Bernini's generation knew the source of that river, and, in fact, Bernini's work preceded Borromini's by several years.

Turn right out of the plaza just north of the Bernini fountain. Cross Corso del Rinascimento and bear left to Via del Salvatore. One block long, it leads to San Luigi dei Francesi, the national church for French Catholics.

Return to Piazza Navona. Cross it and take the last exit on the left one block to twin churches to Mary, Dell'Anima (of the Spirit), a center of German Christian devotion since the fourteenth century, and Della Pace, a shrine to peace dating from the 1100s.

Use the side entrance on Via della Pace to go into Santa Maria dell'Anima.

Santa Maria della Pace and Bramante's cloisters of 1504 beside it at 5 Vicolo della Pace are open Tuesday, Wednesday, and Friday from 10:00 A.M. to noon and 4:00 P.M. to 6:00 P.M., and on Sunday and public holidays from 9:00 A.M. to 11:00 A.M.

There is a choice here: whether to go north to the Via dei Coronari or south to the Campo di' Fiori. For the first, go one block on Via del Volpe to the "street of the rosaries," so called because Via dei Coronari once served as a direct route for pilgrims coming from Piazza del Popolo and Piazza Colonna to the Sant'Angelo bridge and Saint Peter's. It was lined with peddlers of religious articles. Still very much as it was in the time of Pope Sixtus IV (1471–1484), it is a charming thoroughfare lined with antique shops.

To reach the Campo de' Fiori, go south through Piazza Navona or its western parallel, the Via Santa Maria d'Anima, to the Piazza San Pantaleo. Cross the heavily traveled Corso Vittorio Emanuele. Continue south on Via dei Baullari to the three-block-long Campo. A colorful, bustling food market each morning, it is another good place for a sidewalk meal under huge umbrellas. It is also an area of haunting memories. In the center is the statue of the monk Giordano Bruno, burned there at the stake as a heretic on February 17, 1600. Just off the southeast end is where Caesar was murdered in the now largely vanished theater of Pompey.

Janiculum and Trastevere

One of Rome's tallest hills is not one of the ancient seven. It is the Janiculum, on what, in ancient times, was the wrong side of the river, the right bank, Etruscan land. On one side, below it, is the Vatican Hill and Saint Peter's; on the other, the ancient working-class area of

Trastevere. The North American College, in a handsome post–World War II building, is on the middle slope of the Janiculum.

Start the walk high on the hill at the Piazzale Garibaldi with its equestrian statue to Giuseppe Garibaldi, the nineteenth-century conqueror of the papal state and unifier of Italy. Close by was where Garibaldi fought French defenders of Pius IX in an unsuccessful skirmish of 1849. From the plaza there is a sweeping view of Rome and its countryside and the Alban Hills on the East.

Walk southeast on the Passeggiata del Gianicolo to the Piazza di San Pietro in Montorio, with another fine view. Visit the fifteenth-century church of Saint Peter in Montorio with the tombs of exiled Irish nobles of the seventeenth century and, beside it, the "little temple" of Bramante, an exquisite early-sixteenth-century experiment in round dome-topped architecture that influenced much later local Renaissance construction.

Descend the Via Garibaldi and turn left on the Via della Lungara to the Villa Farnesina. A Renaissance gem of 1508–1511, it has masterworks of Raphael. It is open daily except Sunday and public holidays, 9 A.M. to 1:00 P.M.

Trastevere is due south. Take the Via della Lungara and its extension, the Via della Scala, through the Piazza di Sant'Egidio to the Via della Paglia. Turn left into Piazza di Santa Maria in Trastevere, a picturesque square with sidewalk restaurants. Visit the sixteen-century-old church of Santa Maria in Trastevere, the Holy Year church of 1625 and 1700.

From the piazza go southeast down Via di San Francesco di Ripa five blocks to the church of the same name, a Franciscan edifice with Bernini's marble statue of the sixteenth-century Blessed Ludovica Albertoni, a masterful reflection of a saint's final sufferings.

From there go north on Via Anicia, right on Via della Madonna dell'Orto, and left on Via San Michele to the fifth-century Church of Saint Cecilia, with Carlo Maderno's sculpture of the martyr of the year 230.

Continue northeast on Via dei Vascellari. Turn left in Via dei Salumi and then right into the Piazza Piscinula. From there go west two blocks on the Lungaretta to Piazza Sonino and the Church of San Crisogono. Twenty feet beneath it, reached by an iron stairway in the sacristy, there are remains of a fifth-century church altered in the eighth century by Gregory III. There are remnants of paintings of the eighth and tenth centuries. There is a 3,000-lire charge to visit the excavations. They are open 7:00 A.M. to 11:00 A.M. and 4:00 P.M. to 7:00 P.M. and on holidays from 8:00 A.M. to 1:30 P.M. and 4:00 P.M. to 7:00 P.M. Visits are not allowed during services.

To conclude, return on the Lungaretta to Piazza Piscinula, turning north from there across the Lungotevere dell'Anguillara to the first-century B.C. bridge of Cestius. Cross to the island in the Tiber and visit, on the downriver side, the Church of Saint Bartholomew, which was erected by Emperor Otto III at the time of the first millennium. Below it is a temple to Aesculapius, the god of medicine.

Saint Peter's Area

In addition to walks through the Vatican gardens, which can be arranged at the visitors' center in Saint Peter's plaza, and those through the Vatican museums, there are other sights just outside the Vatican state.

With your back to Saint Peter's, leave the plaza and turn left to the Via dei Corridori, the street parallel to Via della Concilizione and just north of it. Turn right into the street and walk beside the tall and impressive remains of the wall Pope Leo IV constructed around the Vatican zone in 847–852 in a dramatic reflection of the turmoil and insecurity of the medieval centuries. The Saracens had invaded Rome on August 23, 846, raiding Saint Peter's and Saint John Lateran, and Leo had decided that massive walls were needed.

Along the top of the wall is the covered passageway Nicholas III added in the thirteenth century to allow besieged popes to flee from the Vatican Palace to the fortress of Castel Sant'Angelo. The wall and passageway lead directly into the castle seven blocks away. In the sixteenth century, when Swiss Guards died defending the Vatican, Giulio de'Medici, Clement VII, profited from the foresight of two-and-one-half centuries earlier, making his way along the walltop to safety in the Castle.

Castel Sant'Angelo is open for visits from 9:00 A.M. to 7:00 P.M., except in winter, when the closing is at sunset. As usual with most monuments, it is closed on New Year's Day, May Day, and Christmas. The last admission is an hour before closing. The charge is 8,000 lire, except for those under eighteen or over sixty, who enter free.

All of the past nineteen centuries are reflected in this astonishing building. Begun as the mausoleum for Emperor Hadrian in the first part of the second century, a generation or so after John wrote the fi-

Saint Peter's Square at Epiphany

nal Gospel, the huge tomb was the burial place of emperors for one hundred years. A half century after Caracalla's entombment, Emperor Valerian thought of another use for it. Barbarians were threatening; he used the great mass as an anchor for his new wall around the city. By the Middle Ages, with the popes exercising civil as well as spiritual rule over central Italy, the great structure served in part as a prison. When Clement fled into it in the sixteenth century, he and several of his successors began installing handsomely decorated Renaissance living areas above the mass. Now operated as an Italian national museum, every phase of the long life of the mausoleum-fortress-palace can be visited.

In front of the mausoleum is the spectacular baroque Ponte Sant'Angelo, the holy angel bridge, with a lively history of its own. Built by Hadrian for cross-Tiber access to his designated burial place, it lost both ends during the centuries but, in contrast to the Ponte Rotto, the missing ends were replaced. Through many of the medieval Holy Years the bridge served pilgrims as their main point of access to the Vatican. In the worst accident of the Holy Year series, it was on this bridge, in 1450, that a panic broke out causing the death of two hundred tightly packed pilgrims.

The statues of Peter and Paul at the left bank side of the bridge were placed there in 1530 by Pope Clement VII. Another Clement, the ninth (1667–1669), lined the bridge with the ten Bernini school statues of angels bearing articles of Christ's Passion, the cross, the crown of thorns, the scourge, the whipping column, Veronica's veil, the soldier's spear, the vinegary sponge, the nails, the mocking sign about the King of the Jews, and Christ's gown and the dice tossed for it by his executioners.

On the castle side of the river, turn west into the plaza at the outset of the Via della Concilizione. The largo is named now for Pope John XXIII and balances the one at the Vatican end dedicated to his immediate predecessor, Pius XII.

Bear left along Lungotevere Vaticano, the riverbank road, and immediately right into Borgo Santo Spirito. Pass on the right a short street named for another twentieth-century pontiff, Saint Pius X (1903–1914), the only pope raised to the altars since Blessed Innocent XI (1676–1689) and the only pontiff canonized since Saint Pius V (1566–1572).

On the left at the corner of Via dei Penitenzieri are the Church of Santo Spirito in Sassia (the Holy Spirit in the Saxon neighborhood) and, beside it, the sprawling Hospital of the Holy Spirit. Each has significance for Holy Year pilgrims, especially for those who are English-speaking.

Continue along the Borgo Santo Spirito toward Saint Peter's. Midway on the left is the world headquarters of the Jesuits, with a helpful information office for pilgrims and tourists.

Via Veneto

From the Church of Santa Susanna at the corner of Via Venti Settembre and Via Leonida Bissolati, it is a short walk to the heartland of much modern American and other foreign activity, something the Paulist Fathers had much in mind when they chose this ancient church in 1922 as the base for their activities as spiritual shepherds of the large American Catholic colony.

To the right is the Grand Hotel used by generations of celebrities. The street out front now bears the name of Vittorio Emanuele Orlando, the last survivor of the Big Four who wrote the World War I Versailles peace treaty.

To the right of the Grand Hotel is the Church of Santa Maria degli Angeli, carved by Michelangelo out of remnants of the immense Baths of Diocletian. It is open 9:00 A.M. to noon and 4:00 P.M. to 6:00 P.M. Beside it, also in the Diocletian ruins, is the excellent Roman National Museum, with a vast collection of Roman and Greek antiquities, including the third-century B.C. bronze of an exhausted pugilist and a statue of Augustus in his fifty-third year, a figure exuding the confidence of the ruler of the civilized world, the man whose decision sent Joseph to Bethlehem.

Just south of the museum is the wide Piazza della Repubblica, also on the site of what was Diocletian's bathhouse. It is a graceful creation of post-1870 Rome, surrounded on two sides by colonnaded walkways of shops and cafés, including the inescapable McDonald's.

As you return northwest through Via Vittorio Emanuele Orlando, just after the Grand Hotel, there is, on the right, a 1587 fountain with Domenico Fontana's marble statue of Moses, a figure that drew some contemporary jeers because the lights of divine inspiration springing from the prophet's head could be mistaken for horns.

Also on the right, across Via Venti Settembre, is the Church of Santa Maria della Vittoria, with Bernini's masterful marble statue of Saint Teresa of Ávila in ecstasy.

Going downhill on Via Bissolati, continue to the American embassy on the right, a palace of 1886, which once was the residence of Queen Margherita, wife of King Umberto I.

Downhill along Via Veneto on the left is the Church of Santa Maria della Concezione, Holy Mary of the Conception, an edifice of 1624, with an extraordinary Capuchin cemetery, the bones and skulls of four thousand friars of 1528 to 1870 arranged in artistic patterns on the walls, a monument to the passing of earthly life.

Continuing downhill, the Via Veneto runs into the Piazza Barberini. Returning uphill, you reach ever-busy outdoor cafés, the center of Rome's indulgent postwar *dolce vita* (sweet life), portrayed in a film of that name by Federico Fellini, one of Italy's great post–World War II directors. A plaque on a building catercorner to the American embassy now records as a fact of Rome's ever-continuing history that Fellini shot *La Dolce Vita* there. At the head of the street is a fine view of the Aurelian walls and a splendid public park, the Villa Borghese.

CHAPTER 18

AS THE ROMANS DO

IT IS FRUITLESS in Rome to worry about why some shops close down at midday for a siesta or why museums seem to have such erratic schedules, but, if you do as Romans do, a great lifetime experience awaits you. Here are some suggestions on how to do in Rome what you must do if your visit is to be what it should be.

Arrival in Rome

A great many of those traveling from afar to take part in the millennium jubilee will touch ground at the Leonardo da Vinci airport, Europe's sixth largest. It is sixteen miles from Rome, thirty minutes away by express train, at least forty-five minutes by car and, at night, an hour by bus.

The fast train leaves every hour from 7:50 A.M. to 10:25 P.M. It goes to Stazione Termini. Return trips to the airport go from the station's Track 22 hourly from 7:00 A.M. to 9:15 P.M. At Stazione Termini, in addition to the ticket office, there is a ticket vending machine at Track 22. Newsstands also sell the tickets. The fare is 13,000 lire.

Buses run hourly from 11:30 P.M. to 6:00 A.M. Labeled Roma, they start from the parking place out in front of the arrivals building. Tickets are on sale at a booth or on the bus. The fare is 7,000 lire.

Cabs are at a stand outside the arrivals building. The charge is about $45. Be sure to use only the yellow or white licensed metered cabs; the cost with freelancers may be much higher. That is true inside Rome as well.

Chauffeured licensed cars also are available for about $50.

Avis, Budget, Hertz, and National/Europcar have counters open until midnight. Think twice about driving yourself in Rome, however. The city is a maze of ancient walls, one-way streets, no-access plazas; and parking spaces, except in Villa Borghese, are hard to come by. If you cannot resist driving, look for the autostrada (A12) signs as you leave the airfield. Go east to the Roma Centro exit. Returning, take A12 west following the airport signs and get off at exit 30.

The Avis phones are 65 01 15 79 and 1678 63063 toll-free in Rome. Budget is 65 01 03 47 and 482 57 26. Hertz is 65 01 15 53 and 1678 22099 toll-free in Rome. National/Europcar is at 65 01 08 79 and 1678 14410 toll-free in Rome.

Housing

With double the annual ten million tourists expected in the Holy Year, early reservations or use of a travel agency are recommended. Many will have to lodge in Florence or Naples, making one-day excursions into Rome for the climactic jubilee events. Good *rapido* connections will help with such trips, and there are plans for tourist buses to drop off passengers at central spots and then to move out of the center until an agreed rendezvous time.

At Stazione Termini there is a hotel booking office. The phone is 48 89 92 55. Rome also has a free telephone reservation service, providing information on two hundred hotels. That number is 699 10 00. The service is available from 7:00 A.M. to 10:00 P.M.

Those on a tight budget are likely to face stiff competition from other pilgrims, especially the many expected from Eastern Europe, but the Holy See is at work with convents, arranging for extra housing. Nuns offer four packages: *camera sola* (room only), *pernotta-mento e prima colazione* (room and breakfast), *mezza pensione* (room, breakfast, and one meal), and *pensione completa* (room, breakfast, and two meals). Not only single women but also married couples, families, and single men are welcome.

For a complete listing of convents and other religious institutions offering low-cost accommodations, write to the Vicariato di Roma, Piazza San Giovanni 6, 00184 Rome, or to the Rome Tourist Board, Via Parigi 11, 00185 Rome. For parish bookings, get in touch with Peregrinatio Ad Petri Sedem in Piazza Pio XII 4, 00120 Vatican City State, phone 6988 48 96, fax 6988 56 17.

Among convents near the Vatican are these:

Suore Teatine, Salita Monte del Gallo 25, 00165 Rome, phone 637 40 84 or 637 46 53, fax 3937 90 50. The range is 44,000 lire with

Saint John Lateran

breakfast to 66,000 for full board. Curfew at 11:00 P.M. Not all rooms have private baths.

The American Order of Franciscan Sisters of the Atonement, Via Monte del Gallo 105, 00165 Rome. All rooms have private baths. English spoken; parking available. 11:00 P.M. curfew encouraged. Price range 42,000 lire with breakfast to 70,000 full board.

Suore Dorotee, Via del Gianicolo 4A, 00165 Rome. Phone 6880 33 49. Fax 6880 33 11. Near the North American College. Half pension 70,000 lire, full 80,000. Some private baths. 11:00 P.M. curfew. Recommended by Vatican Tourist Information Bureau.

Pensione Suore Francescane, Via Nicolo V 35, 00165 Rome. Phone 3936 65 31. Handsome Vatican view. 50,000 lire with breakfast. No full board. No curfew. No private baths. Fluent English.

Domus Aurelia, Suore Orsoline. Via Aurelia 218, 00165 Rome. Phone 636 784. Fax 3937 64 80. Double room, 90,000 lire. Single, 60,000 lire. Room with three beds, 120,000 lire. All rooms have private baths. Breakfast extra charge. 11:30 P.M. curfew.

Suore Pallottini, Viale delle Mura Aurelie 7B, 00165 Rome. Phone 635 697, Fax 635 699. Single room with breakfast 53,000 lire. Double without private bath 90,000 lire. Double with bath 130,000 lire. 10:00 P.M. curfew first night; key provided after that.

Convents near the historic center include these:

Fraternal Dooms, Via di Mount Brains 62, 00186 Rome. Phone 6880 27 27. Fax 683 26 91. It is between Piazza Nova and the Tiber. Price range 40,000 lire with breakfast to 70,000 lire with full board. 18,000 lire supplement for single rooms. All rooms have private baths. Curfew at 11:00 P.M..

Suore di Lourdes, Via Sistina 113, 00187 Rome. Phone 474 53 24. Fax 488 11 44. This shares the elegant Via Sistina with the luxurious Haller Hotel. Without bath 45,000 lire. With private bath 55,000 lire. Breakfast included. Curfew 10:30 P.M..

Suore Brigidine, Piazza Farnese 96, 00186 Rome. Phone 686 57 21 and 686 53 70. Fax 6880 47 80. Near Campo de' Fiori and Piazza Navona. Single room 120,000 lire. Double room 110,000 lire per person. Breakfast included.

Transport Inside Rome

Taxis are few and expensive. Do not expect to flag them down with ease. Use the taxi stands at Piazza Pio XII, opposite Saint Peter's Plaza, at the Vatican, or at such other places as the main hotels, or telephone 3570, 4994, 4157 or 88177. Limit yourself to the licensed and metered white or yellow cabs to avoid the risk of pirate prices. When the cab is summoned by phone, the meter runs immediately, starting at 4,500 lire. After midnight, 5,000 is added. On holidays the surcharge is 2,000. Luggage is extra. Ten percent is an adequate tip.

Rome has a subway, known as the Metro, which some complainers say goes nowhere, and a vast network of often crowded buses. The Metro has two lines, intersecting at Stazione Termini. Among interesting stops it does offer are Piazza di Spagna, Piazza Barberini near Via Veneto, Piazza della Repubblica near Santa Susanna, San Giovanni Laterano, Saint Paul's Outside the Walls, the Pyramid, Circus Maximus, and the Colosseum. The subway runs from 5:30 A.M. to 11:30 P.M.

Most buses run from 5:00 A.M. until midnight, but some stop at 9:00 P.M. Bus maps are available at news kiosks. Prices are modest, 1,500 lire for seventy-five minutes, 6,000 for a full day, and 24,000 for a week. The same ticket serves on buses, trams, and the subway. Enter buses at the rear and use the machine that stamps the beginning of your time period. Inspectors, who pay no attention to hard-luck stories, board the buses, periodically imposing 50,000-lire fines for unstamped tickets.

Buses run to most pilgrim destinations: to Saint John Lateran, 4, 16, 85, 87, and 88; to Saint Peter's, 32, 46, 47, 62, 64, and 77; to Saint Mary Major, 3, 4, 9, 16, 70, 71, and 93; to Saint Paul Outside the Walls, 18, 23, 123, and 223; to San Lorenzo Fuori le Mura and the catacomb of San Lorenzo, 66; to the catacomb of Domitilla, 91, 93 94; to the catacomb of San Pancrazio, 44 and 75; to the catacomb of Sant'Agnese and Sant'Alessandro, 36, 37, 60, and 137; and to the catacomb of Priscilla, 35, 56, 15, and 235. For the catacombs of Saint Calixtus and Saint Sebastian, take Metro A line to Colli Albani, then ATAC bus 660. 1,500 lire.

Trips Out of the Center

To the Youth Hostel at Foro Italico, Metro A to Ottaviano, then ATAC bus 32. 1,500 lire. Hostel phone 323 62 79.

To the extensive ruins of Ostia Antica and to the Ostia Lido. Metro B to Magliana, then the train. Service every thirty minutes. 1,500 lire.

To the magnificent remains of Emperor Hadrian's Villa and the splendid grounds of the Villa d'Este at Tivoli. Metro B to Rebibbia (1,500 lire), then the Cotral bus (3,000 lire). Service to Villa d'Este every ten to fifteen minutes and to Hadrian's Villa every hour.

To the Etruscan remains at Cerveteri, Metro A to Lepanto (1,500 lire), then Cotral bus every half hour (4,900 lire.)

Bus Tours Inside Rome

ATAC bus 110 provides a three-hour tour of Rome. There is no guide, but a leaflet in English identifies Rome's main sights en route. Take the bus from the ATAC information office in Piazza del Cinquecento out front of the Stazione Termini at 3:30 P.M. in summer and 2:30 P.M. in winter. The charge is 15,000 lire.

CIT Viaggi, the city's largest and oldest tourist service, is at 68 Piazza della Repubblica and a dozen other locations. It offers many tours in a range of languages. Phone 47941 or 472172.

Grey Line Tours, 6 Piazza del Esquilino, phone 488 41 51, fax 474 22 14, has some tours in English and offers a night trip around Rome.

The Roma Trolley Tour, 42 Via Banco di Santo Spirito, phone 686 53 75, provides an audio guide. One may get on and off at eleven major sites.

Walks in Rome

Secret Walks at 127 Viale delle Medaglie d'Oro (phone 3972 87 28) and Scala Reale, 46 Via Varese (phone 44 70 08 98 and fax 44 70 08 98), provide guided walks. Secret Walks has a wheelchair tour on the first Saturday of each month.

Information Services

The Ente Provinciale per il Turismo (EPT) provides free maps and Carnet, a monthly English-language listing of events. There are EPT branches between tracks 2 and 3 at Stazione Termini (phone 48 89 92 55) and in the Customs area at Leonardo da Vinci (phone 65 01 02 55). The main office is next to the Grand Hotel at 5 Via Parigi (phone 48 89 91).

Enjoy Rome, at 39 Via Varese, near Stazione Termini, is a private service helping with hotel reservations and tours. Open Monday through Friday 8:30 A.M. to 1:00 P.M. and 3:30 P.M. to 6:00 P.M., and in the morning on Saturday.

City maps are free at McDonald's and at American Express at Piazza di Spagna.

Holidays

Be sure to note these days as you plan your visit. Banks, stores, much transportation, and many museums shut down on these holidays:

New Year's Day, January 1
Epiphany, January 6
Easter Sunday and the day after it, Easter Monday, Pasquetta
Liberation Day, April 25
Labor Day, May 1
The day of the Italian Republic, June 2
The feasts of Saints Peter and Paul, June 29
Ferragosto (Feast of August), Feast of the Assumption, August 15,
     a day when many Romans take off for two weeks
All Saints Day, November 1
Victory Day, November 4
Feast of the Immaculate Conception, December 8
Christmas, December 25
Second Christmas, Saint Stephen's Day, December 26

Hours of Openings

Retail stores generally are open Monday from 4:00 P.M. to 7:30 P.M.; Tuesday through Friday from 10:00 A.M. to 1:00 P.M. and 3:30 P.M. to 7:30 P.M.; Saturday from 10:00 A.M. to 1:00 P.M. In June through August most stores also open Monday morning. Closing time is 8:00 P.M. Department stores and some others downtown are open on Sunday.

Banks are open 8:30 A.M. to 1:30 P.M. and 2:45 P.M. to 3:45 P.M. They are closed Saturdays and Sundays. On Via Veneto near the American Embassy and elsewhere in Rome and Italy ATM (Bancomat) machines are available, with a daily limit of 500,000 lire. Use your ATM card, dial in your PIN number, and money will be drawn immediately from your home account. The machine rate is favorable.

Churches usually are open 7:00 A.M. to noon and 4:00 to 7:00 P.M.

Many restaurants open at 1:00 P.M. for lunch, close in the afternoon, and reopen at 7:30 P.M.

The American Embassy is closed on Presidents' Day (third Monday in February); Memorial Day, last Monday in May; July 4, Independence Day; Labor Day, first Monday in September; Columbus Day, second Monday in October; and Thanksgiving Day, fourth Thursday in November. The Canadian Embassy is closed July 1, Canada Day.

Gas station hours from May to September are 7:00 A.M. to 12:30 P.M. and 3:30 to 7:30 P.M.; in winter, 7:00 A.M. to 12:30 P.M. and 3:00 to 7:00 P.M.

Telephoning

Direct calls from Italy to the United States can be made by dialing 001, the U.S. Area code, and the local number. To avoid hotel surcharges, use calling cards and dial the AT&T operator at 172-1011 or MCI at 172-1022. To reach a long-distance operator for calls to Italian areas outside Rome, dial 10. If the call is to elsewhere in Europe or in North Africa, dial 15. For the U.S. operator, dial 170.

If a line is busy and you must break in, hang up, dial 172, and repeat the number.

For calls in Rome use 100-lire or 200-lire coins or purchase telephone cards for either 5,000 or 10,000 lire at tobacco shops, the *tabaccai*. These are marked by black-and-white signs and the letter "T." They are omnipresent and very useful—providing many services, including the sale of postage stamps.

Mail

Mail is slow, two weeks by air to the States and four to six weeks by surface. The main post office at 19 Piazza San Silvestro is open 9:00 A.M. to 6:00 P.M. weekdays; 9:00 A.M. to 2:00 P.M. Saturdays; and 9:00 A.M. to 6:00 P.M. Sundays. There is full service, registered mail, telegrams, fax communications, parcel post. Branch post offices have much of the same. An alternative is to mail from the Vatican. Some say the papal service is especially efficient. Anyone can use it. Collectors enjoy the stamps with their papal and religious themes.

Restrooms

These pose a problem. There are a few at Saint Peter's plaza, but Rome is largely bereft. Either walk brazenly past the concierge at a hotel or buy a drink in a café for your right of entry. Toilet paper, too, is scarce. Carry a packet of tissues.

Restaurants

Lunch is generally 1:00 P.M. to 3:00 P.M. and dinner 8:00 P.M. to 10:30 P.M. It is wise to reserve, especially on weekends.

Bars

If you are just thirsty, pay the cashier in the bar, then take your receipt to the counter. If you prefer to relax or sightsee at a table an extra charge may be added to the cost of your cappuccino. The good part is that you can stay seated as long as you want.

Tipping

Restaurants often include the service charge. If not, tip at least 10 percent. If the charge is already on the bill, add at least 1,000 lire per person. Tip porters, hotel maids, and conceirges in proportion to the service received. Ushers expect 1,000 lire. So do the self-imposing parking attendants.

Pharmacies

Pharmacies are open 8:30 A.M. to 1:00 P.M. and reopen at 4:30 P.M. They are closed Sundays and on afternoons Saturdays. The pharmacy in Stazione Termini is open all day from 7:30 A.M. to 11:30

P.M. There is twenty-four-hour service at the Internazionale pharmacy at 49 Piazza Barberini, phone 46 29 96, and at the Spinedi pharmacy, 73 Via Arenula, phone 68 80 32 78.

For medical emergencies all hospitals have first aid, *pronto soccorso*. Near the center are Ospedale San Giacomo, 29 Via Antonio Canova, between Vias del Corso and Ripetta (phone 36261); the hospital of the Fatebenefratelli (Do Well Brothers) on the Tiber island (phone 683 72 99); and the Policlinico Umberto I in Viale del Policlinico near Piazza G. Fabrizio (phone 446 23 41). English-speaking staff members are at the Salvador Mundi Clinic, 67 Viale delle Mura Gianicolensi near Via Gabriele Rossetti (phone 58 89 61); the Rome American Hospital, 69 Via Emilio Longoni near the GRA ring road and the Via Prenestina intersection (phone 225 51); and the Clinica Moscati, 506 Via Pineta Sacchetti (phone 350 31)

Holy Year Souvenirs

The Vatican has arranged for special Holy Year commemoratives of special interest to philatelists and numismatists. Making use of its right as a sovereign state to issue its own coins interchangeable with the Italian lire, and to print its own stamps for worldwide postal use, it is issuing a series of jubilee commemoratives of both varieties.

Issuance of the coins in 10,000-lire denominations began in 1995, when two were struck off. They were followed by another two in 1996 and a fifth coin in 1997. Pope John Paul II is on one side of each of the coins and events in the life of Christ on the other: the Annunciation and the Nativity in 1995, Christ's baptism and his preaching to the multitude in 1996, and the calming of the waters in 1997.

For stamp collectors, starting in 1997, the Vatican state is issuing commemorative covers, nine a year for three years, each of them focused on one of the twenty-seven Holy Year pontiffs. Each cover has the picture of one of the jubilee popes, a Vatican postage stamp, and a postmark in Latin, reading "In the 2000 A.D. Jubilee, Christ yesterday, today and always, Vatican Post"; and the date of issuance.

The 1997 covers feature Boniface VIII, Clement VI, and the two Holy Year popes of 1390, Urban VI and Boniface IX, issued on March 10; Boniface IX again for the 1400 jubilee; Martin V and Nicholas V, issued June 10; and Sixtus IV, Alexander VI, and Clement VII, October 10.

Commemorative coins and postal covers can be obtained from

the Ufficio Filatelico e Numismatico, Governatorato, 00120 Citta del Vaticano. For the coins, phone (0039) 6 6988 3708, or use fax (0039) 6 6088 3799. For the postal covers phone (06) 6988 34 06 or fax (06) 6988 53 78.

Shopping

For those with the time, Rome offers many shopping opportunities: antiques, high fashions, jewelry, and clothing in all price ranges.

Many of the shopping opportunities are in the Piazza di Spagna area along Via Condotti, Via Frattina, Via Borgognona, and Via della Carozze, and along the nearby stretch of the Corso. There are glittering displays of clothing, shoes, art objects, the contents of boutiques and jewelry. For women there are handbags, dresses, sweaters, scarves, and shoes at prices within reason.

For fine-quality antiques there is Via del Babuino and, for good value in the same area, Via dei Coronari. Via Sistina and Via Gregoriana offer high fashion. The Via Veneto district has smart shops offering clothing, art objects, and gifts to take home, but prices run high. For more favorable pricing, near the Vatican, there are Via Cola di Rienzo and Via Ottaviano, both of which run from Piazza del Risorgimento.

At the clothing market near Saint John Lateran on Via Sannio, new and second-hand jackets, pants, leather coats, and other items dance in the breeze under broad awnings. Even more spectacular is the Sunday-morning flea market at Porta Portese in Trastavere, just downriver from the island in the Tiber. Everything from old Etruria to modern Africa is on sale. Everyone is busy, especially the pickpockets. It is said that if your watch is lifted as you walk in, you will be able to buy it back as you leave.

Security

Holy Year planners and police have puzzled over how to cope with petty thievery. Even so, the visitor will be wise to take precautions.

Passports, plane tickets, and large cash surpluses should be stored in a hotel safe. Men should carry only enough for the day's needs and that inside a waist pouch or a front pocket. Women are advised to wear purses bandoleer-style across the chest.

The Stazione Termini and all areas of visitor congregation, even papal audiences, are dangerous, not for fear of violence but for loss of property. Buses such as the 64, which runs conveniently from Stazione Termini to Saint Peter's, are notorious for sneak thieves; such vehicles often display signs in several languages warning passengers. Among other perilous buses are 62, 46, and 492. Consular officers are accustomed to hearing horror stories—how thousands of dollars were drawn from credit card accounts in less than an hour. Even local residents have tales of woe—how an apartment was looted despite six locks, an alarm system, and a pit bulldog.

There is an old Roman warning to local girls: Beware of the man with blue eyes. An unreliable foreigner, he is not to be trusted with the heart of a brown-eyed maiden. In distorted fashion, the same sense that well-heeled here-today gone-tomorrow visitors are fair game may motivate some local ne'er-do-wells. It is nothing new. For centuries a Holy See concern has been how to protect jubilee pilgrims from the impious.

Thefts and Losses

Losses should be reported promptly to the Carabinieri or police. The Questura on Via Genova has a special office for foreigners, the *stranieri*. Fill out a *denuncia*. It can serve as a temporary driver's license and can be used to apply for a new passport. Report lost traveler's checks to the American Express office at 38 Piazza di Spagna (toll-free phone, 1678 72000). In the case of credit card losses, inform American Express at 72282, Master Card and Visa at 1678 68086, and Diner's Club at 1678 64064.

It is wise to photocopy all valuable documents—charge cards and driver's licenses—keeping that record in a safe place, such as the hotel.

Towed-Away Cars

If you drive in Rome and your car vanishes, call the Vigili Urbani at 67691. You parked in the wrong place or at the wrong time. Give the police the registration number and the car make, and tell them where you left it. They will tell you where to find it. A *multa*, a fine, will be due. Pay it at the Cassa of the Vigili Urbani, 4 Via della Conciliazione near Castel Sant'Angelo. Use the receipt to reclaim your vehicle.

Consulates and Embassies

American Embassy, 121 Via Vittorio Veneto at Via Buoncompagni, phone 46741. Consulate, 119/A Via Vittorio Veneto, phone 46741.

Australian Embassy, 215 Via Alessandria at Corso Trieste, phone 85 27 21.

British Consulate and Embassy, 80/A Via XX Settembre at Porta Pia, phone 482 54 41, 482 55 51.

Canadian Embassy, 27 Via Giovanni Battista at Via Antonio Nibby, phone 44 59 81. Consulate, 30 Via Zara between Via Nomentana and Corso Trieste, phone 44 59 81 and 841 53 41.

French Embassy, 251 Via Giulia, phone 68 80 64 37.

German Embassy, 25/c Via Po, phone 88741.

Japanese Embassy, 58 Via Sella, phone 48 17 11.

Irish Embassy, 3 Largo Nazzareno, phone 678 25 41.

Israeli Embassy, 12/14 Via Michele Mercati, phone 32 21 44 52.

Mexican Embassy, 16 Via Spallanzani, phone 440 44 00.

New Zealand Embassy, 28 Via Zara, phone 440 29 28.

Museums

In addition to the twenty-nine museums inside the Vatican state, the city of Rome offers another 135, plus a further twenty-one inside the surrounding province of Rome. There is something for everyone. In the city of Rome, there are six additional religious museums, thirty-four dealing with archaeology, fifty-three with medieval and modern themes, twenty concentrating on science, thirteen housing military mememtos, and nine with themes all their own, including one that promises the visitor everything he will wish to know about pasta, that divine dish of every Italian table.

The **spaghetti museum** is in the Palazzo Scanderbeg at 114–120 in the plaza of the same name. Phone 699 1119. The hours are Monday through Friday, 9:30 A.M. to 12:30 P.M. and 4:00 P.M. to 7:00 P.M., Saturday, 9:30 A.M. to 12:30 P.M. The charge is 12,000 lire. The museum traces the way Etruscans first mixed grain and water and then carries forward to 1500, when pasta makers, the *vermicellari*, banded together to promote standards for their profession. Shown are the rudimentary pasta machines of the nineteenth century along with current equipment churning out a bewildering variety of noodles, macaronis and spaghettis.

AMONG THE OTHER MUSEUMS ARE THESE:

The **International Museum of the Christmas Crib,** 31/A Via Tor de' Conti, 6796146, From December 24 to January 16 it is open free from 4:00 P.M. to 8:00 P.M., weekdays and on holidays from 10:00 A.M. to 1:00 P.M. and 3:00 P.M. to 8:00 P.M. More than three thousand cribs and figures from twenty-nine countries including China, Japan, Kenya, and Madagascar are on display, with the Nativity scene represented in a score of materials including wax, ceramics, dough, straw, cork, shells, maize leaves, glass, and sugar.

The **Museum of the Walls,** 18 Via Porta San Sebastiano, phone 70 47 52 84. Open weekdays 9:00 A.M. to 1:30 P.M., Sunday and holidays, 9:00 A.M. to 1:00 P.M. On Tuesday, Thursday, and Saturday there is also an afternoon opening, 4:00 P.M. to 7:00 P.M. Mondays closed. The charge is 3,750 lire. This is inside the Aurelian walls at the Appian Way. In addition to seeing exhibits, the visitor can walk the walltop sentry way as far as Via Cristoforo Colombo.

The **Museum of Folklore,** 1/B Piazza San Egidio, phone 581 6563. Open weekdays 9:00 A.M. to 1:30 P.M. On Thursday it is also open from 5:00 P.M. to 7:30 P.M.; Sunday 9 to 1. The charge is 3,750 lire. Popular Rome, the city of the Trastevere dialect poets, is preserved here, the *scrivano pubblico* who wrote letters for the illiterate in exchange for gifts of food; the *pifferari,* bagpipers who walked the streets of Rome as late as the 1950s at Christmastime playing the haunting "You descended from the Heavens"; and the wine carts that still rolled down from the hills of Frascati in the 1940s.

The **Borghese Museum and Gallery** in Villa Borghese, a few blocks from Via Veneto, phone 854 85 77. Open weekdays, 9:00 A.M. to 7:00 P.M. in summer and 9:00 A.M. to 2:00 P.M. in winter, and on Sunday 9:00 A.M. to 1:00 P.M. Closed Monday. Charge of 4,000 lire. It is a typical example of a well-to-do early sixteenth-century villa. Exhibits include Antonio Canova's marble nude of Napoleon's sister, Paolina Buonaparte, the wife of Prince Camillo Borghese.

The **Napoleonic Museum,** 1 Via Zanardelli, phone 68 80 62 86. Open weekdays, 9:00 A.M. to 2:00 P.M., holidays, 9:00 A.M. to 1:00 P.M. Thursdays also 5:00 P.M. to 8:00 P.M. Charge, 3,750 lire. Included are books Bonaparte had with him on Saint Helena. A room is devoted to Napoleon's sister Paolina.

The **Museum of Musical Instruments,** 9a Piazza Santa Croce in Gerusalemme to the right of the pilgrimage church of that name, phone 701 47 96. Open weekdays, 9:00 A.M. to 2:00 P.M. Closed Sunday. Charge, 2,000 lire. Beginning with the *auloi* (whistle) and rattles, bells and cymbals of ancient Greece and Rome, the collection has a trumpet from 1461, Hans Muller's Leipzig harpsichord of 1537, Bartolomeo Cristofori's piano of 1722, folk instruments from Italy and other parts of Europe, and other exhibits from Africa, the Far East, Oceania, and the Americas.

The **Museum of the Jewish Community of Rome.** It is in the Synagogue on Lungotevere Cenci, opposite the island in the Tiber, phone 656 4648 and 687 5051. Open Monday to Thursday, 9:30 A.M. to 2:00 P.M. and 3:00 P.M. to 5:00 P.M., Friday and Sunday, 9:30 A.M. to 2:30 P.M. Closed Saturday and Jewish holidays. Charge, 4,000 lire, 2,000 for schools. Included is an ornate easy chair of 1870, the Grand Seat of the Prophet Elijah, used for the circumcision rite. There is a large collection of textiles from the time of the walled ghetto. Reproductions of papal bulls and documentation of the Nazi period are included.

The **Franciscan Museum,** at the Historic Institute of the Capuchins, Circonvalazione Occidentale 6850 at the GRA beltway's sixty-fifth kilometer mark, phone 66 15 19 49. Admission is free, but appointments are required. There are 21,195 exhibits, including 515 paintings, 110 sculptures, 420 ceramics and porcelain pieces, and 850 coins and medals illustrating the life of Saint Francis and his followers.

The **Waxworks Museum,** 67 Piazza Venezia, phone 67976. Open daily, 9:00 A.M. to 8:00 P.M. Charge, 5,000 lire. Opened in 1958 in emulation of the waxworks of London and Paris, it offers a grab bag of representations of world history's famous and infamous, Abraham Lincoln, Franklin D. Roosevelt, Hitler, Himmler, Snow White and the seven dwarfs, John XXIII, Christopher Columbus, Italy's humble democratic premier Alcide De Gasperi, and King Solomon. Phone 67976 482. Open daily 9:00 A.M. to 8:00 P.M. Charge, 5,000 lire.

Among Rome's grisliest and least expected is the free **Museum of the Historical Chamber** in the Church of San Giovanni Decollato (Saint John the Baptist Beheaded), 22 Via San Giovanni Decollato near Santa Maria in Cosmedin, phone 67918 90. Open only once a year, on June 24. Exhibits include registers of the executed, large knives and baskets for the heads of the decapitated.

In Ardea: The **Giacomo Manzú collection,** phone 913 5022. Free. Open daily, 9:00 A.M. to 7:00 P.M. Included are 462 of the works of Pope John XXIII's favorite sculptor who did a door for Saint Peter's Basilica in 1965. Manzú lived his final three decades in Ardea, dying there at eighty-three in 1991.

In Carpineto Romano: The museum of the social justice pope, Leo XIII, **Palazzo Pecci,** phone 979 00 20. This village was, in 1810, the birthplace of the future pontiff. Included are his infant crib, souvenirs of the 1900 Holy Year, and vestments worn as cardinal and pope.

In Cerveteri: The **National Cerite Museum** in the Ruspoli family castle, phone 994 13 54. Free. Open 9:00 A.M. to 4:00 P.M. in summer and 9:00 A.M. to 2:00 P.M. in winter. Closed Mondays. Free entry. Remarkable preserved pottery and other objects from all over the Greek world recovered from the area's many Etruscan tombs, some of them dating from the ninth century B.C.

In Fiumicino: The **Museum of Roman Ships,** phone 60 11 10 89 and 652 91 92. Open 9:00 A.M. to 1:00 P.M. On Tuesday and Thursday, open additionally from 2:00 P.M. to 5:00 P.M. Sunday and holidays, 9:00 A.M. to 1:00 P.M. Charge, 2,000 lire. Opened in 1979, this museum exists thanks to the 1960s construction of the Leonardo da Vinci airport. Excavating uncovered the large artificial seaport built by Emperors Claudius and Nero in the first century A.D. The keels of four sunken ships plus fragments of two more were recovered and are on display. Three were cargo ships bringing grain, oil, and wine to ancient Rome. Unique is a fishing boat with nine plugged-up drill holes in the bottom allowing sea water to come in to keep the catch alive, a system still used in Sardinia for lobstering.

In Licenza: The **Museum of Horace** in the Baronial Palace, phone 0774 46031. Request entry from the municipality. In the exhibit are household items and fragments of frescoes from the villa and land occupied by the first-century B.C. poet Horace.

In Nettuno: The **Antiquarium,** 2 Via della Vittoria, phone 980 7114. Open 9:30 A.M. to 12:30 P.M. and, in the afternoon, 4:30 P.M. to 7:30 P.M. in summer, 3:30 P.M. to 6:30 P.M. in winter. Free of charge. There are flint tools and large mammal bones used apparently by *Homo erectus* 400,000 to 200,000 years ago. There are also arrowheads of the late Neolithic period (35,000 to 12,000 years ago) and Copper Age hatchets smoothed from green stones.

Useful Telephone Numbers

Vatican City, 6982

Police emergency, 113.

Fire, 115.

Ambulance, 5510.

Police, Pubblica Sicurezza, 4686.

City police, Vigili Urbani, 67 691.

Carabinieri, 112

Highway police, Polizia Stradale, 5577 905.

Anti-poison center at Gemelli Hospital, 3054 343, and Poison Control, 49 06 63.

Salvator Mundi Hospital 67 Viale della Mura Gianicolensi, 588 961.

Rome American Hospital, 69 Via Emilio Longoni, 22551.

24-hour medical service, 488 2371.

24-hour pharmacy location, 1921.

General information, including museum hours and night pharmacies, 110.

Bus information, 46 95 44 44.

Postal and telegraph information, 160.

Museum hours, 110.

Train information, 4775.

Time, 161.

Wake-up call, 114.

Telephone directory, 12.

Phone operator assistance, 170.

Weather, 1911.

CALENDAR OF EVENTS

1999

Christmas Eve, December 24. Opening of the holy door in Saint Peter's Basilica.

New Year's Eve, December 31. A prayer vigil for passage to the year 2000.

2000

January 2. Children's Day.

January 6. Ordination of bishops.

January 9. Baptism of infants.

January 18. An ecumenical service as part of a week of prayer for Christian unity.

February 2. Jubilee celebration for those in the religious consecrated life.

February 11. The jubilee of the ill and of health care workers.

February 18. Jubilee of artists.

February 20. Jubilee of the permanent deacons.

February 22. Jubilee of the Roman curia, the Holy See staff.

February 25–27. A study convention on carrying out Vatican II Council decisions.

March 8. A request for pardon for past offenses by Church exponents.

March 20. Jubilee of practitioners of the various workaday crafts.

March 25. The Feast of the Annunciation, a liturgical celebration to highlight "the dignity of women in the light of Mary's mission." The main celebration will be at the Basilica of the Annunciation at Nazareth in the Holy Land, with live TV links to major Marian shrines around the world.

April 10. Jubilee of migrants and refugees.

April 18. A communal celebration of the sacrament of Penance, with individual absolution.

April 22. Easter vigil and celebration of the Rite of Christian Initiation of Adults, admission of converts to the Catholic Church.

May 1. May Day, Labor Day, jubilee of workers.
May 7. Ecumenical service at the Colosseum acclaiming the "new martyrs" of many faiths, victims of oppression.
May 18. Jubilee of the clergy.
May 25. Jubilee of scientists.

June 4. Jubilee of journalists.
June 11. Day of prayer for collaboration among religions.
June 18–25. International Eucharistic Congress.

July 9. Jubilee celebration in prisons.

August 5. Prayer vigil on the Feast of the Transfiguration of the Lord, an event held by request of Orthodox Patriarch Bartholomew of Istanbul.
August 15–20. World youth celebration.

September 10. Jubilee of university teachers.
September 15–24. International Marian-Mariological Congress, emphasizing devotion to the Virgin Mary.
September 17. Jubilee of the elderly.

October 3. Day of Jewish-Christian dialogue.
October 8. Jubilee of bishops and dedication of the new millennium to Mary's protection.
October 14–15. Worldwide Encounter of the Holy Father with Families, a jubilee of families and a celebration of the sacrament of matrimony.
October 20–22. International Missionary Congress.
October 29. Jubilee of sports people.

November 5. Jubilee of those working in public life.
November 12. A day of thanks for the gifts of creation and a jubilee of agricultural workers.
November 19. Jubilee of the military and police.
November 24–26. World congress for the Apostolate of the Laity.

December 17. Jubilee of the world of entertainment.
December 31. New Year's Eve, prayer vigil for passage into the third millenium.

2001

January 6. Closing of the holy door in Saint Peter's.

BIBLIOGRAPHY

There are whole libraries on Rome and the Holy See. I found the following books and services especially helpful.

HOLY YEAR HISTORY

Anni Santi, I Giubilei da 1300 al 2000, Francesco Gligora and Biagia Catanzaro, Libreria Editrice Vaticana, Vatican City, 1996.

The Roman Jubilee, History and Ceremonial, Herbert Thurston, S.J., Sands & Co., London, 1925.

Rome and the Holy Year, Milton Gendel, Autostrade, Rome, 1997.

HOLY YEAR 2000

Giubileo Notizie, monthly Holy Year news summary, Radio Televisione Italiana, 1996–2000.

Tertium Millennium, periodical of the Central Committee for the Great Jubilee of the Year Two Thousand, 1996–2000, Rome.

THE VATICAN, PAPACY, AND HOLY SEE

Annuario Pontificio, official directory of the Holy See, 2489 pp., Libreria Editrice Vaticana, Vatican City, 1997.

Guide to Saint Peter's Basilica, Giovanni Giuliani, A.T.S. Italia, Rome, 1995.

Guide to the Vatican Museums and City, Carlo Pietrangeli, Tipografia Poliglotta Vaticano, Vatican City, 1986.

Pontiffs: Popes Who Shaped History, John Jay Hughes, Our Sunday Visitor, Huntington, Indiana, 1994.

The Pope's Back Yard, Curtis G. Pepper, Farrar, Straus & Giroux, New York, 1967.

The Popes: A Concise Biographical History, Eric John, Hawthorn Books, New York, 1964.

Vatican City: Monumenti, Musei e Gallerie, Francesco Roncalli, Tipografia Poliglotta Vaticano, Vatican City, 1989.

Viaggio in Vaticano, Bart McDowell, Touring Club Italiano, National Geographic Society, 1991.

CHRISTIAN ROME

As Romans Do, Church of Santa Susanna, Rome, 1997.

Basiliche e Catacombe a Roma, Ente Provinciale per il Turismo di Roma, Rome.

Christian Rome, Leone Gessi, Ente Provinciale per il Turismo di Roma, Rome, 1958.

City on the Tiber. Rome: A Religious Experience, Willard F. Jabusch, Society of Saint Paul, Staten Island, New York, 1990.

The Pilgrim's Companion in Rome, the Ancient City, Stewart Perowne, Hodder & Stoughton, London, 1964.

A Pilgrim's Guide to Rome, Harry Weedon, Prentice-Hall, New York, 1950.

The Pilgrim's Guide to Rome's Principal Churches, Joseph N. Tylenda, S.J., The Liturgical Press, Collegeville, Minnesota, 1993.

Rome Churches of Special Interest for English-speaking People, Robin Anderson, Libreria Editrice Vaticana, Vatican City, 1982.

Rome: A Jesuit City Too, Elena Bartoli, Jesuit Guest Bureau, Rome, 1995.

SAINTS

Dictionary of Saints, John J. Delaney, Doubleday, New York, 1980.

The One Year Book of Saints, Clifford Stevens, Our Sunday Visitor, Huntington, Indiana, 1989.

Patron Saints, Michael Freze, Our Sunday Visitor, Huntington, Indiana, 1992.

CITY OF ROME

AAA World Traveler: Rome, American Automobile Association, Heathrow, Florida, 1996.

Access Rome, Richard Saul Wurman, Access Press, New York.

The Capitoline Museums, Ente Provinciale per il Turismo di Roma, Rome, 1953.

Itinerari Romani, Ettore della Riccia, Ente Provinciale per il Turismo di Roma, Rome, 1960.

Michelin Rome, Michelin Tyre, Watford Herts, United Kingdom, 1995.

Museums of Rome, Daniela Martellucci, Ente Provinciale per il Turismo di Roma, Rome, 1994.

Roma, Guida d'Italia, 939 pp., Touring Club Italiano, 1993.

ABOUT THE AUTHOR

Barrett McGurn lived in Rome for fifteen years intermittently, from 1939, in the fading days of the Fascist dictatorship, from 1946 to 1952, at the time of Italy's resurrection from the horrors of World War II, from 1955 to 1962, during Italy's brilliant recovery, and from 1966 to 1968. He was chief of the Rome bureau of the New York and International *Herald Tribune* in the 1946–62 period and United States Embassy press attaché in his final two Italian years.

In 1961 and in 1962 he was president of Stampa Estera, an association of four hundred correspondents of forty nations covering Italy and the Holy See. In that capacity he gave an unprecedented address to Pope John XXIII on the difficulties of Vatican media relations and was assured by the pontiff that the Holy See's unique concentration on its diplomatic corps and its ignoring of the world media would end. The promised revolution in Vatican press relations followed.

Barrett McGurn twice received awards as the year's best American foreign correspondent. His alma mater, Fordham University, enrolled him as an honorary doctor of letters. The American Catholic Press Institute gave him its highest annual award. From 1984 to 1990, he was director of communications for the Archdiocese of Washington and publisher of its two weekly newspapers.